William Henry Giles Kingston

Peter Trawl

Or, The Adventures of a Whaler

William Henry Giles Kingston

Peter Trawl
Or, The Adventures of a Whaler

ISBN/EAN: 9783337177362

Printed in Europe, USA, Canada, Australia, Japan

Cover: Foto ©ninafisch / pixelio.de

More available books at **www.hansebooks.com**

PETER TRAWL;

OR

THE ADVENTURES OF A WHALER.

BY
W. H. G. KINGSTON,
AUTHOR OF "THE THREE MIDSHIPMEN," "CLARA MAYNARD,"
"HENDRICKS THE HUNTER," ETC., ETC.

ILLUSTRATED.

New York:
A. C. ARMSTRONG AND SON,
714, BROADWAY.

MDCCCLXXXII.

CONTENTS.

CHAP.		PAGE
I.	MY EARLY DAYS AT HOME	1
II.	HOW A TRUE FRIEND WAS GAINED	10
III.	A SAD CHAPTER IN MY LIFE	23
IV.	A FEARFUL CATASTROPHE	33
V.	A FRIEND LOST AND A FRIEND GAINED	42
VI.	TURNED OUT OF HOUSE AND HOME	51
VII.	HELP COMES WHEN LEAST EXPECTED	60
VIII.	MY FIRST VOYAGE	73
IX.	I EXPERIENCE THE PERILS OF THE SEA	86
X.	ALONE ON THE OCEAN	98
XI.	DANGERS MULTIPLY	110
XII.	PORT REACHED IN AN UNEXPECTED MANNER	121
XIII.	A DISASTROUS VOYAGE	132
XIV.	JIM AND I CARRIED OFF AGAINST OUR WILL	144
XV.	THE VOYAGE OF THE "INTREPID" BEGUN	155
XVI.	WE CROSS THE LINE AND ATTEMPT TO ROUND CAPE HORN	166
XVII.	ROUNDING CAPE HORN	178
XVIII.	OUR FIRST WHALES CAUGHT—I HEAR NEWS OF JACK	189
XIX.	MILES SOPER'S NARRATIVE CONCLUDED	200
XX.	A MUTINY AND ITS CONSEQUENCES	212

CHAP.		PAGE
XXI.	A CRUISE ACROSS THE PACIFIC AND THE ADVENTURES I MET WITH	225
XXII.	A TYPHOON, AND HOW WE GOT THROUGH IT	237
XXIII.	A FEARFUL NARRATIVE—DOINGS AT STRONG'S ISLAND	249
XXIV.	OUR LIFE ON AN UNINHABITED ISLAND	261
XXV.	A PERILOUS VOYAGE IN THE WHALEBOAT	274
XXVI.	MORE STARTLING ADVENTURES	286
XXVII.	THE LOST ONE FOUND AT LAST	298
XXVIII.	ESCAPE FROM THE ISLAND AND THE EVENTS WHICH FOLLOWED	310
XXIX.	ON BOARD OUR OLD SHIP — HER VOYAGE THROUGH EASTERN SEAS	323
XXX.	THE VOYAGE HOME, AND HOW IT ENDED	337

CHAPTER I.

MY EARLY DAYS AT HOME.

BROTHER JACK, a seaman's bag over his shoulders, trudged sturdily ahead; father followed, carrying the oars, spars, sails, and other gear of the wherry, while as I toddled alongside him I held on with one hand to the skirt of his pea-jacket, and griped the boat-hook which had been given to my charge with the other.

From the front of the well-known inn, the " Keppel's Head," the portrait of the brave old admiral, which I always looked at with awe and admiration, thinking what a great man he must have been, gazed sternly down on us as we made our way along the Common Hard of Portsea towards the water's edge.

Father and Jack hauled in the wherry, and having deposited their burdens in her, set to work to mop her out and to put her to rights, while I stood, still grasping the boat-hook, which I held upright with the point in the ground, watching their proceedings, till father, lifting me up in his arms, placed me in the sternsheets.

"Sit there, Peter, and mind you don't topple overboard, my son," he said, in the kind tone in which he always spoke to me and Jack.

I was too small to be of much use, indeed father had hitherto only taken me with him when he was merely going across to Gosport and back or plying about the harbour.

It was a more eventful day to Jack than to me. When I saw mother packing his bag, I had a sort of idea that he was going to sea, and when the next morning she threw her arms round his neck and burst into tears, and Jack began to cry too, I understood that he would be away for a long time.

Jack had been of great use to father, who grieved as much as mother to part with him, but, as he said, he wouldn't, if he could help it, bring him up as a long-shore lubber, and a few voyages would be the making of him.

"He can't get none of the right sort of eddication on shore," observed father. "He'll learn on board a man-of-war what duty and discipline mean, and to my mind till a lad knows that he isn't worth his salt."

The *Lapwing* brig-of-war, fitted out at Sheerness, had brought up at Spithead, and her commander, Captain Rogers, with whom father had long served, meeting him on shore, and hearing that he had a son old enough to go to sea, offered to take Jack and look after him.

When Commander Rogers was a midshipman, he fell overboard, and would have been drowned had not father jumped in and saved him. He was very grateful, but had not till now had an opportunity of practically showing his gratitude. Father, therefore, gladly accepted his offer, being sure that he would do his best for Jack; and as Blue Peter was flying from the masthead of the brig, there was no time to be lost in taking him on board.

At the time I was too young, as I was saying, to understand these matters, but I learnt about them afterwards. All I then knew was that brother Jack was going for a sailor aboard of a man-of-war.

Father and Jack were just shoving off, when two persons who had come out of the "Keppel's Head" were seen hurrying down the Hard with cases and packages in their hands and under their arms. One, as his dress and appearance showed, was a seafaring man; the other wore long toggery, as sailors call the costume of landsmen.

"If you are going out to Spithead, my man, we'll go with you," shouted the first.

"Ay, ay, sir! I'll be glad enough to take you," answered father, happy to get a fare, instead of making nothing by the trip.

"We'll give you five shillings a-piece," said the officer, for such he seemed to be.

"Thank you, sir; that will do. What ship shall I put you aboard?" asked father.

"The *Intrepid*, South Sea whaler—she's lying to the eastward of the men-of-war. We shall see her when we get abreast of Southsea Castle," answered the officer.

"Step aboard, then, sir," said father. "The tide will soon have done making out of the harbour, and there's no time to lose."

The strangers took their seats in the sternsheets, and father and Jack, shoving off, pulled out into the stream.

The officer took the yoke-lines, and by the way he handled them, showed that he knew what he was about. Careful steering is always required where tides run strong and vessels are assembled; but especially was it at that time, when, peace having been just proclaimed, Portsmouth Harbour was crowded with men-of-war lately returned from foreign stations, and with transports and victuallers come in to be discharged; while all the way up towards Porchester Castle lay, now dismantled in vast numbers, those stout old ships with names renowned which had borne the victorious flag of England in many a fierce engagement. Dockyard lighters, man-of-war boats, wherries crowded with passengers, and other craft of various descriptions, were sailing or pulling about in all directions, so that the stranger had to keep his eyes about him to avoid being run down by, or running into, some other boat or vessel.

"We'll step the mast, and make sail while we're in smooth water, sir," said father. "There's a lop of a sea outside, when it wouldn't be pleasant to this gentleman if we were to wait till then," and he gave a look at the landsman, who even now did not seem altogether comfortable.

"The doctor hasn't been used to the sea, but he'll soon get accustomed to it. No fear of that, Cockle, eh?" said the officer, who was, he afterwards told father, second mate of the *Intrepid*.

"I hope I shall, Mr. Griffiths, but I confess I don't much like the thought of going through those foaming waves out there in such a cockleshell of a boat as this," answered the doctor. "No offence to you, my friend," he added, turning to father.

"Ha! ha! ha! That's just what the boat is at present," said the mate, laughing. "Do you twig, doctor? do you twig? She carries you and your fortunes, and if she takes us safe alongside the *Intrepid*—and I see no reason why she shouldn't—we shall be obliged to her and her owner here. What's your name, my man?"

"Jack Trawl, sir; at your service," answered father. "Many's the time I've been out to Spithead in this here wherry when it's been blowing great guns and small arms, and she's ridden over the seas like a duck. The gentleman needn't be afraid."

The doctor, who did not seem to like the mate's joking, or father's remark about being afraid, sat silent for some time.

"I'll take the helm, sir, if you please," said father, who had stepped the mast and hauled aft the sheets. "My wherry likes me to have hold of her, and maybe she mightn't behave as well as she should if a stranger was steering."

"I understand," answered Mr. Griffiths, laughing. "You are wise not to trust any one but yourself. I'll yield to you in handling this style of boat under sail, though I may have been more at sea than you have."

"I doubt that, sir, as I went afloat not long after you were born, if not before, and for well-nigh thirty years seldom set foot on shore," answered father. "All that time I served His Majesty—God bless him—and if there was to come another war I'd be ready to serve him again, as my boy Jack there is just going to do."

"A fine lad he seems, but he'd better by half have joined the merchant service than submitted to the tyranny of a man-of-war," said the mate.

"There are just two opinions, sir, as to that," answered father, dryly. "Haul down the tack, Jack, and get a pull of the foresheet," he sang out.

There was a fresh breeze from the south-east blowing almost up the harbour, but by keeping over on the Portsmouth side, aided by the tide, we stood clear out of it. The wherry soon began to pitch into the seas, which came rolling in round Southsea Castle in a way which made the doctor look very blue. The mate tried to cheer him up, but he evidently didn't like it, especially when the spray came flying over the bows, and quickly wet him and most of us well-nigh through to the skin. Every now and then more than the mere spray came aboard us, and the doctor became more and more uncomfortable.

Father now called Jack aft to bale out the water, and he set to work heaving it overboard as fast as it came in. I laughed, and did not feel a bit afraid, because when I looked up at father's face I saw that there was nothing to be afraid about. At length the mate seemed to think that we were carrying on too long.

"Doctor Cockle is not accustomed to this sort of thing,"

he observed. "Hadn't we better take in a reef or two?"

"Not if you wish to get aboard your ship, sir, before night," answered father. "I know my boat, and I know what she'll do. Trust me, sir, and in less than half-an-hour you'll be safe alongside the *Intrepid*."

The mate seemed satisfied, and began talking to me, amused at the way I sat bobbing, as the spray came aboard, under an old pea-jacket which father had thrown over my shoulders, and grinning when I found that I had escaped the shower by which the others got well sprinkled.

"I'll not forget you, my little fellow," he said, laughing. "You'll make a prime seaman one of these days. Will you remember my name?"

"Yes, sir, I think I shall, and your face too," I answered.

"You are a sharp chap, I see," he observed, in the same tone as before.

"Do you intend to make a sailor of him?" he asked, turning to father.

"Not if I can find a better calling for the boy, sir," answered father. "I've heard say, and believe it, that man proposes and God disposes. It mayn't be in my power to choose for him."

"Ay, ay, you're right there, my friend," said the mate. "If he had been as old as his brother I would have given him a berth aboard the *Intrepid*."

It may seem curious that, young as I was, I should have remembered these remarks, but so it was, and I had reason long afterwards to do so.

Even sooner than father had said we had hooked on to the whaler, a barque of about three hundred tons, her black hull rising high out of the water, and with three boats, sharp at both ends, hoisted up to davits in a line on each side. The good-natured mate having paid the fare and given me a bright shilling in addition, helped the doctor, who wasn't very well able to help himself, up on deck, and we then, shoving off, stood for the man-of-war brig.

Jack almost broke down as we approached her. Not that he was unwilling to go away, but that he was very sorry to part from father and me, and I know that we were very sorry to part with him.

"Jack, my son," said father, and his voice wasn't as firm as usual, " we may never meet again on this side the grave. You may be taken or I may be taken. What I want to say to you is this, and they may be well-nigh the last words you will ever hear me speak. Ever remember that God's eye is upon you, and so live that you may be prepared at any moment to die. I can't say more than that, my boy. Bless you. God bless you."

"I will, father, I will," answered Jack, and he passed the back of his hand across his eyes.

We were soon up to the brig. He gave me a hug and a kiss, and then, having made fast the end of the rope hove to us, he griped father's hand, and sprang up the side of the brig. His bag was hoisted up after him by an old shipmate of father's, who sang out, "All right, Trawl, I'll look after your boy!"

We had at once to shove off, for the brig was rolling considerably, and there was a risk of the wherry being swamped alongside. As we stood away I looked astern. Jack had climbed into the fore-rigging and was waving to us. We soon lost sight of him. When, if ever, should we see him again?

Having the wind and tide with us, we quickly ran back into the harbour. For reasons which will appear by-and-by I ought to say a few words respecting my family, though I don't flatter myself the world in general will be much concerned about the matter. Some people are said to be born with silver spoons in their mouths; if that means, as I suppose it does, that from their earliest days they enjoy all the luxuries of life, then I may say when I first saw the light I must have had a very rough wooden one between my toothless gums. However, as I've often since thought, it isn't so much what a man is born to which signifies, as what he becomes by his honesty, steadiness, perseverance, and above all by his earnest desire to do right in the sight of God.

My father, Jack Trawl (as he spelt his name, or, rather, as others spelt it for him, he being no great hand with a pen), was an old man-of-war's-man. I well remember hearing him say that his father, who had been mate of a merchantman, and had been lost at sea when he himself was a boy, was a Shetlander; and in an old Testament which had belonged to his mother, and which he had treasured as the only relic of either of his parents, I found the name written Troil. The ink was very faint, but I made out the words clearly, "Margaret Troil, given to her by her husband Angus." This confirmed me in the idea I had formed, that both my father's parents had come from the far-off island of Shetland.

My father being a sober, steady man, having saved more of his pay and prize-money than had most of his shipmates, when he left the service bought a wherry, hired and furnished a house, and married my mother, Polly Treherne, the daughter of a bumboat woman who plied her trade in Portsmouth Harbour.

I have no cause to be ashamed of my grandmother, for every one who knew her said, and I am sure of it, that she was as worthy a woman in her line of life as ever lived. She gave good measure and charged honest prices, whether she was dealing in soft tack, fruit, vegetables, cheese, herrings, or any of the other miscellaneous articles with

My Early Days at Home.

which she supplied the seamen of His Majesty's ships; and her daughter Polly, who assisted her, was acknowledged by all to be as good and kind-hearted as she was pretty. No wonder, then, that she won the heart of my brave father when she visited the ship in which he had just come home, or that, knowing his worth, although she had many suitors, she consented to marry him.

For some time all went well, but what happened is a proof that honest, industrious persons may be overtaken by misfortunes as well as other people. Father had no intention that his wife should follow her mother's calling, as he could make enough to keep the pot boiling; but after they had been married a few years, and several children had been born, all of whom died in their infancy, except my eldest brother Jack, and me and Mary, the two youngest, bad times came.

CHAPTER II.

HOW A TRUE FRIEND WAS GAINED.

JUST before we two entered this world of troubles, the bank in which my father had deposited his savings broke, and all were lost. The sails of his wherry were worn out, and he had been about to buy a new suit, which he now couldn't do; the wherry herself was getting crazy, and required repairs, and he himself met with an accident which laid him up for several weeks. Grandmother also, who had lost nearly her all by the failure of the bank, though she had hitherto been hale and hearty, now began to talk of feeling the approach of old age.

One evening, while father was laid up, she looked in on us. " Polly, my girl, there's no use trying to beat up in the teeth of a gale with a five-knot current against one," she exclaimed, as, dropping down into our big arm-chair and undoing her bonnet-strings and the red handkerchief she wore round her neck, she threw her bonnet over the back of her head. " I'm dead beat with to-day's work, and shall be worse to-morrow. Now, my dear, what I've got to say is this, I want you to help me. You know the trade as well as I do. It will be a good thing for you as well as for me; for look you, my dear, if anything should happen to your Jack, it will help you to keep the wolf from the door."

This last argument, with her desire to help the good old lady, made mother say that if father was agreeable she would do as grandmother wished. She forthwith went upstairs, where father was lying in bed, scarcely able to move for the pain his hurt caused him. They talked the matter over, and he, knowing that something must be done for the support of the family, gave, though unwillingly, his consent. Thus it happened that my mother again took to bumming.

Trade, however, wasn't like what it used to be in the war time, I heard grandmother say. Then seamen would have their pockets filled with five-pound notes and golden guineas, which they were eager to spend; now they rarely had more than a few shillings or a handful of coppers jingling in them. Still there was an honest livelihood to be made, and grandmother and mother contrived to make it. Poor grandmother, however, before long fell ill, as she said she should, and then all the work fell on mother. Father got better, and was able sometimes to go out with the wherry, but grandmother got worse and worse, and mother had to attend on her till she died.

When she and father were away from home, Mary and I were left to the care of our brother Jack. He did his best to look after us, but not being skilled as a nursemaid, while he was tending Mary, who, being a girl—she was my twin sister, I should have said—required most of his care, he could not always manage to prevent me from getting into trouble. Fortunately nothing very serious happened.

Dear, kind Jack! I was very fond of him, and generally obeyed him willingly. It would not be true to say that I always did so. He was very fond of Mary and me too, of that I am sure, and he used to show his fondness by spending for our benefit any coppers he picked up by running on errands or doing odd jobs for neighbours. As his purchases were usually brandy-balls, rock, and other sweets, it was perhaps fortunate for us that he had not many to spend. By diligently pursuing her trade, mother, in course of time, saved money enough to enable father to get the wherry repaired, and to buy a new suit of sails, and when he got plenty of employment he bade mother stay at home and look after Mary and me, while Jack went with him. As, however, it would not have been prudent to give up her business altogether, she hired a girl, Nancy Fidget, to take her place, as Jack had done, when she was from home.

I don't remember that anything of importance happened after grandmother's death till Jack went to sea. We missed him very much, and Mary was always asking after him, wondering when he would come back. Still, if I had gone away, she would, I think, have fretted still more. Perhaps it was because we were twins that we were so fond of each other. We were, however, not much alike. She was a fair, blue-eyed little maiden, with flaxen hair and a rosy blush on her cheeks, and I was a broad-shouldered, strongly-built chap, the hue on my cheeks and the colour of my hair soon becoming deepened by my being constantly out of doors, while my eyes were, I fancy, of a far darker tint than my sister's.

After Jack went mother seemed to concentrate all her affections on us two. I don't think, however, that any woman could have a warmer or larger heart than hers, although many may have a wider scope for the exercise of their feelings. She never turned a beggar away from her door without some relief even in the worst of times, and when any of the neighbours were in distress, she always did her best to help them. Often when she had been out bumming for the best part of the day, and had been attending to household matters for the remainder, she would sit up the whole night with a sick acquaintance who was too poor to hire a nurse, and had only thanks to give her, and perhaps of that not very liberally.

I have said that my mother had as warm and generous a

heart as ever beat in woman's bosom. I repeat it. I might give numerous instances to prove the truth of my assertion, and to show that I have reason to be proud of being her son, whatever the world may think about the matter. One will suffice. It had an important effect on my destinies, although at the time no one would have supposed that such would be the case. One evening, as my mother was returning home off the water after dark, she found a female fallen down close to our door, in what seemed to be a fit. Some of the neighbours had seen the poor creature, but had let her lie there, and gone indoors, and several persons passing showed by their remarks what they thought of her character; but mother, not stopping to consider who she was or what she was, lifting her up in her strong arms, carried her into the house, and placed her on the bed which used to be Jack's.

Mother now saw by the light of the candle that the unhappy being she had taken charge of was still young, and once had been pretty, but the life she had led had marred her beauty and brought her to her present sad state. After mother had undressed her and given her food and a cordial in which she had great confidence, the girl slightly revived, but it became more evident than before that she was fearfully ill. She sobbed and groaned, and sometimes shrieked out in a way terrible to hear, but would give no account of herself. At length, mother, mistrusting her own skill, sent Nancy and me off to call Dr. Rolt, the nearest medical man we knew of. He came at once, and shaking his head as soon as he saw the stranger, he advised that she should be removed forthwith to the hospital.

"Not to-night, doctor, surely," said mother. "It might be the death of her, poor young creature!"

"She may rapidly grow worse, and it may be still more dangerous to move her afterwards," remarked Dr. Rolt.

"Then, please God, I'll keep charge of her till she recovers, or He thinks fit to take her," said mother, in her determined way.

"She will never recover, I fear," said the doctor; "but I will do the best for her I can."

Telling mother how to act, and promising to send some medicine, he went away. When father, who had been across to Ryde in the wherry, came home, he approved of what mother had done.

"Why, you see, Jack, what I think is this," I heard her say; "I've no right to point a finger at her, for if I hadn't had a good mother to show me right and wrong, I might have been just as she is."

The next morning the doctor came again. He looked grave when he left the stranger's room. "You are still resolved to let this poor outcast remain in your house, Mrs. Trawl?" he asked.

"Yes, sir, my good man thinks as I do, that we ought," answered mother, positively.

Dr. Rolt returned in the afternoon, accompanied by a gentleman wearing a broad-brimmed hat and a straight-cut broadcloth coat of sombre hue. He smiled pleasantly at mother as he took the seat she offered him without doffing his hat, and beckoning to Mary and me, put his hands on our heads, while he looked into our faces and smiled as he had done to mother.

"I have brought Mr. Silas Gray, a member of the Society of Friends, knowing that I should have your leave, Mrs. Trawl, as he desires to see the poor girl you have taken care of," said Dr. Rolt.

"Verily, sister, thou hast acted the part of the Good Samaritan towards the hapless one of whom friend Rolt has told me, and I would endeavour to minister to her spiritual necessities, the which I fear are great indeed; also with thy leave I will help thee in supplying such creature comforts as she may need," said Mr. Gray.

"Thank you kindly, sir," answered mother. "I couldn't say much on the matter of religion, except to tell her that God cares for her as well as He does for the richest lady in the land, and will pardon her sins if she will but turn to Him through Christ; and as to food, kickshaws fit for sick folk are not much in my way, still I'll——"

"Thou knowest the very gist of the matter, sister," observed Mr. Gray, interrupting her; "but time is precious. I'll go in with friend Rolt and speak to the wandering child." Saying this, Mr. Gray accompanied the doctor into the stranger's room.

He, after this, came again and again—never empty-handed—oftener indeed than the doctor, whose skill failed, as he feared it would, to arrest the poor girl's malady, while Mr. Gray's ministrations were successful in giving her the happy assurance that "though her sins were as scarlet, she had become white as snow," so he assured mother.

"Praise the Lord," was her reply.

So the young stranger died—her name, her history, unknown. Mr. Gray paid the expenses of her funeral, and frequently after that came to see us, to inquire, as he said, how we were getting on.

We had not heard from brother Jack since he went aboard the *Lapwing*. Mother thought that he might have got some one to write for him, though he was no great hand with a pen himself. All we knew was that the brig had gone out to the East Indies, which being a long way off would have accounted for our not often getting letters from him; but just one father hoped he would have contrived to send after he had been a year away; now nearly three years had passed since then. Had the *Lapwing* been fitted out at Portsmouth, we should have got news of him from others, but as none of her crew hailed from our town, there was no one to whom we could go to ask about him. Father had taken lately to talk much about Jack, and sometimes regretted that he had let him go away.

"You acted for the best, and so don't be blaming yourself," observed mother, trying to console him. "There's One aloft looking after him better than we can, and He'll bring our boy back to us if He thinks fit."

Mary and I little knew all the trials father and mother had to go through. Mother's trade was bad, and father was often out all day without bringing a shilling home. Younger men with more gaily-painted boats—he would not acknowledge that they were better—got fares when he could not manage to pick up one. Sometimes also he was laid up with the rheumatics, and was unable to go afloat. One day, while thus suffering, mother fetched Dr. Rolt to see him. Father begged the doctor to get him well as soon as he could, seeing that he wanted to be out in the wherry to gain his livelihood.

"All in good time, my man," answered the doctor. "You'll be about again in a few days, never fear. By-the-bye, I saw our friend Mr. Gray lately, Mrs. Trawl, and he was inquiring for you. He would have come to see your husband had he known that he was ill, but he went away to London yesterday, and may, I fear, be absent for some time. Many will miss him should he be long away."

Sooner than father expected he was about again. I had gone down with father and mother to the Hard, mother to board a ship which had just come in, and father to look out for a fare, while Mary remained at home with Nancy. It was blowing pretty fresh, and there was a good deal of sea running outside, though in the harbour the water was not rough enough to prevent mother from going off. While she was waiting for old Tom Swatridge, who had been with grandmother and her for years to bring along her baskets of vegetables from the market, a gentleman came hurrying down the Hard, and seeing father getting the wherry ready, said,

"I want you to put me aboard my ship, my man. She's lying out at Spithead; we must be off at once."

"It's blowing uncommon fresh, sir," said father. "I don't know how you'll like it when we get outside; still there's not a wherry in the harbour that will take you aboard drier than mine, though there's some risk, sir, you'll understand."

"Will a couple of guineas tempt you?" asked the stranger, thinking that father was doubting about the payment he was to receive.

"I'll take you, sir," answered father. "Step aboard."

I was already in the boat, thinking that I was to go, and was much disappointed when father said,

"I am not going to take you, Peter, for your mother wants you to help her; but just run up and tell Ned Dore I want him. He's standing by the sentry-box."

As I always did as father bade me, I ran up and called Ned, who at once came rolling along down the Hard, glad of a job. When he heard what he was wanted for he stepped aboard.

"I hope to be back in a couple of hours, or three at furthest, Polly," father sang out to mother, as he shoved off the wherry. "Good-bye, lass, and see that Peter makes himself useful."

Mother waved her hand.

"Though two guineas are not to be picked up every day, I would as lief he had stayed in the harbour this blowing weather," she said to herself more than to me, as on seeing old Tom coming we stepped into her boat.

When father first went to sea, Tom Swatridge had been

his shipmate, and had done him many a kind turn which he had never forgotten. Old Tom had lost a leg at Trafalgar, of which battle he was fond of talking. He might have borne up for Greenwich, but he preferred his liberty, though he had to work for his daily bread, and, I am obliged to say, for his daily quantum of rum, which always kept his pockets empty. He had plenty of intelligence, but he could neither read nor write, and that, with his love of grog, had prevented him from getting on in life as well as his many good qualities would otherwise have enabled him to do. He was a tall gaunt man, with iron-grey hair, and a countenance wrinkled, battered, and bronzed by wind and weather.

When he first came ashore he was almost as sober a man as father, and having plenty of prize-money he managed to purchase a small dwelling for himself, which I shall have by-and-by to describe. Old Tom taking the oars, we pulled aboard the *Dartmouth*, forty-two gun frigate, just come in from the Mediterranean. Several of the men had been shipmates with father, and all those belonging to Portsmouth knew mother. They were very glad to see her, and she had to answer questions of all sorts about their friends on shore. It is the business of a bumboat woman to know everything going forward, what ships are likely to be commissioned, the characters of the captains and officers, when they are to sail, and where they are going to. Among so many friends mother drove a brisker trade than usual, and when the men heard that I was Jack Trawl's son they gave me many a bright shilling and sixpence, and kind pats on the head with their broad palms. " He's a chip of the old block, no doubt about that, missus," cried one. " He'll make a smart young topman one of these days," said another. Several gave her commissions to execute, and many sent messages to friends on shore. Altogether, when she left the frigate she was in better spirits than she had been for a long time.

Scarcely had we shoved off, however, when down came the rain in torrents, well-nigh wetting us through.

"It's blowing plaguey hard, missus," observed old Tom, as he tugged away at the oars, I helping him while mother steered. "I hope as how we shall find your good man safe ashore when we gets in."

On reaching the Hard the wherry was not to be seen. After old Tom had made fast the boat, wet as she was mother waited and waited in the hopes that father would come in. Old Tom remained also. He seemed more than usually anxious. We all stood with our hands shielding our eyes as we looked down the harbour to try and make out the wherry, but the driving rain greatly limited our view.

"Hast seen anything of Jack Trawl's wherry?" asked old Tom over and over again of the men in the different boats, as they came in under their mizens and foresails. The same answer was returned by all.

"Maybe he got a fare at Spithead for Gosport and will be coming across soon, or he's gone ashore at the Point with some one's luggage," observed old Tom, trying to keep up mother's spirits; but that was a hard matter to do, for the wind blew stronger and stronger. A few vessels could be seen, under close-reefed canvas, running up the harbour for shelter, but we could nowhere perceive a single boat under sail. Still old Tom continued to suggest all sorts of reasons why father had not come back. Perhaps he had been detained on board the ship at Spithead to which he took the gentleman, and seeing the heavy weather coming on would remain till it moderated. Mother clung to this notion when hour after hour went by and she had given up all expectation of seeing father that evening. Still she could not tear herself from the Hard. Suddenly she remembered me.

"You must be getting wet, Peter," she said "Run home,

my child, and tell Nancy to give you your tea and then to get supper ready. Father and I will be coming soon, I hope."

I lingered, unwilling to leave her.

"Won't you come yourself, mother?" I asked.

"I'll wait a bit longer," she answered. "Go, Peter, go; do as I bid you."

"You'd better go home with Peter, missus," said old Tom. "You'll be getting the rheumatics, I'm afraid. I'll stay and look out for your good man."

I had never seen mother look as she did then, when she turned her face for a moment to reply to the old man. She was as pale as death; her voice sounded hoarse and hollow.

"I can't go just yet, Tom," she said.

I did not hear more, as, according to her bidding, I set off to run home. I found Mary and Nancy wondering what had kept mother so long.

"Can anything have happened to father?" exclaimed Mary, when I told her that mother was waiting for him.

"He has been a long time coming back from Spithead, and it's blowing fearfully hard," I answered.

I saw Nancy clasp her hands and look upwards with an expression of alarm on her countenance which frightened me. Her father and brother had been lost some years before, crossing in a wherry from Ryde, and her widowed mother had found it a hard matter to keep herself and her children out of the workhouse. She said nothing, however, to Mary and me, but I heard her sighing and whispering to herself, "What will poor missus do? What will poor missus do?" She gave Mary and me our suppers, and then persuaded us to go to bed. I was glad to do so to get off my wet clothes, which she hung up to dry, but I could not go to sleep for thinking what had happened to father.

At length mother came in alone. She sat down on

chair without speaking, and her hands dropped by her side. I could watch her as I looked out from the small closet in which my bunk was placed. Even since I had left her her countenance had become fearfully pale and haggard. She shivered all over several times, but did not move from her seat.

"Won't you get those wet duds of yours off, missus, and have some hot tea and supper?" asked Nancy, who had been preparing it.

Mother made no reply.

"Don't take on so, missus," said Nancy, coming up to her and putting her hand affectionately on her shoulder.

"Bless me, you're as wet as muck. I've put Peter and Mary to bed, and you must just go too, or you'll be having the rheumatics and I don't know what. Do go, missus, now do go."

In vain Nancy pleaded, and was still endeavouring to persuade mother to take off her wet garments, when I at last fell asleep. When I awoke in the morning I saw Nancy alone bustling about the room. I soon jumped into my clothes. My first question was for father.

"He's not yet come back, Peter," she answered. "But maybe he will before long, for the wind has fallen, and if he put into Ryde he'd have waited till now to come across."

"Where's mother?" I next asked, not seeing her.

"Hush, Peter, don't speak loud," she said in a low tone. "She's been in a sad taking all night, but she's quiet now, and we mustn't waken her."

On hearing this I crept about as silent as a mouse till Mary got up, and then we sat looking at each other without speaking a word, wondering what was going to happen, while Nancy lit the fire and got breakfast ready. At last we heard mother call to Nancy to come to her, not knowing that Mary and I were on foot.

"I must get up and go and look after my good man," she cried out, in a voice strangely unlike her own. "Just help me, Nancy, will you? What can have come over me? I feel very curious."

She tried to rise, but could not, and after making several attempts, sank back on her bed with a groan. Mary and I now ran into her room.

"What's the matter, mother dear?" asked Mary, in a tone of alarm.

She gazed at us strangely, and groaned again.

"Missus is, I fear, taken very bad," said Nancy. "I must run for a doctor, or she'll be getting worse. I'm sure I don't know what to do; I wish I did. Oh dear! oh dear!"

"Let me go," I said, eagerly. "I know where he lives, and you stay and take care of mother. I can run faster than you can in and out among the people in the streets."

Nancy agreed, and I set off.

CHAPTER III.

A SAD CHAPTER IN MY LIFE.

AS I ran for the doctor I felt that I was engaged in a matter of life and death, for I had never seen mother ill before. In my anxiety for her I almost forgot all about father. On I rushed, dodging in and out among the workmen going to their daily toil—there were not many other persons out at that early hour. Two or three times I heard the cry of "Stop thief!" uttered by some small urchins for mischief's sake, and once an old watchman, who had overslept himself in his box, suddenly starting out attempted to seize hold of me, fancying that he was about to capture a burglar, but I slipped away, leaving him sprawling in the dust and attempting to spring his rattle, and I ran on at redoubled speed, soon getting out of his sight round a corner. At last I reached Dr. Rolt's house and rang the surgery bell as hard as I could pull. It was some time before the door was opened by a sleepy maid-servant, who had evidently just hurried on her clothes.

"Mother wants the doctor very badly," I exclaimed. "Ask him, please, to come at once."

"The doctor can't come. He's away from home, in London," answered the girl. "You'd better run on to Dr. Hunt's. Maybe he'll attend on your mother."

I asked where Dr. Hunt lived. She told me. His house

was some way off, but I found it at last. Again I had to wait for the door to be opened, when, greatly to my disappointment, the maid told me that Dr. Hunt had been out all night and might not be at home for an hour or more.

"Oh dear! Oh dear! who then can I get to see poor mother?" I cried out, bursting into tears.

"There's Mr. Jones, the apothecary, at the end of the next street. He'll go to your mother, no doubt," said the maid. "Don't cry, my boy. Run on now; the first turning to the left. You'll see the red and green globes in his window."

Without stopping to hear more, off I set again. Mr. Jones was in his dispensary, giving directions to his assistant. I told him my errand.

"I'll go presently," he answered. "What's the number?"

Our house had no number, and I could not manage to explain its position clearly enough for his comprehension.

"Then I'll stay, sir, and show you the way," I said.

"Wait a bit, and I'll be ready," he replied.

He kept me waiting, however, a cruel long time, it seemed to me. At last he appeared with his silver-mounted cane in hand, and bade me go on.

"Stop! stop, boy. I can't move at that rate," he cried out, before we had got far. He was a short stout man, with a bald head and grey hair. I had to restrain my eagerness, and walked slower till we reached our house. Nancy was looking out at the door for me, wondering I had not returned.

"How is mother?" I asked.

"Very bad, Peter; very bad indeed, I'm afeard," she answered, almost ready to cry. Then seeing Mr. Jones stop with me, she continued, "Come in, doctor, come in. You'll try and cure missus, won't you?"

"I'll certainly do my best when I know what is the

matter with her," answered Mr. Jones, as he followed Nancy into the house.

Mary was with mother. I stole in after the doctor, anxious to hear what he would say about her. He made no remark in her presence, however, but when he came out of the room he observed in a low voice to Nancy,

"You must keep her quiet. Let there be nothing done to agitate her, tell her husband when he comes in. I'll send some medicine, and pay her another visit in the afternoon."

"But it's about her husband that she's grieving, sir," said Nancy. "He went away to Spithead yesterday morning and has never come back."

"Ah, that's bad," replied Mr. Jones. "However, perhaps he will appear before long. If he doesn't, it can't be helped. You must give her the medicines, at all events. I'll write the directions clearly for you."

Poor Nancy had to confess that she could not read. The doctor then tried to impress upon her how and when she was to give the physic.

"You'll remember, and there can be no mistake," he added, as he hurried off.

I fancied that everything now depended on the arrival of the apothecary's stuff, and kept running to the door looking out for the boy who was to bring it. He seemed very long coming. I had gone half-a-dozen times when I caught sight, as I turned my eyes the other way thinking he might have passed by, of Tom Swatridge stumping slowly up the street. He stopped when he saw me, and beckoned. He looked very downcast. I observed that he had a straw hat in his hand, and I knew that it was father's.

"How is mother?" he asked, when I got up to him.

"Very bad," I answered, looking at the hat, but afraid to ask questions.

"The news I bring will make her worse, I'm afeard," he said, in a husky voice, as he took my hand. "Peter, you had as good a father as ever lived, but you haven't got one now. A cutter just come in picked up this hat off St. Helen's, and afterwards an oar and a sprit which both belonged to the wherry. I went out the first thing this morning to the ship your father was to put the gentleman aboard. He had got alongside all right, for I saw the gentleman himself, and he told me that he had watched the wherry after she shoved off till he lost sight of her in a heavy squall of rain. When it cleared off she was nowhere to be seen. So, Peter, my poor boy, there's no hope, I'm afeard, and we shall never see my old messmate or Ned Dore again."

"Oh, Tom! Tom! You don't mean to say that father's gone!" I cried out.

"I'd sooner have lost another leg than have to say it," answered the old man. "But it must be said notwithstanding, and now how are we to tell mother?"

I could not answer, but kept repeating to myself, "Gone! gone! father gone!" as Tom led me on to the house. We met the boy with the physic at the door.

"Let Nancy give her the stuff first," said the old man, thoughtfully; "maybe it will give her strength, and help her to bear the bad news."

Nancy took in the bottles, while Tom and I remained outside. After some time she came out and told Tom that mother wanted to see him. He went in, shaking all over so much that I thought he would have fallen. I followed, when, seeing Mary, I threw my arms round her neck and burst into tears. She guessed what had happened even before I told her. We sat down, holding each other's hands and crying together, while Tom went in to see mother. What he said I do not know, though I am sure he tried to break the news to her as gently as he could. When she saw the hat, which he still held in his hand, she knew that father was lost. She did not go off into fits, as Tom afterwards told me he thought she would, but remained terribly calm, and just bade him describe to her all that he knew.

"I mustn't give in," she said at length, "I have the children to look after, for if I was to go what would become of them?"

"While I'm able to work they shan't want, missus," answered Tom, firmly.

"I know what you'd wish to do, Tom; but there's one thing won't let you: that thing is liquor," said mother.

"Then I'll never touch another drop as long as I live, missus!" exclaimed Tom. "May God help me!"

"He will help you, Tom, if you ask Him," said mother; "and I hope that, whether I live or die, you'll keep to that resolution."

I believe that conversation with Tom did mother much good; it took her off from thinking of father. She was still, however, very ill, and had to keep her bed. The doctor came again and again; generally twice a day. He of course had to be paid, and a good deal too. There was nothing coming in, and poor mother became more and more anxious to get out and attend to her business. The doctor warned her that she would go at great risk—indeed, that she was not fit to leave her bed. "She had no money left to pay for food and rent and the doctor's bill," she answered, and go she must. Though she had no money, she had, however, ample credit to stock her bumboat.

Very unwillingly Nancy assisted her to dress. Out she would go, taking me with her to lay in a stock of the articles she required. People remarked on her changed looks, and some did not even know her. She acknowledged that she was very tired when we got home, but declared that she should be the better for going on the water.

The next morning old Tom had his boat ready. "I do wish, missus, that you'd stayed at home a few days longer," he remarked, looking at her. "Howsomedever, as you've come, I hopes you'll just take what I say kindly, and not be from home longer than you can help. There's dirty weather coming up from the south-west."

Tom was right. We had two ships to visit. Before we got alongside the second down came the rain. But mother would go on, and consequently got wet through. Tom was very unhappy, but she said that she had done a good trade, and that no harm would come of it. Unhappily she was mistaken; that night she was taken very ill—worse than before. I fetched the doctor; he shook his head and said he wouldn't answer for what might happen. Faithful Nancy was half distracted. Poor mother got worse and worse. At last one day she beckoned with her pale hand to Mary and me to come to her bedside.

"I know that I am going to be taken from you, my dears," she said, in a low voice, for she could not speak loud. "I want you to promise me to be true to each other, to do your duty in God's sight, and always to ask Him to help you."

"I do, mother—I do promise," said Mary, the tears dropping from her eyes.

She could scarcely speak for sobbing.

I promise, too, mother, that I do!" I exclaimed, in a firmer voice; and I sincerely intended to fulfil my promise.

Mother was holding our hands in hers. She said much more to us, anxious to give us all the advice in her power. Nancy came in with her medicine, after which she rallied, and bade us go to bed.

A Sad Chapter in my Life.

I was awakened early in the morning by hearing Nancy cry out,

"Run for the doctor, Peter! run for the doctor! Missus is taken worse."

I slipped into my clothes, and was off like a shot, without asking a question, or even looking into mother's room.

I rang the night-bell, for no one was up. At last the servant opened the door, and said she would call her master.

Mr. Jones soon appeared. He had been paid regularly, and when he saw me he was the more ready to come. Eager as I was to get back, I did not like to run ahead of him; and, to do him justice, he exerted himself to walk as fast as his breath would allow him.

He asked me several questions; then I told him that mother had been again out bumming.

"Bad—very bad. I told her not to go. A relapse is a serious matter," he remarked, panting and puffing between his sentences. "However, we must try what can be done."

Mary met us at the door.

"Mother has been breathing very hard since you went, Peter," she said, "but she is quite quiet now."

The doctor's face looked very serious when he heard this. He hurried into the room.

"I thought so," I heard him remark to Nancy. "I could have done nothing if you had sent for me hours ago. The woman is dead."

"Oh, dear! oh, dear! what shall I do?" cried Nancy, sobbing bitterly.

"The sooner you let any friends the children may have know what has happened the better, and then send for the undertaker," answered Mr. Jones. "The boy is sharp— he'll run your errands. I can do no more than certify the cause of death."

He hurried away without bestowing a look at Mary and me, as we stood holding each other's hands, unable as yet to realise the fact that we were orphans. He had so many poor patients that he could not afford, I suppose, to exercise his compassionate feelings. Even when Nancy afterwards took us in to see mother's body, I would scarcely believe that she herself had been taken from us.

I will not stop to speak of Mary's and my grief.

At last Nancy, her eyes red with crying, sat down, with her hands pressed against her head, to consider what was to be done.

"Why, I ought to have sent for him at once!" she suddenly exclaimed. "Peter, run and find Tom Swatridge, and tell him that poor missus has gone."

I needed no second bidding, and, thank'ul to have something to do, I started away.

On reaching the Hard, where I expected to find old Tom, I heard from some of the watermen that he had gone off with a fare to Gosport, so I had to wait for his return. Many of the men standing about asked me after mother, and seemed very sorry to hear of her death. I saw them talking earnestly together while I waited for Tom. Others joined them, and then went away, so that the news soon spread about our part of the town. I had to wait a long time, till old Tom came back with several persons in his boat. He pocketed their fares, touching his hat to each before he took any notice of me.

"What cheer, Peter? How's the missus?" he asked, stepping on shore and dropping the kedge to make fast his boat. "I feared she wouldn't be up to bumming to-day."

"Mother's dead," I answered.

"Dead! the missus dead!" he exclaimed, clapping his hand to his brow, and looking fixedly at me. "The Lord have mercy on us!"

A Sad Chapter in my Life. 31

"Nancy wants you, Tom," I said.

"I'm coming, Peter, I'm coming. I said I'd be a father to you and Mary, and I will, please God," he replied, recovering himself.

He took my hand, and stumped away towards our house.

"Dick Porter, look after my boat, will ye, till I comes back?" he said to one of the men on the Hard as we hurried by.

"Ay, ay," was the cheerful answer—for Dick knew where old Tom was going.

Not a word did the old man speak all the way. When we got to the house, what was my astonishment to find a number of people in the sitting-room, one of whom, with note-book in hand, was making an inventory of the furniture! Mary was sitting in a corner crying, and Nancy was looking as if she had a mind to try and turn them all out. As soon as Mary saw me she jumped up and took my hand.

"What's all this about?" exclaimed old Tom, in an indignant tone. "You might have stopped, whatever right you may have here, till the dead woman was carried to her grave, I'm thinking."

"And others had carried off the goods," answered the man with the note-book. "We are only acting according to law. Mrs. Trawl has run into debt on all sides, and when the goods are sold there won't be five shillings in the pound to pay them, that I can see, so her children must take the consequences. There's the workhouse for them."

"The work'us, do ye say? Mrs. Trawl's children sent to the work'us!" exclaimed old Tom, and he rapped out an expression which I need not repeat. "Not while this here hand can pull an oar and I've a shiner in my pocket. If you've got the law on your side, do as the law lets you. But all I can say is, that it's got no bowels of compassion in it, to allow the orphans to be turned out of house and home, and the breath scarce out of their mother's body. Nancy, do you pack up the children's clothes, and any school-books or play-things you can find, and then come along to my house. The law can't touch them, I suppose."

"What is that drunken old Swatridge talking about?" said one of the broker's men.

Tom heard him.

"Such I may have been, but I'll be no longer 'drunken old Swatridge' while I have these children to look after," he exclaimed; and giving one hand to Mary and the other to me, he led us out of the house.

CHAPTER IV.

A FEARFUL CATASTROPHE.

LEAVING Nancy, who could well hold her own, to battle with the broker's men, Tom, holding Mary by the hand, and I walked on till we came to his house, which I knew well, having often been there to call him. It consisted of two small rooms—a parlour, and little inner bedchamber, and was better furnished than might have been expected; yet old Tom had at one time made a good deal of money, and had expended a portion of it in fitting up his dwelling. Had he always been sober he would now have been comfortably off.

"Stay here, my dears, while I go out for a bit," he said, bidding us sit down on an old sea-chest on one side of the fireplace. "I haven't got much to amuse you, but here's the little craft I cut out for you, Peter, and you can go on rigging her as I've been doing. No matter if you don't do it all ship-shape. And here, Mary, is the stuff for the sails; I've shaped them, you see, and if you will hem them you'll help us finely to get the craft ready for sea."

Mary gladly undertook the task allotted to her, and even smiled as Tom handed out a huge housewife full of needles and thread and buttons, and odds and ends of all sorts.

"My thimble won't suit your finger, I've a notion, my little maid," he observed; "but I dare say you've got one of your own in your pocket. Feel for it, will you?"

Mary produced a thimble, six of which would have fitted into Tom's.

"Ay, I thought so," he said, and seeing us both busily employed, he hurried out of the house. He soon, however, returned, bringing a couple of plum buns for Mary, and some bread and cheese for me, with a small jug of milk. "There, my dears, that'll stay your hunger till Nancy comes to cook some supper for you, and to put things to rights," he said, as he placed them before us. "Good-bye. I'll be back again as soon as I can," and off he went once more.

Mary and I, having eaten the provisions he brought in, worked away diligently, thankful to have some employment to occupy our attention. But she stopped every now and then, when her eyes were too full of tears to allow her to see her needle, and sobbed as if her dear heart would break. Then on she went again, sewing as fast as she could, anxious to please old Tom by showing him how much she had done. At length Nancy arrived with a big bundle on her back. "I've brought away all I could," she said, as she deposited her load on the floor. "I'd a hard job to get them, and shouldn't at all, if Tom Swatridge and two other men hadn't come in and said they'd be answerable if everything wasn't all square. He and they were ordering all about the funeral, and I've got two women to stay with the missus till she's put all comfortable into her coffin. Alack! alack! that I should have to talk about her coffin!" Nancy's feelings overcame her. On recovering, she, without loss of time, began to busy herself with household duties—lighted the fire, put the kettle on to boil, and made up old Tom's bed with some fresh sheets which she had brought. "You and I are to sleep here, Mary," she said, "and Peter is to have a shakedown in the sitting-room."

"And where is Tom going to put up himself?" I asked.

"That's what he didn't say, but I fancy he's going to stay

at night with an old chum who has a room near here. He said his place isn't big enough for us all, and so he'd made up his mind to turn out."

Such I found to be the case. Nothing would persuade our friend to sleep in his own house, for fear of crowding us. He and several other watermen, old shipmates, and friends of father's, had agreed to defray the expenses of mother's funeral, for otherwise she would have been carried to a pauper's grave. Her furniture and all the property she had possessed were not sufficient to pay her debts contracted during her illness, in spite of all her exertions. We, too, had not Tom taken charge of us, should have been sent to the workhouse, and Nancy would have been turned out into the world to seek her fortune, for her mother was dead, and she had no other relatives. She did talk of trying to get into service, which meant becoming a drudge in a small tradesman's family, that she might help us with her wages; but she could not bring herself to leave Mary; and Tom, indeed, said she must stay to look after her. As father had had no funeral, his old friends wished to show all the respect in their power to his widow, and a score or more attended, some carrying the coffin, and others walking two and two behind, with bits of black crape round their hats and arms, while Mary and I, and Nancy and Tom, followed as chief mourners all the way to Kingston Cemetery. Nancy, with the help of a friend, a poor seamstress, had managed to make a black frock for Mary and a dress for herself, out of mother's gown, I suspect. They were not very scientifically cut, but she had sat up all night stitching at them, which showed her affection and her desire to do what she considered proper.

Some weeks had passed since mother's death, and we were getting accustomed to our mode of life. Tom sent Mary to a school near at hand every morning, and she used to impart the knowledge she obtained to me in the evening, including sometimes even sewing.

During the time Mary was at school Nancy went out charing, or tending the neighbours' children, or doing any other odd jobs of which she was capable, thus gaining enough to support herself, for she declared that she could not be beholden to the old man for her daily food. I always went out with Tom in his boat, and I was now big enough to make myself very useful. He used to make me take the helm when we were sailing, and by patiently explaining how the wind acted on the canvas, and showing me the reason of every manœuvre, soon taught me to manage a boat as well as any man could do, so that when the wind was light I could go out by myself without the slightest fear.

"You'll do, Peter; you'll do," said the old man, approvingly, when one day I had taken the boat out to Spithead alongside a vessel and back, he sitting on a thwart with his arms folded, and not touching a rope, though he occasionally peered under the foot of the foresail to see that I was steering right, and used the boathook when we were going alongside the vessel, and shoving off, which I should have had to do if he had been steering. "You'll now be able to gain your living, boy, and support Mary till she's old enough to go out to service, if I'm taken from you, and that's what I've been aiming at."

Often when going along the Hard a friend would ask him to step into one of the many publics facing it to take a glass of spirits or beer. "No thank ye, mate," he would reply; "if I get the taste of one I shall be wanting another, and I shouldn't be happy if I didn't treat you in return, and I've got something else to do with my money instead of spending it on liquor."

I never saw him angry except when hard pressed by an ill-judging friend to step into a public-house.

A Fearful Catastrophe.

"Would you like to see Jack Trawl's son in a ragged shirt, without shoes to his feet, and his daughter a beggar-girl, or something worse? Then don't be asking me, mate, to take a drop of the poisonous stuff. I know what I used to be, and I know what I should be again if I was to listen to you!" he exclaimed. "Stand out of my way, now! stand out of my way! Come along, Peter," and, grasping my hand with a gripe which made my fingers crack, he stumped along the Hard as fast as he could move his timber toe.

It was a pleasure on getting home to find Mary looking bright and cheerful, with her work or books before her, and Nancy busy preparing supper. The old man and I always took our dinner with us—generally a loaf of bread, with a piece of cheese or bacon or fried fish, and sometimes Irish stew in a basin, done up in a cloth, and a stone bottle of water. I remember saying that I was born with a wooden spoon in my mouth, but when I come to reflect what excellent parents I had, and what true friends I found in Tom Swatridge and Nancy, I may say that, after all, it must have been of silver, though perhaps not quite so polished as those found in the mouths of some infants.

Another change in my life was about to occur. We had taken off a gentleman from Gosport. From his way of speaking, we found that he was a foreigner, and he told us that he wanted to be put on board a foreign ship lying at Spithead.

"Is dere any danger?" he asked, looking out across the Channel, and thinking what a long distance he had to go.

"Not a bit, sir," answered Tom, for the water was as smooth as a mill-pond. There was a light air from the southward, and there was not a cloud in the sky. "We might cross the Channel to France for that matter, with weather like this."

"Oh no, no! I only want to get to dat sheep out dere!"

cried the foreigner, fancying that we might carry him across against his will.

"Certainly, mounseer; we'll put you aboard in a jiffy as soon as we gets a breeze to help us along," said Tom.

We pulled round Blockhouse Point, along shore, till we came off Fort Monkton, when opening Stokes Bay, the wind hauling a little to the westward, we made sail and stood for Spithead. A number of vessels were brought up there, and at the Mother-bank, off Ryde, among them a few men-of-war, but mostly merchantmen, outward bound, or lately come in waiting for orders. It was difficult as yet to distinguish the craft the foreigner wanted to be put aboard.

"It won't matter if we have to dodge about a little to find her, mounseer, for one thing's certain: we couldn't have a finer day for a sail," observed old Tom, as we glided smoothly over the blue water, shining brightly in the rays of the unclouded sun.

He gave me the helm while he looked out for the foreign ship.

"That's her, I've a notion," he said at length, pointing to a deep-waisted craft with a raised poop and forecastle, and with much greater beam than our own wall-sided merchantmen. "Keep her away a bit, Peter. Steady! That will do."

The tide was running to the westward, so that we were some time getting up to the ship.

"You'll be aboard presently, if that is your ship, as I suppose, mounseer," said Tom.

"Yes, yes; dat is my sheep," answered the foreigner, fumbling in his pockets, I fancied, for his purse.

He uttered an exclamation of annoyance. "Ma monie gone! Some villain take it, no doubt. You come aboard de sheep, and I vill give it you, my friend," he said. "One half guinea is de charge, eh? I have also letter to write; you take it and I vill give two shillings more."

"All right, mounseer, I will wait your pleasure, and promise to post your letter," answered Tom.

As there were several boats alongside, he told me to keep under weigh till he should hail me to come for him, and as he was as active as any man, in spite of his wooden leg, taking the foreigner by the hand, he helped him up on deck. I then hauled the tacks aboard and stood off to a little distance. I waited and waited, watching the ship, and wondering why Tom was so long on board.

The wind at last began to drop, and afraid of being carried to leeward, I was on the point of running up alongside when I heard a fearful roaring thundering sound. A cloud of black smoke rose above the ship, followed by lurid flames, which burst out at all her ports; her tall masts were shot into the air, her deck was cast upwards, her sides were rent asunder; and shattered fragments of planks, and of timbers and spars, and blocks, and all sorts of articles from the hold, came flying round me. I instinctively steered away from the danger, and though huge pieces of burning wreck fell hissing into the water on either side, and far beyond where I was, none of any size touched the wherry. For a minute or more I was so confounded by the awful occurrence that I did not think of my old friend. I scarcely knew where I was or what I was doing. The moment I recovered my presence of mind I put the boat about, getting out an oar to help her along, and stood back towards the burning wreck, which appeared for a moment like a vast pyramid of flame rising above the surface, and then suddenly disappeared as the waters closed over the shattered hull.

I stood up, eagerly gazing towards the spot to ascertain if any human beings had survived the dreadful catastrophe, though it seemed to me impossible that a single person could have escaped. One boat alone was afloat with some people in her, but they were sitting on the thwarts or lying at the bottom, not attempting to exert themselves, all more or less injured. The other boats had been dragged down, as the ship sank. All about were shattered spars and pieces of the deck, and some way off the masts with the yards still fast to them. Here and there was a body floating with the head or a limb torn off. One man was swimming, and I saw another in the distance clinging to a spar, but the former before I could get up to him sank without a cry, and I then steered for the man on the spar, hoping against hope that he might be old Tom. I shouted to him that he might know help was coming, but he did not answer. Meantime boats from the various ships lying around were approaching. I plied my oar with all my might, fearing that the man I have spoken of might let go his hold and be lost like the other before I could reach him. The nearer I got the more I feared that he was not Tom. His face was blackened, his clothes burnt and torn. Then I saw that he had two legs, and knew for certain that he was not my old friend. Still, of course, I continued on till I got up to the spar, when I tried to help the poor man into my boat, for he was too much hurt to get on board by himself. But my strength was insufficient for the purpose, and I was afraid of letting go lest he should sink and be lost. There was no small risk also of my being dragged overboard. Still, I did my best, but could get him no higher than the gunwale.

"Well done, youngster! Hold fast, and we'll help you," I heard a voice sing out, and presently a man-of-war's boat dashing up, two of her crew springing into the wherry quickly hauled the man on board.

"We must take him to our ship, lads, to let the surgeon attend to him," said the officer, a master's mate in charge of the man-of-war's boat.

The man was accordingly lifted into her. It appeared to

A Fearful Catastrophe.

me, from his sad condition, that the surgeon would be unable to do him any good.

"What, did you come out here all by yourself, youngster?" asked the officer.

"No, sir, I came out with old Tom Swatridge, who went on board the ship which blew up," I answered.

"Then I fear he must have been blown up with her, my lad," said the officer.

"I hope not, sir, I hope not," I cried out, my heart ready to break as I began to realise that such might be the case.

CHAPTER V.

A FRIEND LOST AND A FRIEND GAINED.

IT seemed but a moment since the ship blew up. I could not believe that old Tom had perished.

"Some people have been picked up out there, sir, I think," observed the coxswain to the officer, pointing as he spoke to several boats surrounding the one I had before remarked with the injured men in her. "Maybe the old man the lad speaks of is among them."

"Make the wherry fast astern, and we'll pull on and ascertain," said the officer.

"If he is not found, or if found is badly hurt, I'll get leave for a couple of hands to help you back with your boat to Portsmouth."

"I can take her back easily enough by myself if the wind holds as it does now; thank you all the same, sir," I answered.

I felt, indeed, that if my faithful friend really was lost, which I could scarcely yet believe, I would rather be alone; and I had no fear about managing the wherry single-handed.

As may be supposed, my anxiety became intense as we approached the boat. "Is old Tom Swatridge saved?" I shouted out.

No answer came.

"Tom! tell me, Tom, if you are there!" I again shouted.

A Friend Lost and a Friend Gained. 43

"Step aboard the boat and see if your friend is among the injured men," said the good-natured officer, assisting me to get alongside.

I eagerly scanned the blackened faces of the men sitting up, all of whom had been more or less scorched or burnt. A surgeon who had come off from one of the ships was attending to them. They were strangers to me. Two others lay dead in the bottom of the boat, but neither of them was old Tom. He was gone; of that I could no longer have a doubt.

With a sad heart I returned to the wherry. The other boats had not succeeded in saving any of the hapless crew. The ship had been loaded with arms and gunpowder, bound for South America, I heard some one say.

"Cheer up, my lad!" said the officer; "you must come aboard the *Lapwing*, and we'll then send you into Portsmouth, as we must have this poor fellow looked to by our surgeon before he is taken to the hospital."

The name of the *Lapwing* aroused me; she was the brig in which my brother Jack had gone to sea. For a moment I forgot my heavy loss with the thoughts that I might presently see dear Jack again. But it was only for a moment. As I sat steering the wherry towed by the man-of-war's boat my eyes filled with tears. What sad news I had to give to Jack! What would become of Mary and Nancy? For myself I did not care, as I knew that I could obtain employment at home, or could go to sea; but then I could not hope for a long time to come to make enough to support them. My chief feeling, however, was grief at the loss of my true-hearted old friend.

Soon after we got alongside the brig of war the master's mate told me to come up on deck, while one of the men took charge of the wherry. He at once led me aft to the commander, who questioned me as to how I came to be in the wherry by myself. I described to him all that had happened.

"You acted a brave part in trying to save the man from the ship which blew up. Indeed, had you not held on to him he would have been lost," he observed. "I must see that you are rewarded. What is your name?"

"Peter Trawl, sir," I answered, and, eager to see Jack, for whom I had been looking out since I got out of the boat, thinking that we should know each other, I added, "I have a brother, sir, who went to sea aboard this brig, and we have been looking out for him ever so long to come home. Please, sir, can I go and find him?"

The commander's countenance assumed a look of concern. "Poor fellow! I wish that he was on board for his sake and yours, my lad," he answered. "I cannot say positively that he is dead, but I have too much reason to believe that he is. While we were cruising among the islands of the East Indian Archipelago he formed one of a boat's crew which was, while at a distance from the ship, attacked by a large body of Malay pirates. When we got up we found only one man, mortally wounded, in the bottom of the boat, who before he died said that, to the best of his belief, the officer in charge and the rest of the men had been killed, as he had seen several dragged on board the proas, and then hacked to pieces and hove overboard.

"We chased and sank some of the pirate fleet, and made every possible search for the missing men, in case any of them should have escaped on shore, to which they were close at the time of the attack, but no traces of them could be discovered. I left an account of the occurrence with the vessel which relieved me on the station, and should any of the poor fellows have been found I should have been informed of it. It was my intention, as soon as I was paid off the *Lapwing*, to come down to Portsmouth to break the news to his father. Say this from me, and that I yet hope to see him shortly."

Commander Rogers seemed very sorry when I told him that father and mother were both dead. He asked me where I lived. I told him, as well as I could describe the house, forgetting that, too probably, Mary and I and Nancy would not be long allowed to remain there.

"When I commission another ship, would you like to go with me, my lad?" he asked.

"Very much, sir," I answered. "But I have a sister, and I couldn't go away with no one to take care of her; so I must not think of it now Tom Swatridge has gone. All the same, I thank you kindly, sir."

"Well, well, my lad; we will see what can be done," he said, and just then a midshipman came up to report that the boat was ready to carry the rescued man, with the surgeon, to the shore.

I found that the master's mate, Mr. Harvey, and one of the men were going in my boat, and of course I did not like to say that I could get into the harbour very well without them. I touched my hat to the commander, who gave me a kind nod—it would not have done for him, I suppose, to shake hands with a poor boy on his quarter-deck even if he had been so disposed—and then I hurried down the side.

I made sail, and took the helm just as if I had been by myself, Mr. Harvey sitting by my side, while the seaman had merely to rig out the mainsail with the boathook, as we were directly before the wind.

"You are in luck, youngster," observed Mr. Harvey; "though you have lost one friend you've gained another, for our commander always means what he says, and, depend on it, he'll not lose sight of you."

He seemed a very free-and-easy gentleman, and made me tell him all about myself, and how we had lost father and mother, and how Tom Swatridge had taken charge of Mary and me. His cheerful way of talking made me dwell less on my grief than I should have done had I sailed into the harbour all alone.

"I should like to go and see your little sister and the faithful Nancy," he said, "but I must return to the brig as soon as that poor man has been carried to the hospital, and I have several things to do on shore. Land me at the Point, you can find your way to the Hard by yourself, I've no doubt."

"The boat would find her way alone, sir, she's so accustomed to it," I answered.

We ran in among a number of wherries with people embarking from the Point or landing at it. The Point, it should be understood by those who do not know Portsmouth, is a hard shingly beach on the east side, at the mouth of the harbour, and there was at that time close to it an old round stone tower, from which an iron chain formerly extended across to Blockhouse Fort, on the Gosport side, to prevent vessels from coming in without leave.

"Here, my lad, is my fare," said Mr. Harvey, slipping half a guinea into my hand as he stepped on shore, followed by the seaman; "it will help to keep Nancy's pot boiling till you can look about you and find friends. They will appear, depend on it."

Before I could thank him he was away among the motley crowd of persons thronging the Point. I was thankful that no one asked me for old Tom, and, shoving out from among the other boats, I quickly ran on to the Hard.

When I landed the trial came. A waterman had gained an inkling of what had occurred from one of the crew of the *Lapwing's* boat, and I was soon surrounded by people asking questions of how it happened.

"I can't tell you more," I answered, at length breaking

from them. "Tom's gone, and brother Jack's gone, and I must go and look after poor Mary."

It was late by the time I reached home. Nancy had got supper ready on the table, and Mary had placed old Tom's chair for him in a snug corner by the fire. They saw that something was the matter, for I couldn't speak for a minute or more, not knowing how to break the news to them. At last I said, with a choking voice, pointing to the chair, "He'll never sit there more!"

Dear me, I thought Mary's and Nancy's hearts would break outright when they understood what had happened. It was evident how much they loved the rough old man—I loved him too, but in a different way, I suppose, for I could not ease my heart by crying; indeed I was thinking about what Mary and Nancy would do, and of brother Jack's loss. I did not like to tell Mary of that at first, but it had to come out, and, strange as it may seem, it made her think for the time less about what was to us by far the greater loss. Supper remained long untasted, but at last I felt that I must eat, and so I fell to, and after a time Nancy followed my example and made Mary take something.

Nancy then began to talk of what we must do to gain our living, and we sat up till late at night discussing our plans. There was the wherry, and I must get a mate, and I should do very well; then we had the house, for we never dreamed that we should not go on living in it, as we were sure Tom would have wished us to do. Nancy was very sanguine as to how she could manage. Her plain, pock-marked face beamed as she spoke of getting three times as much work as before. Short and awkward as was her figure, Nancy had an heroic soul. Mary must continue to attend school, and in time would be able to do something to help also.

We talked on till we almost fell asleep on our seats. The next morning we were up betimes. Nancy got out some black stuff we had worn for mother, a piece of which she fastened round my arm to show respect to old Tom's memory, and after breakfast I hurried out to try and find a mate, that I might lose no time in doing what I could with the wherry. I had thought of Jim Pulley, a stout strong lad, a year or two older than myself, who, though not very bright, was steady and honest, and I knew that I could trust him; his strength would supply my want of it for certain work we had to do. Jim was the first person I met on the Hard. I made my offer to him; he at once accepted it.

"To tell the truth, Peter, I was a-coming to say, that if thou hadst not got any one to go in the place of Tom Swatridge, I would help thee till thou art suited for nothing, or if thou wilt find me in bread and cheese I'll be thankful."

In a few minutes after this Jim and I were plying for hire in the harbour, and we had not long to wait before we got a fare. The first day we did very well, and I gave Jim a quarter of what we took, with which he was perfectly content.

"I wouldn't ask for more, Peter," he said, "for thou hast three mouths to feed, and I have only one."

The next few days we were equally successful; indeed I went home every evening in good spirits as to my prospects. I made enough for all expenses, and could lay by something for the repairs of the wherry.

Though Jim and I were mere boys, while the weather was fine people took our boat as willingly as they did those of grown men. Sometimes we got parties to go off to the *Victory*, at others across to the Victualling Yard, and occasionally up the harbour to Porchester Castle.

We worked early and late, and Jim or I was always on the look out for a fare.

When I got home at night I had generally a good account to give of the day's proceedings. Now and then I asked

A Friend Lost and a Friend Gained. 49

Jim in to take a cup of tea, and many a hearty laugh we had at what the ladies and gentlemen we had taken out had said and done. Seeing that we were but boys they fancied that they could talk before us in a way they wouldn't have thought of doing if we had been grown men.

It must not be supposed that we were able to save much, but still I put by something every week for the repairs of the boat. I had got enough to give her a fresh coat of paint, which she much wanted, and we agreed that we would haul her up on Saturday afternoon for the purpose, so that she would be ready for Monday.

We carried out our intentions, though it took every shilling I had put by, and we lost more than one fare by so doing. But the wherry looked so fresh and gay, that we hoped to make up for it the next week. Jim went to chapel on the Sunday with Mary and Nancy and me, and spent most of the day with us. He was so quiet and unassuming that we all liked him much. As we had put plenty of dryers in the paint, and the sun was hot on Sunday, by Monday forenoon we were able to ply as usual. We had taken a fare across to Gosport, when a person, whom we supposed to be a gentleman from his gay waistcoat and chains, and his top-boots, and hat stuck on one side, came down to the beach and told us to take him over to Portsea. We soon guessed by the way he talked that, in spite of his fine clothes, he was not a gentleman.

"I say, you fellow, do you happen to know whereabouts an old chap, one Tom Swatridge, lives?" he asked of Jim.

"He doesn't live anywhere; he's dead," answered Jim.

"Dead! Dead, do you say?" he exclaimed. "Who's got his property?"

"He had no property that I knows on," answered Jim; "except, maybe——"

"Oh yes, he had and if the old fellow had lived he

would have been the possessor of a good round sum; but, as I am his nephew, that will be mine, and everything else he left behind him, the lawyer, Master Six-and-eightpence, as I call him, tells me."

All this time I had not liked to say anything, but the last remark made me feel very uncomfortable. The speaker presently took a letter out of his pocket, and, reading it, said, "Ah! I see Mr. Gull is the man I've got to go to. Can you show me where Mr. Gull, the attorney, lives?" he asked of Jim; "he'll settle up this matter."

Jim made no answer, for we were getting near the shore, and had to keep out of the way of two craft coming up the harbour. We soon ran up to the Hard, when the man, stepping out, offered Jim a sixpence.

"A shilling's the fare, sir," said Jim, keeping back his hand.

"No, no, you young rascal! I know better; but I'll give you another sixpence if you will show me the way to Mr. Gull's."

"You may find it by yourself," answered Jim, indignantly, as he picked up the sixpence thrown to him by our fare, who walked off.

"Half a loaf is better than no bread, Peter, so it's as well not to lose the sixpence," said Jim, laughing. "But no gentleman would have offered less than a shilling. I wonder whether he really is old Tom's nephew?"

CHAPTER VI.

TURNED OUT OF HOUSE AND HOME.

WE had just landed the gaily-dressed individual who had announced himself the nephew of old Tom Swatridge. Thinking that he might possibly be the person he said he was, and not knowing what tricks he might play, I was intending to row home, when a gentleman, with two young ladies and a boy, who I knew by their dress to be Quakers, came down, wishing to take a row round the harbour, and afterwards to visit the Victualling Yard.

After we had pulled off some way, I asked if they would like to go aboard the *Victory*.

"No, thank thee, young friend, we take no pleasure in visiting scenes, afloat or on shore, where the blood of our fellow-creatures has been shed," answered the gentleman.

As he spoke I thought by his look and the tone of his voice that he must be Mr. Silas Gray, who had come to our house when the poor girl mother took in was dying, but I did not like to ask him. The young people called him father. At last he began to ask Jim and me questions, and how, young as we were, we came to have a boat by ourselves.

"I suppose thy father is ill on shore?" he said.

Then I told him how he was lost at Spithead, and mother had died, and old Tom had been blown up, and I had taken his wherry, seeing there was no one else to own her; and how Mary and Nancy and I lived on in his house.

"And art thou and this other lad brothers?" he inquired.

"No, sir; but Jim Pulley and I feel very much as if we were," I answered. "My name is Peter Trawl."

"And was thy mother a bumboat-woman, a true, honest soul, one of the excellent of the earth?" he asked.

"Ay, ay, sir! that was my mother," I said, my heart beating with pleasure to hear her so spoken of.

Then he told me that he was Mr. Silas Gray, and asked if I remembered the visits he used to pay to our house. Of course I did. The young ladies and his son joined in the conversation, and very pleasant it was to hear them talk.

We were out the whole afternoon, and it was quite late when we got back to Portsea. Mr. Gray said that he was going away the next morning with his family to London, but that when he returned he would pay Mary a visit, and hoped before the summer was over to take some more trips in my wherry. He paid us liberally, and he and the young people gave us kind smiles and nods as they stepped on shore.

While we were out I had not thought much about the fare we had brought across from Gosport in the morning, but now, recollecting what he had said, I hurried home, anxious to hear if he had found out the house. I had not to ask, for directly I appeared Nancy told me that while Mary was at school an impudent fellow had walked in and asked if old Tom Swatridge had once lived there, and when she said "Yes," had taken a note of everything, and then sat down and lighted his pipe, and told her to run out and bring him a jug of ale.

"'A likely thing, indeed!' I answered him," said Nancy; "'what! when I come back to find whatever is

worth taking carried off, or maybe the door locked and I unable to get in!' The fellow laughed when I said this—
—a nasty sort of a laugh it was—and said, 'Ay! just so.' I didn't know exactly what he meant, but presently he sang out, 'What! are you not gone yet, gal?' 'No, and I shan't,' I answered; 'and when Peter and Jim come in you'll pretty quickly find who has to go.' On this he thundered out, trying to frighten me, ' Do you know that I am old Tom Swatridge's nephew and heir-at-law, [I think that's what he called himself], 'and that this house and everything in it is mine, and the wherry, and any money the old chap left behind him? I'll soon prove that you and your brother are swindlers, and you'll be sent off to prison, let me tell you.' He took me for Mary, do you see, Peter; and I was not going to undeceive him? I felt somewhat nonplussed when he said this, but without answering I walked to the window, working with my needle as I was doing when he came in, and looked out as if I was expecting you and Jim to be coming. I would give him no food, nor even a drink of water; so at last he grew tired, and, saying I should see him again soon, swinging his cane and whistling, he walked away."

"What do you think, Peter? Can he really be old Tom's nephew?" asked Mary, when Nancy ceased speaking.

"One thing is certain, that if he proves himself to be so we shall be bound to turn out of this house, and to give up the wherry," I answered.

"Oh, Peter! what shall we do, then?" exclaimed Mary.

"The best we can, my sister," I said. "Perhaps the man may not be able to prove that he is what he calls himself. I have heard of impostors playing all sorts of tricks. We'll hope for the best. And now Nancy, let us have some supper."

Though I tried to keep up the spirits of Mary and Nancy, I felt very anxious, and could scarcely sleep for thinking on the subject. Whatever might happen for myself I did not care, but I was greatly troubled about what Mary and Nancy would do. I naturally thought of Commander Rogers, from whom all this time I had heard nothing, though he had promised to come and see after Mary and me. Mr. Gray had said that he was going away again, so that I could not obtain advice from him. "I have God to trust to, that's a comfort," I thought, and I soon dropped off to sleep.

The next morning I remained at home to a later hour than usual. Just as I was going out a man came to the door, who said he was sent by Lawyer Gull, and put a paper into my hand, which he told me was a something I could not exactly make out, to quit the house within twenty-four hours. "His client, the owner of the property, wishes not to act harshly, so refrains from taking stronger measures at present," said the clerk, who, having performed his task, went away. I stopped a few minutes to talk with Mary and Nancy. Mary said quietly that if we must go we must, and that we had better look out for cheap lodgings at once. Nancy was very indignant, and declared that we had no business to turn out for such a scamp as that. Old Tom had never spoken of having a nephew; she did not believe the fellow was his nephew, and certainly, if he was, Tom would not have left his property to him. She advised me, however, to go out and try to get advice from some one who knew more about the law than she did. I accordingly set off for the Hard, where I was sure to find several friends among the watermen. I had not got far when I met Jim Pulley, looking very disconsolate.

"What is the matter, Jim," I asked.

"We've lost the wherry!" he exclaimed, nearly blubbering. "Two big fellows came down, and, asking what boat she was, told me to step ashore: and when I said I wouldn't for them, or for any one but you, they took me, crop and heels, and trundled me out of her."

"That is only what I feared," I said. "I was coming down to find some one to advise us what to do."

"Then you couldn't ask any better man than Bob Fox, he's been in prison half a score of times for smuggling and such like, so he must know a mighty deal about law," he answered.

We soon found Bob Fox, who was considered an oracle on the Hard, and a number of men gathered round while he expressed his opinion.

"Why, you see, mates, it's just this," he said, extending one of his hands to enforce his remarks; "you must either give in or go to prison when they brings anything agen you, and that, maybe, is the cheapest in the end; or, as there's always a lawyer on t'other side, you must set another lawyer on to fight him, and that's what I'd advise to be done in this here case. Now I knows a chap, one Lawyer Chalk, who's as sharp as a needle, and if any man can help young Peter and his sister to keep what is their own he'll do it. I'm ready to come down with some shiners to pay him, for, you see, these lawyer folk don't argify for nothing, and I'm sure some on you who loves justice will help Jack and Polly Trawl's children; so round goes the hat."

Suiting the action to the word, Bob, taking off his tarpaulin, threw a handful of silver into it, and his example being followed by a number of other men, he grasped me by the hand, and set off forthwith to consult Lawyer Chalk.

We quickly reached his office. Mr. Chalk, a quiet-looking little man, with easy familiar manners, which won the confidence of his illiterate constituents, knowing Bob Fox well, received us graciously. His eyes glittered as he heard the money chink in Bob's pocket.

"It's all as clear as a pikestaff," he observed, when he heard what I had got to say. "They must prove first that this fellow who has turned up is Tom Swatridge's nephew; then that he is his heir-at-law, and finally that the house and boat belonged to the deceased. Now possession is nine-tenths of the law; you've got them, and you must hold them till the law turns you out."

"I couldn't, sir, if another has a better right to them than I have," I answered. "I lived on in the house and used the wherry because I was sure that old Tom would have wished me to do so, but then I didn't know that he had any relation to claim them."

"And you don't know that he has any relation now," said Mr. Chalk; "that has to be proved, my lad. The law requires proof; that's the beauty of the law. The man may swear till he's black in the face that he is the deceased's nephew, but if he has no proof he'll not gain his cause."

Bob Fox was highly delighted with our visit to the lawyer.

"I told you so, lad; I told you so!" he exclaimed, rubbing his hands; "t'other chap will find he has met his match. Bless you! old Chalk's as keen as a razor."

As I could not use the wherry, I went home feeling in much better spirits than before about our prospects. I was able even to cheer up Mary and Nancy. I told them that, by Lawyer Chalk's advice, we were not to quit the house, and that he would manage everything. No one appeared during the day. The next morning we had breakfast as usual, and as the time went by I was beginning to hope that we should be unmolested, when two rough-looking men came to the door, and, though Nancy sprang up to bar them out, in they walked. One of them then thrust a paper out to her, but she drew back her hand as if it had been a hot iron. The man again attempted to make her take it. "One of you must have it," he growled out.

"No, no! I couldn't make head or tail of it if I did," answered Nancy, still drawing back.

"Let me have it," I said, wishing to know what the men really came for.

"The sum total is, that you and the rest of you are to move away from this, and if you don't go sharp we're to turn you out!" exclaimed the bailiff, losing patience at the time I took to read the document. "It's an order of ejectment, you'll understand.

"Don't you mind what it is, Peter!" exclaimed Nancy; "Mr. Chalk said we was to stay here, and stay we will for all the scraps of paper in the world!" And Nancy, seating herself in a chair, folded her arms, and cast defiant looks at the officers of the law.

They were, however, up to the emergency. Before either she or I were aware of what they were about to do, they had secured her arms to the back of the chair, and then, lifting it and her up, carried her out of the house and deposited her in the street, in spite of the incautious attempt I made to effect a rescue. The moment I got outside the house one of the bailiffs, turning round, seized me in a vice-like grasp, and the other then entering, led out Mary, who saw that resistance was hopeless. He next walked back, took the key from the door, and, having locked it, released Nancy and re-entered the house with the chair. Before Nancy could follow him he had shut himself in, while his companion, letting me go with a shove which sent me staggering across the street, walked off, I concluded to tell the lawyer who sent him and his mate that they had got possession of the house.

Nancy was standing, with her fists clenched, too much astonished at the way she had been treated to speak. Mary was in tears, trembling all over.

"Oh, Peter, what are we to do?" she asked.

"I'll go to Lawyer Chalk and hear what he says," I answered. "If the house and boat ought to be ours, he'll get them back; if not, I can't say just now what we must do. Meantime do you and Nancy go to Widow Simmons's, and wait there. She was always a friend of mother's, and will be glad to help you."

Mary agreed, but Nancy, who at length found her tongue, declared that she wasn't going to lose sight of the house, and that she would stay where she was and watch and tell the folks who passed how we had been treated. As nothing I could say would induce her to move, I accompanied Mary to the widow's, where I left her, and hastened on to Mr. Chalk's. The lawyer made a long face when I told him how we had been treated.

"I told you that 'possession is nine-tenths of the law,' my lad, and now they are in and you are out," he answered. "It's a bad job—but we'll see what can be done. We must obtain at all events your clothes, and any other private property you may possess. Now go, my lad, and call upon me in a week or two; I shall see Bob Fox in the meantime."

Soon after leaving the lawyer's I met Jim Pulley. Having seen Nancy, he was fuming with indignation at our having been turned out of our home, and proposed trying to break into the house to regain possession, but I had sense enough to know that we must abide by the law, whichever way that decided. I found Nancy still keeping watch before the door, and vehemently appealing to all who would stop to listen to her. It was with some difficulty that I at length persuaded her to go with me to Mrs. Simmons's. The kind widow was willing to give us shelter, and as Mary had fortunately my savings in her pocket, we had sufficient to pay for our food for some days. The next morning Mary went as usual to school; Nancy left the house, saying that she was going to look for work, and I set out, hoping to find employment in a wherry with one of the men who knew me.

CHAPTER VII.

HELP COMES WHEN LEAST EXPECTED.

I FOUND it more difficult to obtain employment with wages sufficient to support Mary and me, not to speak of Nancy, than I had expected. Jim and I tried to hire a boat, but we could not obtain one to suit us for any sum we could hope to pay. Ours, for so we still called her, had been carried off, and locked up in a shed at Portsmouth. He and I picked up a sixpence or a shilling now and then, but some days we got nothing. There was a great risk of our becoming what my father had so strongly objected to "long-shore loafers." I would not desert Jim, who had served me so faithfully, and so we tried, as far as we could, to work together. Sometimes he talked of going off to sea, but as I could not leave Mary his heart failed him at the thought of going without me. At the time appointed I called on Lawyer Chalk.

"Sorry to say we are beaten, my lad," were the words with which he greeted me. "I fought hard, but there's no doubt that Mr. Gull's client is the nephew of Tom Swatridge, who died intestate, consequently his nephew is his heir. Had the old man wisely come to me I would have drawn up a will for him, securing his property to you or any one he might have desired. I am very sorry for you, but law is law, and it can't be helped. I hope that you will find employment somewhere soon. Good-day to you." And he waved me out of his office.

Help Comes when Least Expected.

In consequence of his failure in my cause, Lawyer Chalk sank considerably in the estimation of Bob Fox and his friends, who declared that the next time they wanted legal advice they would try what Lawyer Gull could do for them. I should have said that a day or two before he had sent a clerk armed with due authority to accompany Nancy and Mary, who brought away our clothing and all the articles which we had purchased with our own money. Curiously enough, I did not again set eyes on Mr. Eben Swatridge, who was, I understood, the son of a younger brother of old Tom, who had gone into business in London and made money. Some property having been left to the two brothers, or to the survivor of either, Eben had been compelled to make inquiries respecting his long unrecognized uncle, and had thus been induced to pay the visit to Portsea which had produced such disastrous results to Mary and me.

The house and furniture and wherry were sold, and directly afterwards he disappeared from Portsmouth. Perhaps he thought it wise to keep out of the way of Bob Fox and the other sturdy old salts who supported me. Not that one of them would have laid a finger on him, and Mary and I agreed that, far from having any ill-feeling, we should have been ready, for his uncle's sake, to have been friends if he had explained to us at the first who he was and his just rights in a quiet way. We had now a hard struggle to make the two ends meet. Mrs. Simmons fell ill, and Mary, who could no longer go to school, had to attend on her, and I had to find food and, as it turned out, to pay her rent, she being no longer able to work for her own support. I did not grumble at this, for I was grateful to her for her kindness to us; but though we stinted ourselves to the utmost, we often had not a sixpence in the house to buy fit nourishment for the poor old lady. Nancy was ready to slave from morning to night, but was often unsuccessful in obtaining work, so that she made scarcely enough to support herself; she might have got a situation, but she would not leave Mary. Whenever honest Jim Pulley could save a shilling he brought it, as he said, for the widow, though I knew that besides his wish to help her he was much influenced by his regard for us. I often thought when the winter came what he and I should do then. I did not say anything to Mary about the future, but tried to keep up her spirits, for I saw that her cheek was becoming pale, and she was growing thinner and thinner every day. At last one morning, when I had got up just at daylight, and having taken a crust of bread and a drink of water for breakfast, was about to go out in search of work, Nancy came into the room, and said,

"I don't know what has come over Mary, but she has been talking and talking ever so strangely all night, and her cheek is as hot as a live cinder."

I hurried into the little back room Mary and Nancy occupied next to the widow's. A glance told me that my dear little sister was in a high fever. My heart was ready to burst, for she did not know me. Mrs. Simmons was too ill to get up and say what she thought of its nature.

"I must run for the doctor, Nancy," I exclaimed; "there's not a moment to lose;" and snatching up my hat I rushed out of the house, assured that Nancy would do her best in the meantime.

I had caught sight of Dr. Rolt passing along the street on the previous day, so I knew that he was at home, and I felt more inclined to go to him than to Mr. Jones. I ran as I had not run for a long time, and no one ventured to stop me now. The doctor was on foot, early as was the hour. He remembered mother and Mary and me the moment I mentioned my name.

"I'll come to see your little sister directly," he said.

Help Comes when Least Expected.

I waited for him, fearing that he might not find the house. He was soon ready, and, considering his age, I was surprised how well he kept up with me. I eagerly ushered him into the house. He had not been long with Mary before he sent me off to the chemist to get some medicine, for which I had fortunately enough in my pocket to pay. When I came back he gave it to her himself, and said that he would send some more in the evening; but he would not tell me what he thought of her.

I will not dwell on this unhappy time. The doctor came twice every day and sometimes oftener, but Mary seemed to be getting no better. I had to go out to get work, but all I could make was not sufficient for our expenses, and I had to run into debt, besides which the widow's rent was due, and she could not pay it.

One day Jim brought me a few shillings, which he said the watermen had given him, but times were bad with most of them, and they could do but little. This enabled me to get some things absolutely necessary for Mary and food for the rest of us. The landlord called two or three times for rent, and at last said that he must put in a distress if it was not paid. The thought of what the consequence of this would be to Mary made me tremble with fear. Ill as she and Mrs. Simmons were, their beds might, notwithstanding, be taken from beneath them. The widow might be carried off to the workhouse, and we should be turned into the street. I begged hard for delay, and promised that I would do all I could to raise the money. The landlord replied that he would give us two days more, but would not listen to anything further I had to say. The doctor had just before called, so that I could not then tell him of our difficulty. He had not yet given me any assurance that he thought Mary would recover. Nancy could not leave the house, as she was required every moment to attend on her and Mrs. Simmons. I was not likely to find Dr. Rolt till the evening, so I determined to consult Jim and Bob Fox. I soon met Jim; he was ready to cry when I told him. He scratched his head and rubbed his brow, in vain trying to suggest something.

"Bob can't help us either," he said, at length. "He's got into trouble. Went away three days ago over to France in a smuggling lugger, the *Smiling Lass*, and she was catched last night with tubs aboard, so he's sure to want all the money he can get to pay Lawyer Chalk to keep him out of prison, if that's to be done, but I'm afeared even old Chalk will be nonplussed this time."

"I wonder whether Lawyer Chalk would lend me the money," I said.

"Might as well expect to get a hen's egg out of a block of granite," answered Jim.

On inquiry I found that all my friends from whom I had the slightest hope of assistance were away over at Ryde, Cowes, or Southampton.

"I tell you, Peter, as I knowed how much you wanted money, I'd a great mind to go aboard the *Smiling Lass* t'other day, when Bob axed me. It's a good job I didn't, isn't it?"

"I am very glad you didn't, not only because you would have been taken, but because you would have broken the law," I answered. "Father always set his face against smuggling."

"Yes, maybe he did," said Jim, who did not see that smuggling was wrong as clearly as I did. "But now what's to be done?"

"We'll go down to the Hard, and try to pick up a job," I answered. "A few pence will be better than nothing."

We each got a job in different boats. The one I was in took some passengers over to Ryde, and thence some others to Spithead and back, so that it was late when I got home with a shilling and a few pence in my pocket. Mary was no better. The doctor had been, and Nancy had told him of the landlord's threats, but he had made no remark.

"I'll tell you what I'll do, Nancy," I said; "I'll offer the landlord this shilling when he comes to-morrow to show that I am in earnest, and perhaps he will let us off for another day or two."

"Better hear what the doctor thinks when he comes in the morning. I don't think that he'll allow Mary and Widow Simmons to have their beds taken from under them. Cheer up, Peter! cheer up!"

I did cheer up a little when Jim came in and brought another shilling, his day's earnings, declaring that he'd had a good dinner, and had still some coppers in his pocket to pay for the next day's breakfast. He, however, could not resist eating some bread and cheese which Nancy pressed on him before he went away.

I could scarcely close my eyes for thinking of what the morrow might bring forth. About midnight Nancy came in and told me that Mary was sleeping more calmly than she had done since she was taken ill. Hoping that this was a good sign my mind became less disquieted, and I fell asleep. The next morning the usual hour for the doctor's coming passed and he did not appear. We waited and waited, anxious to know whether Mary really was better. At last there came a knocking at the door, and in walked the landlord, with a couple of men at his heels.

"Have you the rent ready, good people?" he asked, in a gruff tone.

"No, sir; but I have two shillings, and I promise to pay as much as I can every day till you've got what you demand," I said, as fast as I could speak.

The men laughed as I said this.

"Two shillings! that won't go no way, my lad," cried the landlord. "Let me see, why this old pot and kettle and the cups and plates, and table and chairs, and everything in this room won't sell for more than half my demands, so we must have the bedsteads and bedding and a chest of drawers or so; and as the old woman in there won't ever be able to pay me more rent, she and all of you must turn out with what remains! So now, Crouch and Scroggins, do your duty."

The moment he had entered the house Nancy, passing behind me, had locked Mary's and Mrs. Simmons's doors, and having put the keys in her pocket, had slipped into the scullery or little back kitchen, where we often cooked in summer. One of the men was in the act of placing one chair upon another, and his companion was approaching Mary's room, when suddenly Nancy rushed out of the back kitchen with a red-hot poker in her hand, and placing herself before it, exclaimed,

"Step an inch nearer if ye dare, ye cowards! Out on ye, Mr. Grimes, to come and disturb a fever-sick girl and an old dying woman for the sake of a few filthy shillings! Peter here has offered you some, and has promised to pay you more when he can get them, and I promise too; and now let me see if one of you dare to lay a finger on any of Missus Simmons's things! Get out of this house! get out of this house, I say!"

And she began flourishing her poker and advancing towards the intruders in a way which made them beat a rapid retreat towards the door, Mr. Grimes scrambling off the first, and shouting out,

"Assault and battery! I'll make you pay for this, you young vixen!"

"I don't mind your salt and butter, nor what you call me either," cried Nancy; and she was just slamming the door

Help Comes when Least Expected.

behind them, when two persons appeared as if about to enter, one of whom exclaimed, in a voice which I recognised as that of Dr. Rolt,

"Why, my good girl, what is all this about?"

"They said that they was a-going to take Mary's and the widow's beds and all the things away, sir, and I wouldn't let them," she answered, panting and still grasping the hot poker.

"Verily, daughter, thou hast taken a very effectual way of preventing them," said the other person, who I now saw to my great joy was Mr. Silas Gray. He and the doctor at once entered the house.

"Now listen to me, damsel," he continued. "Thou hast been prompted by affectionate zeal to defend thy friends, I doubt not, but nevertheless thou hast acted illegally, and the consequences to thyself may be serious; however, I will say no more on the subject at present. Put back thy weapon into the fireplace and attend on friend Rolt, who desires to see his patients."

I saw Mr. Gray and the doctor exchange smiles as Nancy, producing the keys from her pocket, unlocked the doors. He now, observing me, said,

"Tell me, my lad, how all this happened. I thought that thou wast doing well with thy wherry."

So while the doctor was seeing Mary and Mrs. Simmons, I gave him an exact account of all that had happened since the day he and his family were out with Jim and me on the water. I had just finished, when the doctor came into the room.

"I can give you a favourable account of your young sister, my lad," said Dr. Rolt. "Her patience and obedience, aided by Nancy's care, have been much in her favour, and she will, I trust, shortly recover. As soon as she has gained sufficient strength our friend Mr. Gray wishes her to be removed to his house, and Nancy can remain here to look after the poor widow, whose days on earth are numbered."

"Oh, thank you, gentlemen; thank you!" I exclaimed, my heart swelling so that I could scarcely utter the words.

"And what about yourself, my son?" asked Mr. Gray.

"Oh, Jim and I will try to rub on together, and I'll try to pay the widow's rent as I promised, if you'll speak a word, sir, to Mr. Grimes and get him not to press for payment," I answered.

"Set thy mind at rest on that point. I will satisfy the demands of the widow's landlord," said Mr. Gray; and he then added, "Come to my house to-morrow, and I will meantime consider what can be done to put you in the way of gaining your daily bread. I desire to show thee that I am pleased with thy conduct, but it were small kindness were I to enable thee to live in idleness."

Again thanking Mr. Gray from the bottom of my heart, I said, "What I want, sir, is work. Help me to get that, and it will be all I ask."

Before going away Mr. Gray saw Mary for a short time, and paid a long visit to poor Mrs. Simmons, which she said did her heart good.

I had never felt so happy in my life, and could not resist going out to tell Jim Pulley.

"Ask him to set thee up with a wherry and we'll go out together again as we used to do. That will be fine, and we'll be as merry as two crickets!" he exclaimed.

"I think I ought to leave it with him," I answered. "A wherry costs a lot of money, and he has already been very generous, though I should like him to do as you propose, and I promise you, Jim, whatever he proposes, to stick by you."

"That's all I care for," answered my friend.

He accompanied me to the door, but would not come in for fear of disturbing Mary.

The next day I went to see Mr. Gray, who lived in a pretty house some way out of Portsmouth. He and his daughters received me very kindly. He had, he said, been considering what he could do for me. He would obtain a wherry for me, but he considered that the life of a waterman was not suited to a lad like me, and he then said that he was a shipowner, and was about to despatch a brig in a few days to the coast of Norway for timber, and that, if I pleased, he would send me on board her as an apprentice. Also, as he considered that I was already a seaman, he would give me a trifle of pay. Remembering what my father used to say about not wishing Jack " to become a long-shore lubber," I at once replied that I would thankfully have accepted his offer, but that I could not desert Jim Pulley, who would well-nigh break his heart, if I were to go away without him.

" Nor need thee do that, my son," he answered. " I will provide a berth also for thy friend on board the *Good Intent*, and he and thou need not be parted. I approve of thy constancy to him and of his faithfulness to thee. A long-shore life, such as thou wouldst lead if thou wast owner of a wherry, would be dangerous if not demoralising, albeit thou might live comfortably enough."

" But, sir, what will my sister do without me when she recovers and leaves you, and where will Nancy go when the widow dies ? "

" I will be chargeable for both of them. Set thy mind at rest on that point. Should I be called away—and no man knows how long he has to live—I will direct my daughters to watch over them. Thou and thy friend Jim can, in the meantime, follow thy vocation of watermen, so that thou mayest eat the fruit of thy labours, which is sweeter far to brave hearts like thine than food bestowed in charity."

I did my best to thank Mr. Gray as I ought, and hastened back to tell Mary and Nancy and Jim.

"I'd have gone with thee, Peter, even if it had been to Botany Bay, or any of them outlandish parts," exclaimed Jim, when I told him what Mr. Gray had promised. "I am glad; yes, I am glad!"

We both tried at once to get employment, and did very well that afternoon and on the two following days.

When I got home on the evening of the last I found that a message had been left by Mr. Gray when he visited the widow and Mary, directing Jim and me to go the next morning at nine o'clock on board the *Good Intent*, which had just come into the Commercial Dock. I hastened off to tell Jim at once. As may be supposed, we were up betimes, and as we got to the dock before the hour appointed we were able to examine the *Good Intent* at our leisure. She was a fair enough looking craft, but as she was deep in the water, having only just begun to discharge a cargo of coals brought from the north, and had a dingy appearance, from the black dust flying about, we could not judge of her properly.

As the bells of St. Thomas's Church began to strike nine we stepped on board, and directly afterwards Mr. Gray, followed by a short, broad, oldish man, who had not a bit the look of a skipper, though such I guessed he was, came out of the cabin.

"Right! Punctuality saves precious hours," said Mr. Gray, with an approving nod. "These are the lads I desire to commit to thy care, Captain Finlay. Instruct them in their duties, so that they may become able seamen, and they will repay thy teaching."

"I'll act justly by the laddies, Mr. Gray, but there's an auld saying that ' ye canna make a silk purse out of a sow's ear.' If they dinna keep their wits awake, or if they ha' na wits to keep awake, all the teaching in the world will na make them sailors."

"They are fair sailors already, and thou wilt find them handy enough, I hope," observed Mr. Gray.

After putting a few questions, Captain Finlay told us to come aboard the next day but one with our bags, by which time the cargo would be discharged. We set off home greatly pleased, though puzzled to know how we should obtain a decent kit. With Nancy's help, I might be pretty well off, but poor Jim had scarcely a rag to his back besides the clothes he stood in. In the evening, however, a note came from Mr. Gray with an order on an outfitter to give us each a complete kit suited to a cold climate. We were not slow to avail ourselves of it. The next day Dr. Rolt considered Mary sufficiently well to be removed, and Mr. Gray sent a closed carriage to convey her to his house. The doctor told me to be ready to accompany her, and kindly came himself. It was the first time I had ever been in a coach, and the rolling and pitching made me feel very queer. The young ladies received us as if we had been one of themselves, and Mary was carried up into a pretty, neat room, with white dimity curtains to the bed, and the fresh air blowing in at the open window.

"I'll leave her to you, now, Miss Hannah," said the doctor. "This is all she requires, with your watchful care."

After I had had a short talk with Mary alone I took my leave, and Miss Hannah told me to be sure to come back and see them before the *Good Intent* sailed. It was not likely I should forget to do that.

Jim and I now went to live on board the brig. We had plenty of work, cleaning out the hold and getting rid of the coal-dust, and then we scrubbed the deck, and blacked down the rigging, and painted the bulwarks and masts, till the change in the appearance of the dingy collier was like that of a scullery-maid when she puts on her Sunday best. We did not mind the hard work, though it was a good deal harder than any we had been accustomed to, but the master and the rest of the crew set us a good example. There was little grumbling, and what surprised me, no swearing, such as I had been accustomed to hear on the Hard. Captain Finlay would not allow it, and the mate supported him in checking any wrong expressions which some of the men had been in the habit of uttering.

I got leave to run up and see Mary and to bid Nancy and Mrs. Simmons good-bye. Miss Hannah and her sisters seemed to be making a great deal of Mary. It was evident they liked her much, and I was not surprised at that. The widow I never expected to see again. Nancy would scarcely let me go.

"Oh, Peter, Peter! what should us do if anything was to happen to ye out on the cruel sea!" she cried, as she held my hand and rubbed her eyes with her apron.

The next day the *Good Intent* went out of harbour, and I began in earnest the seafaring life I was destined to lead.

CHAPTER VIII

MY FIRST VOYAGE.

WIND south-south-west. The North Foreland had been rounded; the countless craft, of all sizes and rigs, generally to be found off the mouth of the Thames, had been cleared, and the *Good Intent*, with studding sails alow and aloft, was standing across the German Ocean.

Jim and I soon found our sea-legs, and were as well able to go aloft to reef topsails as the older hands. We were already well up to the ordinary duties of seamen, and could take our place at the helm with any of them.

"Mr. Gray was not mistaken about thee, laddie," said the captain to me one day as I came aft to the wheel. "Go on as thou hast begun; obey God, and thou wilt prosper."

I was much pleased with this praise, for the old man was not given to throwing words away. While I steered he stood by telling me not only what to do then, but how to act under various circumstances. At other times he made me come into the cabin and gave me lessons in navigation to fit me to become a mate and master. Jim, being unable to read, and showing no aptitude for learning, had not the same advantages. We both of us lived forward with the men, some of whom were a little jealous of the favour I received, and not only played me tricks, ordered me to do all sorts of disagreeable jobs, and gave me a taste of the rope's-end on the sly, but tried hard to set Jim against me. They soon, however, found out that they were not likely to succeed, for though Jim did not mind how they treated him, he was always ready to stick up for me.

The forecastle of the *Good Intent* was thus not a paradise to either of us. The greater number of the men were, however, well disposed, and it was only when they were on deck that the others dared to behave as I have described, while, as we would not complain, the mate knew nothing of what was going forward below. I remember thinking to myself, "If these sort of things can be done on board a ship, with a well-disciplined crew and a good captain and mate, how hard must be the lot of the unhappy boys serving in a craft where the captain, officers, and men are alike brutal!" Jim was always ready to oblige, and I did my best to win over my enemies by trying to show that I did not mind how they treated me, and I soon succeeded.

We were, I should have said, bound out to Bergen, on the coast of Norway, for a cargo of hides, tallow, salt fish, and spars, which we were to carry to London. The weather had hitherto been fine, a great advantage to Jim and me, as we had time to learn our duties and to get accustomed to going aloft before our nerves and muscles were put to any severe test.

But though the sea was smooth, the breeze, which had at first carried us briskly along, shifted to the northward, so that we made but slow progress. Now we stood on one tack, now on the other, the wind each time heading us. At last the grumblers began to declare that we should never make our port.

"The old craft has got a run of ill-luck, there's something worse a-going to happen," said Sam Norris, one of my chief persecutors, as during his watch below he sat with his arms folded on his chest in the fore-peak. "I seed a black cat come aboard the night afore we left the docks, and no one knows that she ever went ashore again."

Some of the men looked uncomfortable at Sam's statement, but others laughed.

"What harm could the black cat do, if she did come aboard?" I inquired. "Probably she came to look for rats, and having killed all she could find, slipped ashore again unseen by any one."

"I didn't say a she-cat. It looked like a big tom-cat; but who knows that it was really a cat at all?" said Sam.

"If it wasn't a tom-cat, what was it?" asked Bob Stout, a chum of Sam's.

"Just what neither you nor I would like to meet if we had to go down into the hold alone," said Sam, in a mysterious tone.

Just then the watch below was summoned on deck to shorten sail. Not a bit too soon either, and we were quickly swarming aloft and out on the yards.

To reef sails in smooth water is easy enough, but when the ship is pitching into the fast rising seas and heeling over to the gale, with the wind whistling through the rigging, blocks rattling, ropes lashing about, the hard canvas trying to escape from one's grip, and blatters of rain and sleet and hail in one's face, it is no pleasant matter. We had taken two reefs in the topsails, and even then the brig had as much canvas on her as she could stand up to, and we had all come down on deck, with the exception of Jim, who had been on the foreyard, when the mate, seeing a rope foul, ordered him to clear it. Jim performed his duty, but instead of coming down as he ought to have done, remained seated on the foreyard, holding on by the lift to get accustomed to the violent motion, in which he seemed to take a pleasure. The mate, not observing this, came aft to speak to the captain, who shortly afterwards, finding that the brig was falling off from the wind, which had before been baffling, having shifted ahead, ordered her to be put about.

"Down with the helm," cried the captain.

I saw the men hauling at the braces, when, looking up, I caught sight of Jim at the yardarm. I shrieked out with terror, expecting that the next instant, as the yardarm swung round, he would be dashed to pieces on the deck, or hove off into the raging sea. The kind-hearted mate, recollecting him, came rushing forward, also believing that his destruction was certain, unless he could be caught as he fell. My heart beat, and my eyes were fixed on my friend as if they would start out of my head. I wildly stretched out my hands, yet I felt that I could do nothing to save him, when he made a desperate spring, and catching hold of the backstay, came gliding down by it on deck as if nothing particular had happened, scarcely conscious, indeed, of the fearful danger he had escaped. The mate rated him in stronger language than he generally used for his carelessness, winding up by asking:

"Where do you think you would have been, boy, if you hadn't have jumped when you did or had missed your aim?"

"Praise God for His great mercy to thee, laddie, and may thou never forget it all the days of thy life," said the old captain, who had beckoned Jim aft to speak to him.

Jim, touching his hat, answered, "Ay, ay, sir!" but he was, perhaps, less aware of the danger he had been in than any one on board.

The gale increased; several heavy seas struck the old brig, making her quiver from stem to stern, and at last one heavier than the rest breaking on board, carried the starboard bulwarks forward clean away. Some of the men were below; Jim and I and others were aft, and the rest, though half drowned, managed to secure themselves. To avoid the risk of another sea striking her in the same fashion, the brig was hove to under a close-reefed fore-topsail. As we had plenty of sea room, and the brig was tight as a bottle, so the mate affirmed, there was no danger; still, I for one heartily wished that the weather would moderate. I had gone aft, being sent by the cook to obtain the ingredients of a plum-pudding for the cabin dinner. Not thinking of danger, on my return I ran along on the lee side of the deck, but before I reached the caboose I saw a mountain sea rolling up with a terrific roar, and I heard a voice from aft shout, "Hold on for your lives!" Letting go the basin and dish I had in my hands, I grasped frantically at the nearest object I could meet with. It was a hand-pike sticking in the windlass, but it proved a treacherous holdfast, for, to my horror, out it came at the instant that the foaming sea broke on board, and away I was carried amid the whirl of waters right out through the shattered bulwarks. All hope of escape abandoned me. In that dreadful moment it seemed that every incident in my life came back to my memory; but Mary was the chief object of my thoughts. I knew that I was being carried off into the hungry ocean, and, as I supposed, there was no human aid at hand to save me, when the brig gave a violent lee lurch, and before I was borne away from her side I felt myself seized by the collar of my jacket, and dragged by a powerful arm, breathless and stunned with the roar of waters in my ears, into the galley.

The cook, who had retreated within it when the sea struck the brig, had caught sight of me, and at the risk of his life had darted out, as a cat springs on her prey, and saved me. I quickly recovered my senses, but was not prepared for the torrent of abuse which my preserver, Bob Fritters, poured out on me for having come along on the lee instead of the weather side of the deck.

Two or three of the watch who had been aft and fancied

that I had been carried overboard, when they found that I was safe, instead of expressing any satisfaction, joined the cook in rating me for my folly. Feeling as I suppose a half-drowned rat might do, I was glad to make my escape below, where, with the assistance of Jim, I shifted into dry clothes, while he hurried on deck to obtain a fresh supply of materials for the captain's pudding. Shortly after this the gale abated, and the brig was again put on her course.

I had been sent aloft one morning soon after daybreak to loose the fore-royal, when I saw right ahead a range of blue mountains, rising above the mist which still hung over the ocean. I knew that it must be the coast of Norway, for which we were bound.

"Land! land!" I shouted, pointing in the direction I saw the mountains, which I guessed were not visible from the deck.

The mate soon came aloft to judge for himself.

"You are right, Peter," he said. "We have made a good landfall, for if I mistake not we are just abreast of the entrance to the Bay of Jeltefiord, at the farther end of which stands Bergen, the town we are bound for."

The mate was right. The breeze freshening we stood on, and in the course of the morning we ran between lofty and rugged rocks for several miles, through the narrow Straits of Carmesundt into the bay—or fiord rather—till we came to an anchor off the picturesque old town of Bergen. It was a thriving, bustling place; the inhabitants, people from all the northern nations of Europe, mostly engaged in mercantile pursuits.

We soon discharged our cargo and began taking on board a very miscellaneous one, including a considerable quantity of spars to form the masts and yards of small vessels. The day seemed to me wonderfully long, indeed there was scarcely any night. Of course, we had plenty of hard work, as we were engaged for a large part of the twenty-four hours in hoisting in cargo. I should have thought all hands would have been too tired to think of carrying on any tricks, but it seemed that two or three of them had conceived a spite against Jim because he would not turn against me.

One of our best men, Ned Andrews, who did duty as second mate, had brought for his own use a small cask of sugar, as only molasses and pea-coffee were served out forward. One morning, as I was employed aft under the captain's directions, Andrews came up and complained that on opening his cask he found it stuffed full of dirty clouts and the sugar gone. I never saw the captain so indignant.

"A thief on board my brig!" he exclaimed; "verily, I'll make an example of him, whoever he is."

Calling the mate, he ordered him forthwith to examine all the men's chests, supposing that the thief must have stowed the sugar in his own.

"Go, Peter, and help him," he added, "for I am sure that thou, my son, art not the guilty one."

I followed the mate into the fore-peak. Having first demanded the keys from the owners of those which were locked, he examined chest after chest, making me hold up the lids while he turned out the contents or plunged his hands to the bottom. No sugar was found in any of them. He then came to my chest, which I knew was not locked, and the idea came into my head that the stolen property would be there. I showed some anxiety, I suspect, as I lifted up the lid. The mate put in his hands with a careless air, as if he had no idea of the sort. Greatly to my relief he found nothing. There was but one chest to be examined. It was Jim's.

Scarcely had I opened it when the mate, throwing off a jacket spread over the top, uttered an exclamation of surprise. There exposed to view was a large wooden bowl procured the day before by the steward for washing up glasses and cups, and supposed to have fallen overboard, cram full of sugar.

"Bring it along aft," cried the mate. "I did not think that of Pulley."

"And I don't think it now, sir," I answered, in a confident tone, as I obeyed his order.

"What's this? where was it found?" inquired the captain, as we reached the quarter-deck.

The mate told him.

"I'll swear Jim never put it there, sir; not he!" I exclaimed.

"Swear not at all, my son, albeit thou mayest be right," said the captain. "Send James Pulley aft."

Jim quickly came.

"Hast thou, James Pulley, been guilty of stealing thy shipmate's sugar?" asked the captain.

"No, sir, please you, I never took it, and never put it where they say it was found," answered Jim, boldly.

"Appearances are sadly against thee, James Pulley," observed the captain, with more sorrow than anger in his tone. "This matter must be investigated."

"I am sure that Jim speaks the truth, sir," I exclaimed, unable to contain myself. "Somebody else stole the sugar and put it in his chest."

The crew had gathered aft, and two or three looked thunder-clouds at me as I spoke.

"Thine assertion needs proof," observed the captain. "Was thy cask of sugar open, Andrews?"

"No, sir, tightly headed up," answered Andrews.

"Then it must have been forced open by some iron instrument," said the captain. "Bring it aft here."

The empty keg was brought.

"I thought so," remarked the captain. "An axe was

used to prise it open. Did any one see an axe in the hands of James Pulley?"

There was no reply for some time. At last, Ben Grimes, one of the men who had always been most hostile to Jim and me, said, "I thinks I seed Jim Pulley going along the deck with what looked mighty like the handle of an axe sticking out from under his jacket."

"The evidence is much against thee, James Pulley," said the captain. "I must, as in duty bound, report this affair to Mr. Gray on our return, and it will, of course, prevent him from bestowing any further favours on you."

"I didn't do it. I'd sooner have had my right hand cut off than have done it," cried Jim. "Let me go ashore, sir, and I'll try to gain my daily bread as I best can. I can't bear to stay aboard here to be called a thief; though Peter Trawl knows I didn't take the sugar; he'd never believe that of me; and the mate doesn't, and Andrews himself doesn't."

"I am sorry for thee, lad. Thou must prove thine innocence," said the captain, turning away.

Poor Jim was very unhappy. Though both he and I were convinced that one of the men for spite had put the sugar in his chest, we could not fix on the guilty person. I did my best to comfort him. He talked of running from the ship, but I persuaded him not to think more of doing so foolish a thing.

"Stay, and your innocence will appear in due time," I said.

As we went about the deck we heard Grimes and others whispering, "Birds of a feather flock together."

They bullied Jim and me worse than ever, and took every occasion to call him a young thief, and other bad names besides. They saw how it vexed him, and that made them abuse him worse than before. The day after this we sailed

Poor Jim declared that if he could not clear himself he would never show his face in Portsmouth. I was sure that Andrews and the other good men did not believe him to be guilty, but they could not prove his innocence; and, as he said, the others would take care to blabber about him, and, worst of all, Mr. Gray would think him a thief.

An easterly breeze carried us clear of the harbour, but the wind then shifted to the southward, and then to the south-west, being very light, so that after three days we had not lost sight of the coast of Norway. There seemed every probability of our having a long passage. Some of the men said it was all owing to the black cat, and Grimes declared that we must expect ill-luck with such a psalm-singing Methodist old skipper as we had. Even Andrews prognosticated evil, but his idea was that it would be brought about by an old woman he had seen on shore, said by everyone to be a powerful witch. As, however, according to Andrews, she had the power of raising storms, and we had only to complain of calms and baffling winds, I could not see that she had had any influence over us.

At last we got so far to the westward that we lost sight of the coast of Norway, but had not made good a mile to the southward—we had rather indeed drifted to the northward. Meantime, the captain hearing from the mate how the men were grumbling, called all hands aft.

"Lads, I want ye to listen to me," he said. "Some or ye fancy that we are having these calms and baffling winds on one account, and some on another, but this I know, that He who rules the seas does not allow any other beings to interfere with His plans. Ye have heard, maybe, however, of the prophet Jonah. Once upon a time, Jonah, when ordered by God to go to a certain place and perform a certain duty, disobeyed his Master, and trying to escape from Him took passage on board a ship, fancying that he

My First Voyage.

could get out of God's sight. Did he succeed? No! God had His eye on Jonah, and caused a hurricane which well-nigh sent the ship to the bottom. Not till Jonah was hove overboard did the tempest cease. Now, lads, just understand there are some aboard this brig who are disobeying Him and offending Him just as much as Jonah did, and it's not for me to say that He does not allow these calms, so unusual in this latitude, to prevail in consequence. That's all I've got to say, lads, but ye'll just think over it; and now go forward."

Whether or not the men did think over it, or exactly understood what the old man meant, I cannot say, but the next morning the carpenter came aft to the captain and said that he had had a dream which made him remember that the evening before Andrews's sugar was found to have been stolen, Ben Grimes had borrowed an axe from him, on examining which afterwards he discovered that a small piece had been broken off on one side, and that Grimes acknowledged he had done it by striking a nail in a piece of wood he was chopping up. On hearing this the captain again summoned all hands aft, and ordered Andrews to bring his sugar cask. There in the head was found a piece of iron which exactly fitted the notch in the axe which the carpenter produced.

"Now, lads, say who stole Andrews's sugar and concealed it in Pulley's chest?" asked the skipper.

"Grimes! Grimes! no doubt about it!" shouted all the men, with the exception of the individual mentioned and one other.

"You are right, lads, and Pulley is innocent," said the skipper.

"As the babe unborn," answered the men, and they all, except Grimes and his chum, following my example, gave Jim a hearty shake of the hand.

I thought that he would have blubbered outright with pleasure. Though I was sure that Jim had never touched the sugar, I was thankful that the captain and the rest were convinced of his innocence.

Before noon that day a dark bank of clouds was seen coming up from the southward. In a short time several black masses broke away from the main body, and came careering across the sky.

"Away aloft and shorten sail," cried the skipper. "Be smart, lads!"

We hurried up the rigging, for there was no time to be lost.

"Two reefs in the fore-topsail! Furl the main-topsail! Let fly topgallant sheets!"

These orders came in quick succession. The captain, aided by the mate, was meantime lowering the mainsail. He at first, I believe, intended to heave the brig to, but before the canvas was reduced the gale struck her—over she heeled—the top-gallant sails, with their masts, were carried away just as Jim and I were about mounting the rigging, he the fore and I the main, to furl them; the mainsail, only half lowered, flying out, nearly knocked the mate overboard. I had got down on the weather side of the main-topsail yard to assist the hands on it, when the straining canvas broke loose from our grasp, and at the same instant the topgallant rigging, striking the two men on the lee yardarm, hurled them off into the foaming ocean.

To lower a boat was impossible; we had not strength sufficient as it was to clear away the top-gallant masts, and to hand the topsails. A grating and some spars were hove to them by the mate, who then, axe in hand, sprang aloft to assist us. None too soon, for we could do nothing but cling on to the yard till the top-gallant rigging was cleared away. The men on the foreyard were more successful, and

I saw Jim gallantly using his knife in a fashion which at length cleared away the wreck and enabled them to secure the sail. The mate succeeded also in his object, and we were expecting them to assist us in attempting to furl the main-topsail, when the captain, seeing that we were not likely to succeed, calling us down, ordered the helm to be put up and the yards squared away, and off we ran before the fast-increasing gale, leaving, we feared, our two shipmates, the carpenter and Grimes, to perish miserably.

CHAPTER IX.

I EXPERIENCE THE PERILS OF THE SEA.

THE *Good Intent* ran on before the increasing gale. The fast-rising seas came rolling up astern, threatening every instant to poop her, for, having a full cargo, she was much deeper in the water than when we sailed from Portsmouth. We quickly lost sight of the grating and spars thrown to our hapless shipmates, and they themselves had before then disappeared.

The first thing now to be done was to get the main-topsail stowed, for, flying wildly in the wind, it seemed as if about to carry away the main-topmast. The mate, Andrews, and two other men were on the point of going aloft to try and haul it in, in spite of the danger they ran in so doing, when a report like that of thunder was heard, and the sail, split into ribbons, was torn from the bolt-ropes. The fragments, after streaming out wildly in the wind, lashed themselves round and round the yard, thus saving us the hazardous task of attempting to furl the sail.

The brig flew on, now plunging into the roaring and foaming seas, now rolling from side to side so that it was difficult to keep our feet. The fore-staysail and jib had been stowed in time, and the flying jib had been blown away, so that the fore-topsail was the only sail set.

Thus hour after hour passed. Had we been running in

I Experience the Perils of the Sea. 87

the opposite direction we should have been making good progress, but we were now going farther and farther from our destination, to be driven into even worse weather, and perhaps to have to make our way south round the Irish coast. To avoid this, the captain was anxious to heave the brig to, and I saw him and the mate consulting how it could be done. It was a dangerous operation, they both knew, for should she not quickly come up to the wind, a sea might strike her on the broadside and sweep over her deck, or throw her on her beam-ends.

"If we get a lull it must be done," said the captain.

"Ay, ay, sir!" answered the mate; and he ordered the men to stand ready to brace round the fore-topsail-yard as the brig came up to the wind.

Still we watched in vain for the wished-for lull. In spite of the roaring seas I felt wonderfully sleepy, and could scarcely keep my eyes open as I held on to a stanchion at the after-part of the deck. Jim was much in the same condition, for we had both been on foot since the morning watch had been called, and we had had no food all day.

The kind captain, observing the state we were in, instead of abusing us, as some skippers would have done, ordered us to go below to find something to eat and to lie down till we were wanted. We were making our way forward when he shouted out,

"Go into the cabin, laddies. There is some bread and cheese in the pantry, and ye'll be ready at hand when I call ye."

We quickly slipped below, and he again closed the companion-hatch which he had opened to let us descend. The other hatches had been battened down, for at any moment a sea might break on board, and if they had not been secured might fill the vessel.

Not a ray of light came below, but Jim and I, use of

about, found the bread and cheese we were in search of and soon satisfied our hunger. We then, thankful to get some rest, lay down on the deck of the cabin—which landsmen would call the floor—for we should have considered it presumptuous to stretch ourselves in one of the berths or even on the locker; and in spite of the rolling and pitching of the brig we were quickly fast asleep.

I seldom dreamed in those days, but, though tired as I was, my slumbers were troubled. Now I fancied that the brig was sinking, but that, somehow or other, I came to the surface, and was striking out amid the raging billows for the land; then I thought that I was again on board, and that the brig, after rushing rapidly on, struck upon a huge reef of black rocks, when, in an instant, her timbers split asunder, and we were all hurled into the seething waters. Suddenly I was awoke by the thundering, crashing sound of a tremendous blow on the side of the vessel, and I found myself hove right across the cabin, clutching fast hold of Jim, who shouted out, "Hillo, Peter, what is the matter? Are we all going to be drowned?"

Before I could answer him there came from above us—indeed, it had begun while he was speaking—a deafening mingling of terrific noises, of rending planks, of falling spars, the rush and swirl and roar of waters, amid which could be heard the faint cries of human voices.

The brig had been thrown on her beam-ends; of that there could be no doubt, for when we attempted to get on our feet we found the deck of the cabin almost perpendicular.

"Do you think the brig will go down?" shouted Jim.

The hubbub was so great that it was impossible to hear each other unless we spoke at the very top of our voices.

"We must, at all events, get on deck as soon as we can, and do our best to save ourselves," I answered.

I Experience the Perils of the Sea.

Though I said this, I had very little hope of escaping, as I thought that the vessel might at any moment founder. Even to get on deck was no easy matter, for everything in the cabin was upside down—boxes and bales, and casks and articles of all sorts, thrown out of the lockers, mixed with the furniture which had broken adrift, were knocking about, while all the time we were in complete darkness. The dead lights had fortunately been closed at the commencement of the gale, and the companion-hatch remained secure, so that, as yet, no water came below.

Getting on our feet we were endeavouring to grope our way to the companion-ladder when we heard two loud crashes in quick succession, and directly afterwards, the brig righting with a violent jerk, we were thrown half across the cabin, bruised and almost stunned, among the numberless things knocking violently about. After a time, on recovering our senses, we picked ourselves up and made another attempt to get on deck. I now began to hope that the brig would not go down as soon as I had expected, but still I knew that she was in a fearfully perilous condition. I was sure from the crashing sounds we had heard that both her masts were gone: that very probably also she had sprung a leak, while we were far to the northward of the usual track of vessels.

At last we found our way to the cabin door, but groped about in vain for the companion-ladder, till Jim suggested that it had been unshipped when the vessel went over. After some time we found it, but had great difficulty, in consequence of the way the brig was rolling, to get it replaced. As soon as it was so I mounted and shouted as loud as I could to some one to come and lift off the hatch.

No voice replied. Again and again I shouted, fancying that the people might have gone forward for some reason or other and had forgotten us.

"What can have happened?" cried Jim, in a tone of alarm.

I dared not answer him, for I feared the worst.

Feeling about, I discovered an axe slung just inside the companion-hatch, on which I began hammering away with all my might—but still no one came.

"Jim, I'm afraid they must all be gone," I cried out at last.

"Gone!" he exclaimed. "What, the old captain, and mate, and Andrews, and the rest?"

"I am afraid so," I answered.

Again I shouted and knocked. Still no one came.

"We must break open the hatch," I said, and I attempted to force up the top with the axe, but did not succeed.

"Let me try," cried Jim; "my arm is stronger than yours."

I got down the ladder and gave him the axe. He took my place and began working away at the part where the hatch was placed. I could hear him giving stroke after stroke, but could see nothing, for the hatch fitted so closely that not a gleam of light came through it.

Presently I heard him sing out, "I've done it," and I knew by the rush of cold damp air which came down below that he had got off the hatch.

Still all was dark, but looking up I could distinguish the cloudy sky. Not till then did I know that it was night. We had gone to sleep in broad daylight, and I had no idea of the number of hours which had passed by since then. I sprang up the companion-ladder after Jim, who had stepped out on deck.

The spectacle which met my eyes was appalling. The masts were gone, carried away a few feet from the deck—only the stumps were standing—everything had been swept clear away, the caboose, the boats, the bulwarks; the brig was a complete wreck; the dark foam-topped seas were rising up high above the deck, threatening to engulf her.

The masts were still alongside hanging on by the rigging, their butt ends every now and then striking against her with so terrific a force that I feared they must before long drive a hole through the planking. As far as I could make out through the thick gloom, some spars which had apparently fallen before the masts gave way lay about the deck, kept from being washed away by the rigging attached to them having become entangled in the stanchions and the remaining portions of the shattered bulwarks.

Not one of our shipmates could we see. Again we shouted, in the faint hope that some of them might be lying concealed forward. No one answered.

"Maybe that they have gone down into the fore-peak," said Jim; "I'll go and knock on the hatch. They can't hear our shouts from where we are."

I tried to persuade Jim not to make the attempt till daylight, for a sea might break on board and wash him away.

"But do you see, Peter, we must try and get help to cut away the lower rigging, which keeps the masts battering against the sides?" he answered.

"Then I'll go with you," I said. "We'll share the same fate, whatever that may be."

"No, no, Peter! You stay by the companion-hatch; see, there are plenty of spars for me to catch hold of, and I'll take good care not to get washed away," answered Jim, beginning his journey forward.

Notwithstanding what he said, I was following him when I fancied that I heard a faint groan. I stopped to listen. It might be only the sound produced by the rubbing of two spars together or the working of the timbers. Again I heard the groan. I was now sure that it was uttered by one of our shipmates. It came from a part of the deck covered by a mass of broken spars and sails and rigging. Though I could not see as far, I knew that Jim had reached the forehatchway by hearing him shouting and knocking with the back of the axe.

"Are any of them there?" I cried out.

"No! Not one, I'm afeared," he answered.

"Then come and help me to see if there is any person under these spars here," I said.

Of course we had to bawl out to each other at the top of our voices on account of the clashing of the seas, the groaning and creaking of the timbers and bulk-heads, and the thundering of the masts against the sides.

Jim soon joined me. We had to be very cautious how we moved about, for besides the risk there was at any moment of a sea sweeping across the deck, we might on account of the darkness have stepped overboard. We lost no time in crawling to the spot whence I heard the groans proceeding.

On feeling about we soon discovered a man, his body pressed down on the deck by a heavy spar, and partly concealed by the canvas.

"Who are you?" cried Jim. "Speak to us,—do."

A groan was the only answer.

"Do you try and lift the spar, Jim, and I'll drag him out," I said.

Jim tried to do as I told him, but though he exerted all his strength he could not succeed in raising the spar.

"Oh, dear! oh, dear! the poor fellow will die if we cannot get him free soon," I exclaimed, in despair.

"This will do it," cried Jim, who had been searching about, and now came with the broken end of a top-gallant-yard to serve as a handspike. By its means he prised up the spar, while I as gently as I could dragged out the man by the shoulders. No sooner did I feel his jacket than I

I Experience the Perils of the Sea.

was almost sure that he was no other than our good old skipper. He was breathing heavily, and had apparently been rendered unconscious by a blow on the head. I at length got him out from under the spar.

"We must carry him below before another sea breaks on board," I said. "Come, help me, Jim."

Together we lifted the old man, and staggering along the slippery deck, reached the companion-hatch in safety. To get him down without injury was more difficult. I going first and taking his legs, and Jim holding him by the shoulders, we succeeded at last. While Jim supported him at the bottom of the ladder, I hunted about till I found a tinder-box and matches and lighted the cabin lamp. It showed us, as I had supposed, that the person I had rescued was our captain. He was pale as death, and bleeding from a wound in the head. The light also exhibited the utter confusion into which the cabin had been thrown. I managed, however, to clear a way to the state cabin, to which we carried the captain, and then getting off his wet clothes placed him between the blankets in his berth. Fortunately, there was a cask of water in the pantry, which enabled us to wash and bind up his head, so as to staunch the blood flowing from it. The operation was performed but roughly, as all the time the sound of the masts thundering like battering rams against the side of the vessel warned us that we must try to cut them adrift without delay. I feared that already they had done some serious damage. Even before we left the captain he seemed to have somewhat recovered his consciousness, for I heard him mutter, "Be smart, lads. Tell mate—cut away wreck."

Of course we did not let him know that besides himself we alone of all the crew were left alive. In the cabin I found another axe, and Jim and I, going on deck, began the difficult and dangerous task we had undertaken.

The lower rigging, on what had been the weather side, had entirely given way, so that we had only to cut that on the opposite side, but in leaning over to reach the shrouds at the chains we ran a fearful risk of being carried off by the sea as the vessel rolled from side to side.

We first tried to clear the mainmast. We had cut two of the shrouds, when a sea, having driven the butt end against the side with fearful force, lifted it just as the brig rolled over, and it came sweeping along the deck, nearly taking Jim and me off our legs. With the greatest difficulty we escaped.

"It shan't do that again," cried Jim; and dashing forward with axe uplifted he cut the last shroud, and the mast was carried away by the next sea.

We had still to get rid of the foremast and bowsprit, which were doing as much damage as the mainmast had done, by every now and then ramming away at the bows with a force sufficient, it seemed, to knock a hole through them at any moment. I felt anxious to return to the cabin to attend to our old captain, but the safety of the vessel required us not to delay a moment longer than could be helped in cutting away the remaining masts and bowsprit.

I observed soon after the mainmast had gone that the wind had fallen, and that there was somewhat less sea running, and in a short time the light began to increase. I do not think that otherwise we should have accomplished our task. Jim sprang forward with his axe, taking always the post of danger, and hacking away at rope after rope as he could manage to reach them.

I followed his example. O'ten we had to hold on for our lives as the seas washed over us. At length the work was accomplished. We gave a shout of satisfaction as, the last rope severed, we saw the mass of wreck drop clear of the brig. But our work was not done. There we were in the midst of the North Sea, without masts or canvas or boats, our bulwarks gone, the brig sorely battered, and only our two selves and our poor old captain to navigate her. To preserve his life our constant attention was required.

"We'll go below and see how the old man gets on," I said. "There's nothing more for us to do on deck that I can see at present."

"Not so sure of that, Peter," answered Jim. "You go and look after the skipper, and I'll just see how matters are forward and down in the hold."

As I felt sure that the captain ought not to be left longer alone, I hurried into the cabin. He was conscious, but still scarcely able to speak. I told him that we had cleared away the wreck of the masts, and that the weather was moderating.

"Thank God!" he murmured. Then, getting some more water, I again dressed his wounded head, and afterwards proposed lighting the cabin fire and trying to make him some broth.

"Water! I only want water," he said, in the same low voice as before.

I procured some in a mug. He drank it, and then said, "Get up jury-masts and steer west," not understanding as yet, I suppose, that the crew were lost.

"Ay, ay, sir," I answered, being unwilling to undeceive him, though I wondered how Jim and I could alone obey his orders; yet, if we were ever to reach a port, jury-masts must be got up.

As I could do nothing more just then for the captain, I was going on deck, when I met Jim at the companion-hatch, his face wearing an expression of the greatest alarm.

"Things are very bad, Peter," he exclaimed. "The

water is coming in through a big hole in the bows like a mill-sluice, and I'm much afeared that before long the old craft will carry us and the captain to the bottom."

"Not if we keep our wits awake, Jim," I answered. "We must try to stop the hole. Come along."

Hurrying forward, we dived down into the fore-peak. We could now venture to leave the hatch off, so as to give light below. Sure enough the water was coming in terribly fast, but not quite so fast as Jim described, though already the men's chests and other articles were afloat.

The largest hole was, I saw, in the very centre of a bunk, so that we could easily get at it. Dragging out all the blankets from the other bunks, I rammed them into the hole.

"Hand me a board or the top of a chest—knock it off quick!" I sang out.

Jim, leaping on a chest, wrenched off the lid and gave it me.

"Now that handspike."

There was one close to him. By pressing the board against the blankets, and jamming the handspike down between it and the outer corner of the bunk, the gush of water was stopped.

"Here's another hole still more forward, I can see the water bubbling in," cried Jim, holding a lantern, which he had lit that he might look round, to the place.

We stopped it as we had the first.

"It will be a mercy if there are no other holes in the side under the cargo," he said. "We'll try the well."

We returned on deck, and Jim sounded the well.

"Six feet of water or more," he said, in a mournful tone, as he examined the rod.

"Then we must rig the pumps and try to clear her!" I exclaimed. "It will be a hard job, but it may be done, and we must not think of letting the old craft sink under our feet."

We set to work, and pumped and pumped away, the water coming up in a clear stream, till our backs and arms ached, and we felt every moment ready to drop, but we cheered each other on, resolved not to give in as long as we could stand on our legs.

CHAPTER X.

ALONE ON THE OCEAN.

"ARE we gaining on the leaks, think you, Jim?" I at length gasped out, for I felt that if our efforts were producing some effect we should be encouraged to continue them, but that if not it would be wise before we were thoroughly exhausted to try and build a raft on which we might have a chance of saving our lives.

My companion made no reply, but giving a look of doubt, still pumped on, the perspiration streaming down his face and neck showing the desperate exertions he was making. I was much in the same condition, though, like Jim, I had on only my shirt and trousers. I was the first to give in, and, utterly unable to move my arms, I sank down on the deck. Jim, still not uttering a word, doggedly worked on, bringing up a stream of water which flowed out through the scuppers.

It seemed wonderful that he could go on, but after some time he also stopped, and staggered to where he had left the rod.

"I'll try," he said.

I gazed at him with intense anxiety.

"Three inches less. We're gaining on the leaks! he exclaimed.

I sprang to my feet and seized the brake. Jim struck out with his arms "to take the turns out of the muscles," a he said, while he sat for a minute on the deck, and again went at it.

All this time the wind was falling and the sea going down. As we laboured at the pumps we looked out anxiously for the appearance of a vessel which might afford us assistance, but not a sail appeared above the horizon. We must depend on our own exertions for preserving our lives. Though a calm would enable us the better to free the brig of water and to get up jury masts, it would lessen our chance of obtaining help. Yet while the brig was rolling and tumbling about we could do nothing but pump, and pump we did till our strength failed us, and we both sank down on the deck.

My eyes closed, and I felt that I was dropping off to sleep. How long I thus lay I could not tell, when I heard Jim sing out,

"Hurrah! we've gained six inches on the leak," and clank, clank, clank, went his pump.

I cannot say that I sprang up, but I got, somehow or other, on my feet, and, seizing the brake, laboured away more like a person in his sleep than one awake.

I saw the water flowing freely, so I knew that I was not pumping uselessly. Presently I heard Jim cry out,

"Hillo! look there!"

Turning my eyes aft, I saw the captain holding on by the companion-hatch, and gazing in utter astonishment along the deck. His head bound up in a white cloth, a blanket over his shoulders, his face pale as death, he looked more like a ghost than a living mam.

"Where are they, lads?" he exclaimed at length, in a hollow voice.

"All gone overboard, sir," answered Jim, thinking he ought to speak.

The old man, on hearing this, fell flat on the deck.

We ran and lifted him up. At first I thought he was dead, but he soon opened his eyes and whispered,

"It was a passing weakness, and I'll be better soon. Trust in God, laddies; go on pumping, and He'll save your lives," he said.

"We'll take you below first, sir. You'll be better in your berth than here," I answered.

"No, no! I'll stay on deck; the fresh air will do me good," he said; but scarcely had he uttered the words than he fell back senseless.

"We must get him below, or he'll die here," I said; so Jim and I carried him down as before, and got him into his bed.

"He wants looking after," said Jim; "so, Peter, do you tend him, and I'll go back to the pumps."

Thinking that he wanted food more than anything else, I lighted the cabin fire, and collecting some materials from the pantry for broth in a saucepan, put it on to boil.

Though I had been actively engaged, I felt able once more to work the pumps. Jim said that he was certain the water in the hold was decreasing, while, as the brig was steadier, less was coming in. This increased our hopes of keeping her afloat, but we should want rest and sleep, and when we knocked off the water might once more gain on us.

We did not forget, however, what the captain had said. When I could pump no longer I ran below, freshly dressed the old man's head, and gave him some broth, which was by this time ready. It evidently did him good. Then, taking a basin of it myself, I ran up on deck with another for Jim.

"That puts life into one," he said, as, seated on the deck with his legs stretched out, he swallowed it nearly scalding hot. A draught of water which he told me to bring, however, cooled his throat, and he again set to, I following his example.

By this time the day was far advanced, and even Jim confessed that he must soon give in, while I could scarcely stand.

The wind had continued to go down, but the sea still rolled the vessel about too much to enable us to get up jury-masts, even if we had had strength to move, before dark.

"It's no use trying to hold out longer, I must get a snooze," sighed Jim.

He looked as if he were half asleep already.

"We had better go and lie down in the cabin, so that we may be ready to help the captain," I answered; "but I'll tell you what, we'll take a look into the fore-peak first, to see how the leaks are going on there."

"Oh, they are all right," said Jim. "We shouldn't have lessened the water so much if anything had given way."

Still I persisted in going forward, and Jim followed me. Just then the vessel gave a pitch, which nearly sent me head first down the fore-hatchway. As we got below I heard the sound of a rush of water. The handspike which secured the chief leak had worked out of its place, and the blankets and boards were forced inwards. It required all our remaining strength to put them back. Had we been asleep aft the brig would have filled in a few minutes. Jim wanted to remain forward, but I persuaded him to come aft, being sure that he would sleep too soundly to hear the water coming in should the leaks break out afresh, and might be drowned before he awoke. Having done all we could to secure the handspikes, we crawled rather than walked to the cabin.

We were thankful to find that the captain was asleep, so, without loss of time, Jim crept into one of the side berths, and I lay down on the after locker. In half a minute I had forgotten what had happened and where I was. As the old captain and we two lads lay fast asleep on board the demasted brig out there in the wild North Sea, a kind Providence watched over us. We might have been run down, or, the leaks breaking out afresh, the vessel might have foundered before we awoke.

A voice which I supposed to be that of the captain aroused me. The sun was shining down through the cabin skylight. The vessel was floating motionless. Not a sound did I hear except Jim's snoring. I tried to jump up, but found my limbs terribly stiff, every joint aching. I made my way, however, to the old man's berth.

"How are you, Captain Finlay?" I asked.

He did not reply. I stepped nearer. His eyes were closed. I thought he was dead; yet I heard his voice, I was certain of that. I stood looking at him, afraid to ascertain if what I feared was the case. A feeling of awe crept over me. I did not like to call out to Jim, yet I wanted him to come to me. At last I staggered over to the berth in which Jim was sleeping. "Jim! Jim!" I said, "I am afraid the captain is taken very bad."

Jim did not awake, so I shook him several times till he sat up, still half asleep and rubbing his eyes.

"What's the matter?" he asked. "Oh—ay, I know. We'll turn to at the pumps, Peter."

I repeated what I had said. He was on his feet in a moment. He moved at first with as much difficulty as I had done. "Come along," I said, and together we went over to the state cabin. We looked at the old man without speaking. After some time Jim mustered courage to touch his hand. To my great relief the captain opened his eyes.

"Praise God, who has preserved us during the night, my lads!" were the first words he spoke, and while we stood by his side he offered up a short prayer.

He then told us to go on deck and learn the state of the weather.

We hurried up. The sun was shining brightly; the sea was smooth as glass, unbroken by a single ripple. Jim did not forget the leak; he sounded the well.

"We must turn to at the pumps, Peter," he exclaimed. "She's made a good deal of water during the night, and it will take us not a few hours to get it out of her, but we'll not give in."

"I should think not, indeed," I answered. "But I'll go down and hear what the captain wants us to do."

Before I had got half way down the companion-ladder I heard the clank of the pump. Jim had lost no time in setting to work.

I hastened to the state-room. I was startled by the changed appearance of the captain's countenance during the short time I had been on deck. His eyes were turned towards me with a fixed look. I spoke, but he did not answer; I leant over him, no breath proceeded from his lips; I touched his brow, then I knew that the good old man was dead. Presently I closed his eyes, and with a sad heart returned on deck.

"He's gone, Jim," I cried.

"Gone! the captain gone! Then I am sorry," answered Jim, as he stopped pumping for a moment, though he still held the brake in his hands. "Then, Peter, you and I must just do our best to take the brig into port by ourselves."

"I was thinking the same, Jim," I said. "He told us to get up jury-masts and steer west, and that's just what we must do if the wind will let us."

The death of our good captain made us feel very sad, for we had learned to look upon him as our true friend. It caused us also to become more anxious even than before about ourselves. With his assistance we had had little doubt, should the weather remain fine, of reaching a port, but as we were neither of us accustomed to the groping charts, and did not know how to take an observation, we could not tell to what port we should steer our course.

We had both, however, dauntless spirits, and had been accustomed from our childhood to trust to our own resources. Our grand idea was to steer west, if we could manage to get sail on the brig, but before this could be attempted we must pump her free of water.

There was no time to mourn for our old captain, so without delay we turned to at the pumps. My arms and legs and every part of my body felt very stiff. Jim saw that I should not be able to continue long at it.

"Peter, do you go below and look out for some spars to serve as jury-masts," he said; "I'll meantime keep on. We shall soon get the water under; it's only a wonder more hasn't come in."

Jim and I never thought who was captain; if I told him to do a thing he did it, or if he gave an order I did not stop to consider whether or not he had the right to command. We worked together as if we had but one will.

It was "a long pull, a strong pull, and a pull both together."

There were plenty of spars below, and I soon selected some which I thought would serve for the masts and yards we required. I had to call Jim to help me get them up on deck.

"There'll be no use for these till we can find some canvas to spread on them," I observed.

"Nor till we get a breeze to fill the sails," said Jim. "However, we'll get them set while the calm lasts, and no doubt you'll find as many as we can carry in the sail-room."

This was right aft, down a small hatchway. While Jim went again to his pump, I hunted about and hauled out two top-gallantsails and royals, a fore-staysail, a second jib, and a main-trysail. If we could set all these we should do well, supposing we got a fair breeze. It would be no easy job, however, I knew, to get up the masts. We had one advantage. The proper masts had been carried away some six or seven feet from the deck, so that we might lash the spars to them. Before setting to work I again went below to hunt for rope. I got more than I expected from different parts of the vessel, and we had also saved some of the rigging, which had been entangled in the bulwarks.

"We shall want every scrap of rope we can find!" cried Jim, panting and still pumping away.

"I'll take a spell with you," I said. "Then we'll turn to and rig the ship."

I pumped till I could pump no longer, and then, after a short rest, we commenced in earnest. We first lashed a short spar, with a tackle secured to its head, to the stump of the foremast, and then, having fitted two shrouds on a side, with a forestay and backstays, and blocks for the halliards, to the spar we had chosen for a foremast, we swayed it up my means of the short spar and tackle. We could not possibly in any other way have accomplished our object. We next lashed the spar to the stump of the mast. No time was lost in setting up the standing rigging. Our foremast being thus fixed, we surveyed it with infinite satisfaction, and then turned to and fitted the brig with a mainmast in the same fashion. This we made somewhat stronger, as we intended it to carry a mainsail should we have to haul on a wind. Our work, as may be supposed, was not especially neat—indeed, we had to knot most of the shrouds, as it was necessary to keep all the longer lengths of rope for halliards, and we had none to spare.

I cannot stop to explain how we accomplished all this; we could not have done it without employing tackles, which we brought to the windlass, and thus gained twenty times as much power as we by ourselves possessed.

We were now pretty well tired and hungry, for, except some bread and cheese and a jug of cold water, we had taken nothing all day.

It was with a feeling of awe that we went down into the cabin where the old captain lay. Jim, however, closed the door of the state-room, so that we could not see him. We then lighted the fire and cooked some dinner—or rather supper, for evening was drawing on. Anxious to be again at work, we hurried over the meal.

"I say, Peter, don't you think we ought to bury the skipper?" asked Jim, after a long silence.

"Not for some days to come," I answered; "I hope that we may get into port first, so as to lay him in a grave on shore."

"I don't think it will make much odds to him; and, to say the truth, now he's dead, I'd rather he were out of the ship," said Jim; "they say it's unlucky to have a dead man on board."

I had some difficulty in persuading Jim of the folly of such a notion, but we finally agreed that we would try to carry the captain's body to land.

Before bending sails we took a look down forward to see the condition of the leaks. The handspikes were in their places, and, except a slight moisture round the holes, we could not discover that any water was getting in. Still there was a great deal too much in the brig for safety, so we took another spell at the pumps before going on with the rigging.

Darkness found us hard at work. We were too tired and sleepy to attempt keeping a look-out, but I bethought me of hoisting a lantern at each masthead, which would save us from being run down should a breeze spring up during the night. Jim thought the idea capital, and promised to get up and trim the lamps.

Fortunately, the nights were short, so that there was not

much necessity for that. Our chief wish now was that the calm would continue for a few hours during the next day, that we might get the brig to rights.

"One spell more at the pumps!" cried Jim.

We seized the brakes, worked till we could work no longer, then went below, ate some food from the pantry, and lying down in the two larboard berths in the cabin, were fast asleep in a few seconds.

People talk of sleeping like tops. A hard-worked shipboy will beat any top in the world at sleeping soundly.

For a second night the brig lay becalmed. I doubt that if even a fierce gale had sprung up it would have awakened us. The sun was shining when I opened my eyes. It might have been shining for hours for what I could tell.

I roused up Jim, and we sprang on deck, vexed at having, as we supposed, lost so much precious time. By the height of the sun above the horizon, however, we judged that it was not so late as we had at first fancied. The clock in the cabin had been unshipped when the brig went over, and the captain's watch had stopped, so that we had otherwise no means of knowing how the hours passed by. It was still perfectly calm. We looked round in all directions. Not a sail was in sight.

"We must get ready for the breeze, Jim, when it does spring up," I said. "It will come before many hours are over, I've a notion."

I had observed some light clouds just under the sun.

"May be; but we must take a spell at the pumps first," he answered—his first thought was always of them.

We turned to as before, till our arms ached, and then we ran down and got some breakfast. We knew the value of time, but we couldn't get on without eating, any more than other people.

On returning to the deck we lowered the lanterns, which

had long since gone out, finished bending the sails, fitting braces, tacks, sheets, and bowlines, and were then ready to hoist away. We at once set all the sails we had ready, to see how they stood. To our satisfaction, they appeared to greater advantage than we had expected.

"They'll do!" cried Jim, as we surveyed them; "only let us get a breeze from the right quarter, and we'll soon make the land."

Fortunately, the rudder had been uninjured when the brig went over, and the wheel was in order. I stood at the helm, longing for the time when I should see the brig moving through the water. I may say, once for all, that at very frequent intervals Jim and I went to the pumps, but he stood longer at the work than I did. There was urgent necessity for our doing so, as, notwithstanding all our exertions, we had but slightly diminished the water in the hold.

When not thus occupied we did various things that were necessary about the brig; among others we got life-lines round the shattered bulwarks, so that should a heavy sea get up, we might run less risk of being washed overboard. We also went to the store-room, and brought to the cabin various descriptions of provisions, that we might have them at hand when wanted. We knew that when once we got a wind we should have no time to do anything besides navigating the vessel.

I had gone below to get dinner ready, the only hot meal we took in the day, leaving Jim pumping, when I heard him sing out down the companion-hatchway,

"Here it comes, and a rattling breeze, too."

I sprang on deck and went to the helm, while Jim stood ready to trim sails. Looking astern I could see a line of white foam sweeping along towards us over the surface of the ocean. Before it was up to us the sails bulged out, the brig gathered way, and presently she was gliding at the rate of three or four knots through the water.

Jim and I shouted with exultation—we forgot the past—we thought not of the future. We believed that we were about to reap the fruit of our labours.

For several hours we ran on with the wind right aft, steering due west. I steered for most of the time, but Jim occasionally relieved me. So eager were we that we forgot all about eating, till he cried out,

"I must have some food, Peter, or I shall drop."

I was running below to get it, feeling just as hungry as he did, when the wind hauled more to the southward. We took a pull at the starboard braces, and I then hurried below to bring up what we wanted. Just as I was cutting some meat which had been boiling till the fire went out, I heard a crash. I sprang up on deck. The brig was again dismasted, and Jim was struggling in the waves astern.

CHAPTER XI.

DANGERS MULTIPLY.

FOR a moment I could not believe my senses. I felt like a person in a dreadful dream. What, Jim gone! The brig again dismasted, and I left alone on board her with the body of our dead captain! I was recalled to myself by hearing a faint shout, and looking over the stern I saw my old friend struggling amidst the waves some distance off.

My first impulse was to leap into the sea and swim to his rescue, but then the thought happily came to me that if I did we should be unable to regain the vessel; so, instead, crying out, "Keep up, Jim—keep up, I'll help you!" I did what was far more likely to prove effectual—I unrove the peak-halliards, cutting them clear with my knife, and fastened one end to the wooden grating over the cabin sky-light. This I threw overboard, and as I feared that the halliards would not prove long enough, I bent on another rope to them. The grating appeared to be dropping astern very fast; and yet Jim, who was swimming strongly, seemed to be nearing it very slowly, by which I knew that the brig must still, urged on by the impetus she had before received, be moving through the water. Securing the line, I therefore put down the helm, and completely stopped her way. All was done faster than I have described it.

Springing back to the tafferel, with straining eyes I watched Jim, for more I could not do to help him, except to give an occasional shout to cheer him up. The dreadful thought came that there might be sharks about, or that his strength might fail him before he could reach the grating. I did more than cheer, though—I prayed to God with all my soul that Jim might be saved. Often he seemed scarcely to be moving through the water—now he threw himself on his back to rest—then he once more struck bravely out, replying as he did so to my cheer. At length he got near the grating. My heart gave a bound of joy as I saw him seize it, when he gradually drew himself up and lay flat on its surface, the best way for making it afford him support.

With a shout to Jim to hold on, I began to haul in the raft till I brought it under the quarter.

"Wait a minute, Jim, while I get a tackle ready to haul you on board," I cried out.

This did not take me the time I said, and forming a bowline I lowered it to him. He seemed so exhausted that I was afraid lest in trying to pass it over his shoulders he might slide off the grating; and I was about to go down to assist him, when, seeing the rope, he slipped his arms through it and exclaimed, "Haul away, Peter."

I was not long in obeying him, it may be supposed, and I almost cried with joy as I had him at length safe on deck. I knew that the first thing now to be done was to get off his wet clothes, and to give him a restorative, but I had a hard job to carry him below, as he could not help himself.

"Never mind, Peter," he said, faintly; "I shall soon be all to rights again." But I was not going to leave him in the cold air on deck, so going first, I let him slip gradually down the companion-ladder, and then stripping off his clothes, in a short time had him snug between the blankets. I then quickly relighted the fire and warmed up the broth I had before cooked, while I hung up Jim's clothes to dry.

The hot broth seemed greatly to restore him, but as he

was pretty well worn out before he had gone overboard, it is no wonder that as soon as the basin was emptied he fell fast asleep. I had not stopped to ask him how the accident had occurred, but I suspected, as I afterwards found was the case, that as the masts fell a rope had somehow or other caught his legs and whisked him overboard. He was, however, never very clear how it happened.

Having performed my duties below, and taken some food, which I greatly needed, I went on deck. It was still blowing fresh, but there was not much sea on, and the brig lay like a log on the water. To my great relief I found that none of the spars or sails had been lost, all of them having fallen inboard, so I set to work to secure them as well as I could, knowing that till Jim was strong enough to help me I could do nothing towards getting up the masts again.

I did not for a moment contemplate giving up the struggle. I next went down into the forepeak to see if our arrangements for keeping out the water were secure. Nothing had moved. Still, as I knew that the water must be coming in and might gain upon us dangerously, I took a spell at pumping. This pretty well exhausted all my remaining trength, yet before turning in to get some rest there was another thing to be done. We might be in the track of some vessel or other, and should the night prove dark might be run down and sent to the bottom while we were asleep. I therefore trimmed the lamp in one of the lanterns, and with great labour having lashed a spar to the stump of the foremast, hoisted the lantern to the top of it. This done I could do no more, and crawling into my cabin was soon fast asleep in my berth.

I slept tranquilly, knowing that He who had hitherto preserved us was watching over us still. I was awakened by the clanking sound of the pump. It was broad daylight; Jim was not in his berth, and on springing on deck there I saw him in his shirt and trowsers hard at work, forcing up the water at a great rate.

"I'm all to rights, Peter," he said, in a cheerful tone, "and as I guessed that you had been up long after I went to sleep, I thought as how I would take a spell at the pump before rousing you up."

Thanking him for his thoughtfulness, I seized the other brake and pumped till my arms ached.

"Now, Peter, we must see about getting up the masts again," he said, when he saw me knock off.

"You want some breakfast first, and so do I," I answered. "We'll then set to work with a will."

We took some food, which rested and refreshed us, and then commenced the task we had undertaken.

The wind had again fallen. What there was of it was fair, and the sea was almost as smooth as a millpond. Had it been rough we could scarcely have attempted the work. We had first to unreeve all the ropes, and unbend all the sails. We then selected two much stouter spars than before for fresh masts, got the standing rigging over their heads, and by means of tackles got them set up to the stumps of the fore and main masts, next securing them much more effectually we hoped than the former jury-masts had been, with light spars of different lengths lashed round them, and additional backstays.

We made such good progress that by night we were almost ready to hoist the sails, having all the time rested only for a few minutes to obtain some food and then going on again.

Nature, however, at last gave way, and if we stopped for a moment we went fast asleep with a rope or marlinespike in our hands.

"It's no use trying to keep awake, Jim," I said.

He in a sleepy voice, agreed, and having again hoisted

the lantern we went below to get the rest we so much needed.

The next morning I heard as before the pump going. It was still dark, but Jim had awoke, and this was always his first thought. I joined him, and we laboured on till there was light enough to enable us to bend sails. The wind being fair we soon had them hoisted, and I went to the helm, Jim pulling and hauling to trim them as required.

It must be understood that everything was done in a rough-and-ready fashion, but it was the best we could do.

Once more the brig glided on towards the west at the rate, as we supposed, of three or four knots an hour. Jim, having done all that was required, took my place at the helm while I went below to get some food for breakfast. As I was unwilling to be off the deck a moment longer than was necessary, without stopping to light the fire I brought up a supply of provisions and water to last us for some time, as also some cloaks and blankets. We agreed that we must content ourselves with cold water, and ham, and cheese, and bread, and be thankful, remembering how many poor fellows had been much worse off than we were.

We ate a hearty meal, I feeding Jim while he steered. He did not appear to have suffered from his long swim, except that he complained of being very sleepy. I therefore advised him to lie down on the coats and blankets I had brought on deck to get some rest, while I took his place at the helm, promising to call him should the breeze freshen and it become necessary to shorten sail. He agreed and I steered on, now looking at the compass, now at the canvas, and now all around on the chance of a vessel appearing from which we might learn our position. I own that I should have been very unwilling for any one to have come on board to take the brig into harbour, for we both thought how proud we should feel if we could carry her in ourselves without help. Still, for the sake of the owners we could not, we had agreed, refuse assistance should it be offered us. At last my eyes began to close, and it was with the greatest difficulty that I could keep them open, or prevent myself from sinking down on the deck. I was, therefore, very thankful when I saw Jim begin to move. I uttered his name. He was on his feet in an instant.

"I'll take a spell at the pump first," he said, rubbing his eyes and looking round, especially ahead; "then I'll come to the helm."

Talking to him aroused me a little, and I was able to hold on till he relieved me. I was almost asleep before I sank down on the blanket, only just hearing him say, "We must keep a bright look-out ahead, for we ought soon to be making the land."

That sleep did me a great deal of good. We agreed that we would both take as much as we could during the day, that we might be more wide-awake at night. I had observed that there was something on Jim's mind, and while we were at supper, soon after sunset, I asked him what it was.

"Why, you see, as I said afore, I wish that our old skipper was, somehow or other, out of the ship. Now if you are willing, Peter, I'll sew him up all comfortable like in an old sail, with a pig of iron at the feet; and as you are a better scholar than I am, you can say the prayers over him while we lower him overboard, and to my mind he'll be just as well off as he would be ashore."

I reminded Jim that he had before consented to our keeping the body as long as we could, but knowing that his superstitious ideas induced him to make the proposal, and that he was really uncomfortable, I agreed to bury our skipper at the end of three days if we did not by that time sight the land.

The night and another day went by, the wind still holding

fair. I pointed out to Jim how thankful we should be for this, as I was certain that in the latitude where we were there was seldom so long a continuance of fine weather. He, however, was far from easy in his mind. He was sure, he said, that we ought to have seen the land before this, and was continually, when not working the pump, going forward to look out for it.

"I knows that England is an island, as the song says, 'Our right little, tight little island;' and don't you think that somehow we may have passed to the nor'ard of it, and be going away into the Atlantic?"

"I hope not," I answered; "for if so we shall not get into port till we have run right across it; but I am sure the captain never intended us to do that when he told us to steer west; I think rather that we have not been going as fast as we supposed. I'll heave the log and try, though it will be a difficult job to do so."

I got out the reel and glass. The latter I gave to Jim to hold with one hand, while he steered with the other. The handle of the reel I managed to put into a hole in the shattered bulwarks, so that it could run round easily. I then took the log-ship in my right hand and hove it.

"Turn!" I cried.

"Turn!" said Jim.

The line ran slowly out.

"Stop!" cried Jim.

I examined the line.

"Two knots and a half was all it showed. Jim thought we were going four. I was thus certain that we had run a much shorter distance than he supposed, but he was not convinced that I was right.

Day and night, between the intervals of pumping, he went forward to look out. Another day went by. It was again night. Jim had been a long time pumping when he said that he would go forward and look out till it was his turn to take the helm. I advised him rather to lie down, as I was sure that he must be tired, but he would not, and away he went into the darkness towards the bows.

I every now and then hailed him and he answered. I had not hailed for some time when I felt the breeze freshen. The maintopsail and mainsail bulged out, straining at the sheets, and the masts began to complain.

"Jim! Jim!" I shouted, "shorten sail, be smart about it."

But Jim did not answer. I dared not leave the helm lest the brig should broach to and our masts again be carried overboard.

Once more I shouted, "Jim! Jim!" Still he did not come, and the dreadful idea arose in my mind that he had fallen overboard.

At last I could withstand the desire no longer of rushing forward to ascertain what had become of him. What mattered it, if he were lost, what else might happen? I made a dash forward, keeping my eye on the stars. I had got as far as the mainmast when I saw that the brig's head was moving round, so I sprang back to right the helm.

Again and again I shrieked out my companion's name at the top of my voice, springing forward, but had only got a little farther than before when I had to return.

The wind continued to get up. The masts would go, I saw, if sail were not shortened. I let go the main-topsail, and throat and peak halliards. The sails flapped loudly in the wind, but as the brig now kept more steadily before it, I thought that I should be able to reach the forecastle, though I had very little hope of finding Jim.

I was still shouting his name, when what was my joy to hear him cry out, "Hillo! what's the matter?" and I saw his head rise from just before the windlass. I never in my life felt more inclined to abuse him for the fright he had given me, thankful as I was that no harm had happened to him. I did not even tell him how much I had been alarmed, but merely cried out, "Come, be smart, Jim, we must stow the canvas." We were beginning to do so, when the wind fell, and instead we again hoisted the fore-topsail. Jim owned that while he fancied he was looking out his legs gave way and that he had sunk down on the deck.

"Take care that the same doesn't happen when you are steering, or worse consequences may follow," I remarked.

He now let me take my nap, and when I awoke he said that we had had a famous run; but towards noon the wind dropped, and it became towards evening a stark calm. This lasted all night and far into the next day.

"Peter, do you know if there's a prayer-book aboard?" asked Jim.

The question surprised me. I was nearly certain that there was not.

"Well then, you can say some prayers without one," he continued. "For, Peter, there's no use talking longer about it; we must bury the skipper."

Reluctantly I agreed. Jim got a piece of canvas, a sailmaker's needle, and some twine, with a pig of iron ballast which had been used in one of the boats. As there was no sign of a breeze, with these he went below, and for the first time since his death opened the captain's state-room. We brought the corpse into the main cabin, and placing it on the canvas, without loss of time Jim began sewing it up. The old man's kind face had scarcely changed. We took one respectful last look at it, and then Jim, drawing the canvas over it, shut it out from sight.

We had now to get the body on deck, but without a tackle this we could not have done. At last we managed to haul it up the companion-ladder. When Jim went below for more canvas and twine to fasten on the pig of iron to the feet, we had been longer about our task than we had supposed. Looking astern, I saw that the sky was darkened by heavy masses of clouds, while a line of foam came hissing over the surface of the deep towards us.

"Quick! quick! Jim," I shouted; "shorten sail, or the masts will be over the side!"

I ran as I spoke to the halliards; he followed; we had to be smart about it, and even thus the gale was on us before we could get the canvas stowed. That was not to be done in a hurry. First one sail got loose, then another, and we had to hurry to secure them. The sea rose with unusual suddenness, and the brig was soon tossing about in a way which made us fear that another leak would be sprung, or the old ones break out. We managed at length to set the fore-topsail, closely reefed, and I going to the helm, we ran before the gale.

If Jim was before anxious about our being near the land, he was more so now. His eyes were nearly always turned ahead, but I began to think more about the leaks. I asked him what he thought.

"We'll try the well," he answered.

No sooner had he examined the rod than he exclaimed,

"We must turn to at the pumps, Peter, if we don't want to go to the bottom."

We no longer thought of burying the captain, or doing anything but keeping the brig afloat. The night began; Jim worked away as hard as his failing strength would allow. I shouted to him to let me take a spell.

"No, no; you keep at the helm, Peter," he answered; "I'll work till I drop."

He only stopped now and then to take a look-out ahead.

The gale seemed to be increasing; the brig pitched and rolled more and more. Suddenly there came a loud clap.

The foresail had given way. Jim ran forward, and lowered it on deck.

As I could no longer be of use at the helm, I ran to his help, and we tried to set it again, but all our efforts were in vain. Every moment, too, the seas now raging round the vessel threatened to break on board.

"Peter, the water is coming in as fast as we get it out, and if we don't keep pumping it will gain upon us," said Jim.

For fear of being carried away, we made ourselves fast to some stanchions near the pumps, so that we could reach the brakes, and worked away till we were both ready to drop. Now and then we had to stop to draw breath and regain our strength. The hard battered brig pitched and rolled and tumbled, the seas dancing up wildly on every side of her. Again we had stopped, when Jim exclaimed, "Hark! I hear the breakers."

I listened. The dreaded sound reached my ears. The brig was driving rapidly towards them.

CHAPTER XII.

PORT REACHED IN AN UNEXPECTED MANNER.

THE sound of the breakers grew louder and louder. Every instant we expected to find the brig sent crashing on the rocks, and to have the furious seas breaking over us.

"There's no use pumping any longer, Peter," said Jim. "We must cling to whatever we can get hold of, and hope for the chance of being hove up on the beach, if there is one."

"A poor chance that," I could not help answering. "Perhaps the brig may be driven in between some rocks, and will hold together till the morning; if not we must be prepared to die."

And I spoke to him as I think my mother would have spoken to me. Clinging to the shattered bulwarks, we waited for the dreadful event with all the resignation we could muster. Still the crash did not come, though the vessel appeared to be tossed about even more violently than before.

"Peter, the breakers don't sound so loud as they did just now," exclaimed Jim, after some time.

"Let's look at the compass," I said, casting off the rope round my waist.

"I'll go too," cried Jim, doing the same. "What happens to you shall happen to both."

Together we made our way to the binnacle, in which the lamp was still burning. As we eagerly examined the compass we found that the wind had shifted to the south-west, and if there was land, as we supposed, to the westward, was blowing partly off shore. We must have drifted past a headland, on which we had heard the seas breaking. Had the foresail stood we should have run on it, and we had cause, therefore, to be thankful that it had given way. Now, however, as it was important to keep off the land, we attempted to secure the clew and tack, and hauling together succeeded in again hoisting it. I then ran to the helm, and found that I could steer east by north or thereabouts. Though the brig moved very slowly, still I believed that we were getting away from the dreaded shore. We ran on for some time, when once more the wind shifted to the eastward of south, and blew with greater fury than before.

"It's drawing more and more to the east," said Jim, looking at the compass.

We hauled down the foresail, as it would only, we believed, drive us the faster to destruction. The brig tumbled and rolled and pitched about in a way that made it difficult for us to keep our feet, and every now and then the seas, washing over the deck, would have swept us off had we not again lashed ourselves to the stanchions near the pumps. These we worked as vigorously as our failing strength would allow. We had resolved not to give in while the brig remained afloat. How we longed for daylight, that we might see where we were, and judge how we could best try to save ourselves!

That we were again driving towards the terrible rocks we knew too well, and several times Jim stopped pumping to listen for the sound of the breakers. At length he exclaimed, "I hear them, Peter! In less than ten minutes the brig will be in pieces! Good-bye, if the sea gets us;

but we'll have a fight for it; so the moment she strikes we'll cast ourselves off from the stanchions."

We were shaking hands while he spoke. I was not quite certain that I did hear the breakers, the noises on board the tumbling vessel making it difficult to distinguish sounds. Shortly after this there came a lull, but we thought it only the prelude to another squall.

The wind fell more and more.

"I see day breaking!" cried Jim, looking eastward.

Faint yellow and red streaks were visible in that direction under the dark mass of clouds. The light increased, and to the westward, fringed by a line of rugged black rocks, a green island gradually rose before our sight. There were grassy slopes, and cliffs, and high, steep, round-topped hills, with clear streams running between them, forming lakelets near the beach, glittering in the rays of the rising sun, now bursting through the dissolving clouds. Far as our eyes could reach not a tree was visible, nor could we discover a single cottage or other habitation of man. As the light increased we found that we were about half a mile away from the entrance of a narrow gulf, which extended apparently far inland. Not a boat floated on the surface of the gulf, not a sail was to be seen along the coast.

" I'm greatly afeared that yonder is a dissolute island " (meaning a desolate island), " and if no help comes to us from the shore we may be blown out to sea, and be worse off than before," said Jim.

The wind had fallen to an almost perfect calm, but what there was blew out of the gulf, so that we could not hope to take the vessel up it, while the breakers still burst in sheets of foam on the rocks, and we lay tossed up and down by the glassy rolling seas. We were utterly helpless.

While we were at breakfast a thought occurred to me.

"I'll tell you what we'll do, Jim," I said; "we'll build a

raft, put the poor old captain on it, take him ashore, and bury him. If we can find no people or houses we'll go off again. The brig won't drift far away in the meantime. If the wind will let us we'll run into the gulf, or if it shifts to the northward we'll steer along shore to the south and look out for another harbour. From what the captain said we may be sure there is one not far off where we shall find people to help us."

Jim jumped at my proposal.

"That's it, Peter; when once the dead man is out of the brig things will go better with us," he answered.

I did not stop to argue the point, but turned to at once with him to form the proposed raft. We had plenty of spars below, so that our undertaking was not so difficult as it would have been had we not had a good supply. We first cut them into lengths with a saw we found below, and having placed them side by side, lashed others across on the top of them.

Eager as we were to finish our task, we had more than once to stop and rest, for we were both very weak, and I felt a sensation of weariness I had not ever before experienced. In fact, we were thoroughly knocked up from the hard work we had gone through, and the little time we had had for rest.

Having completed the raft and formed some paddles, we launched it overboard and secured it alongside.

"Now, Jim," I said, "we must take some provisions, in case there are no people on the island, as we may have a longer pull back than we may like, and we have to bring up the captain and put him on the raft."

We quickly collected some provisions, and I took the empty water-jar from the pantry.

"What's that for?" asked Jim. "There's water enough on shore, surely."

"Yes, but if we have a long pull back to the brig we shall be thankful for water," I answered.

While thus employed we heard a voice coming from no great distance hail "Ship ahoy!".

My heart leapt within me at the sound, and running to the side we saw a boat with five men in her pulling towards us. An oldish man of portly figure, who looked like a sea captain, was steering.

"Are ye the only people aboard?" he sang out as he saw us.

"The only live ones, sir," answered Jim.

There was no time to exchange more words before the boat was alongside, and the old gentleman and his men stepped on board. He gave a look of surprise as he saw the captain's body, and he then, turning to us, appeared more surprised still.

"Why, my laddies, what has happened? How did this craft come here?" he asked, in a kind tone.

I briefly told him how the masts had been carried away and the people washed overboard, and how the captain had been struck down and afterwards had died, and how we had kept him to bury him decently on shore, adding,

"He told us to steer west, sir, and so we did, but we don't know what country we've come to."

"Why, surely, to Shetland, laddies," he answered. "But if ye had kept a little farther to the north ye would have passed our islands and run into the Atlantic, and it's weel for ye that ye did na do that. And now my men and I will take your craft up the voe and anchor her in safety. We might carry her to Lerwick, but the weather is unsettled, and she's na weel fitted to encounter another gale, no discredit to ye, laddies."

Our new friend evidently compassionated our forlorn condition; indeed, now that the necessity for exerting ourselves was over, we both sank down utterly exhausted on the deck.

The Shetlanders would have carried us below, but we begged to remain where we were, that we might see what was going forward. They therefore left us, and having placed the captain's body on the main hatch, covered by a flag, they proceeded to pull our raft to pieces and to hoist the spars composing it on board. This done, the four men jumped into the boat, and going ahead began to tow the brig, while the old gentleman went to the helm to steer.

Before long, however, a breeze from the eastward springing up, the boat returned alongside, the men hoisted the canvas, and we stood in towards the voe, as the gulf, we found, was called. I could just distinguish the high green hills, with here and there grey cliffs and rocks jutting out from these on either side, as we sailed up the voe, but my eyes grew dimmer and dimmer till the brig's anchor was dropped, and I was just aware that we were being placed in the boat to be carried on shore.

When I came to myself I found that I was in a comfortable bed with curtains round it, the sun shining brightly through the open window of the room, which looked neater and prettier than any I had ever slept in.

Hearing a footstep, I peered through the curtains, and saw a lady and a little girl come in, carrying in their hands some things which they placed on the table.

"I think the poor boy is awake, auntie," whispered the little girl. "I heard him move."

"Perhaps he was only moving in his sleep, but I will see," answered the lady, and she approached the bed.

I was looking all the time at the little girl, who seemed to me like an angel or a fairy, or some being altogether brighter than I had ever seen before—even than my sister Mary.

"Yes, marm, I am awake, thank you," I said, as she opened the curtains, "and please, I want to get up and go aboard the brig to look after her and to see that our old captain is buried."

"He was buried by the minister the day you came, and the brig is taken very good care of," she answered. "My father, Mr. Angus Troil, has written to the owners to inform them of what has happened to her and of your brave conduct. He hopes soon to hear from them."

"Thank you, marm," I again said, puzzled to know what the lady meant about hearing soon from Mr. Gray, for I had supposed that Shetland was a long way from England. My first thought, however, had been about Jim.

"Please, marm, where is the other boy, my shipmate?" I asked.

"He was very ill only for three or four days, and is now well enough to go down to the brig with my father," she replied. "But I must not let you talk too much. You were to have some food, the doctor said, when you came to yourself. Here, Maggie, bring the broth and toast."

Thereon the little girl brought the tray to the bedside and gazed compassionately at me, while the lady put the food into my mouth, for I was too weak to do so myself.

It now dawned on me from what the lady said that I must have been in a state of unconsciousness for many days, and such I found was the case. I recollected nothing that had passed since I was placed in the boat. I could not speak much, but when I had finished the basin of broth I said,

"I am very thankful to you and your little daughter, marm, for all you have done for me."

"You deserve to be taken care of, my boy," she answered; "but this little girl is not my daughter. Her father was my brother. He was lost at sea while captain of a ship, and her mother has since died, so that she is very precious to us."

I looked at little Maggie with even more interest than before, and I said,

"My father was also drowned, and so was my grandfather, and I believe his father before him, for I come of a seafaring family."

"That has been likewise the fate of many of the Troils," said the lady; "but I must not let you talk more now. Before long my father and your young shipmate will be returning, and they will be glad to hear from your own lips how you feel. In the meantime try to go to sleep again. The doctor says that the more you sleep the sooner you will regain your strength. Saying this, the lady, followed by the little girl, left the room.

I thought over what she had said to me, and kept repeating to myself, "Margaret Troil! Margaret Troil! I know that name, I am sure!" but I did not think long before I forgot where I was and what had happened.

I saw Maggie's sweet face peeping in at me when I woke, but as soon as she saw that my eyes were open she ran off, and shortly afterwards Mr. Troil and Jim came into the room. The old gentleman spoke very kindly; told me that I must consider myself at home, and that though he hoped I should soon get well, I must be in no hurry to go away. He then went out, saying to Jim, "I can let you stay only five minutes with your friend. When the time is up I must call you."

Jim could at first scarcely speak for joy at seeing me so much better. He then told me how highly Mr. Troil spoke of me and him for the way we had kept the brig afloat, and brought her to the coast of Shetland.

"I told him as how it wasn't us who did it," continued Jim, "but that God sent the wind as blew us here; and he says to me, 'To be sure, that was the case in one way, but then that God rewarded your efforts, and thus you deserve great credit for what you did.' He promises to see that we are rewarded, and to do all he can for us himself. I told him as how you were really captain, and that I couldn't have done anything by myself, except pump, and that I had done with a will, seeing I am bigger and stronger than you."

I was inclined to smile at Jim's modesty, though I felt very grateful to him for speaking so well of me, and was about to ask him what Mr. Troil said in return, when our host called him out of the room. I was thus left to myself, except when the lady, who Jim had told me was Miss Troil, the old gentleman's daughter, or little Maggie looked in to see if I wanted anything. Two days after this I was able to dress and sit out in front of the house, enjoying the sun and air, looking down on the voe in which lay our brig, with a small sloop and several fishing vessels and boats. On that side, looking to the south, there was a view of the voe and the opposite bank, but on all the others the house, a square stone building, was protected by a high wall close to it, built to keep off the biting cold winds and snow of winter. Jim was out with Mr. Troil, and as Miss Troil was engaged, Maggie came and sat by me with a book, and read and talked to me for a long time, getting me to tell her all about myself and our perilous voyage, till her aunt summoned her to attend to some household affairs. When I returned to my room I found that my chest had been brought on shore and placed there. Miss Troil came in and took out the things, which, having become damp and mildewy, she wished to dry. While doing so she came upon my old Testament, which, chancing to open, she examined the inside of the cover with intense curiosity.

"Why, Peter, how did you come by this?" she asked.

The family had got by this time to call me Peter.

I told her that it had belonged to my father's mother, and then for the first time since I came to Shetland I recollected that the name in it was spelt in the same way as that of my host.

"I must ask my father about this!" she exclaimed. "He had an uncle called Angus, after whom he was named, and who married a Margaret Halcro. There are none of the family remaining in Shetland, though at one time they were numerous. Peter, I should not be surprised if it turns out that you are a kinsman of ours. Should you like to be so?"

"Indeed I should!" I answered; "I feel as if I were one already, from the kind way you have treated me, even before you thought I might be a relative."

When Mr. Troil came in he listened attentively to what his daughter told him, and, having examined the handwriting in the Testament, asked me the ages of my father and grandmother, and all other particulars I could tell him.

"I have no doubt about your being a near relative of ours, Peter, and I rejoice to find you one, my dear boy," he said; "though why my aunt Margaret Troil did not come back to her husband's relatives after her husband's death I cannot tell."

"Perhaps she had not the means to make the journey, or my father had gone away to sea, and she was afraid that he might be unable to find her on his return if she left her home; or, now I think of it, I remember my father saying that she died soon after my grandfather was lost, when he himself was a little chap."

"Well, all is ordered for the best, though we don't see how," said Mr. Troil. "And now you have come you must stay with us and turn back into a Shetlander. What do you say to my proposal?"

"Oh, do stay with us, Cousin Peter!" exclaimed Maggie, taking my hand and looking up in my face.

"Indeed, I should like very much to do so," I answered, "but there is my sister Mary, and I cannot desert her, even though I know that she is well off with Mr. Gray."

"Then Peter must go and fetch her!" exclaimed Maggie. "Oh, I should so like to have her here! I would love her as a sister."

"A bright idea of yours, Maggie," said Mr. Troil. "What do you say to it, Peter? I will furnish you with ample funds, and you can be back here in a month, as I feel very sure that your friend Mr. Gray will willingly allow Mary to come."

I need not say that I gladly accepted my generous relative's proposal, and it was arranged that as soon as I had quite recovered my strength I should go south in the first vessel sailing from Lerwick, accompanied by Jim, who wanted to see his friends, and hoped to be able to work his passage both ways, so that he might not be separated from me.

CHAPTER XIII.

A DISASTROUS VOYAGE.

I WAS soon myself again, and ready for the proposed voyage southward. Accordingly, Mr. Troil having received directions from Mr. Gray to send the *Good Intent* to Lerwick to be refitted, Tom and I, bidding farewell, as we hoped, only for a short season to Miss Troil and Maggie, went on board the brig to assist in carrying her there, intending to proceed by the first vessel sailing after our arrival. Mr. Troil sent us a pilot and a good crew to navigate the vessel, and accompanied her himself in his sloop, that he might assist us if necessary.

The wind was fair and the sea smooth, and thus without accident we arrived in that fine harbour called Brassa Sound, on the shore of which Lerwick, the capital of the islands, stands. We there found a vessel shortly to sail for Newcastle. Having taken in a cargo of coals, she was thence to proceed to Portsmouth. This so exactly suited our object that Mr. Troil at once engaged a passage on board her for Jim and me.

After Portsmouth the town appeared small, but the inhabitants have large warm hearts, and were very kind to Jim and me. As he remarked, it is better to have large hearts and live in a small place than small cold hearts and to live in a large place. They seemed never to tire of asking us questions about our voyage in the *Good Intent*, and how we two boys alone managed to rig jury-masts and to keep her afloat.

"By just knowing how to do our work and sticking to it," answered Jim, to one of our friends.

If we had remained much longer at Lerwick we should ave begun to fancy ourselves much more important persons than we really were; but the brig *Nancy*, Captain Gowan, was ready for sea, and wishing farewell to my kind relative, Mr. Troil, who set sail in his ship to return home, we went on board. We soon afterwards got under way with a fair breeze, and before night had left Sumburgh Head, the lofty point which forms the southern end of the Shetland Islands, far astern.

The *Nancy* was a very different sort of craft from the *Good Intent*. She was an old ill-found vessel, patched up in an imperfect manner, and scarcely seaworthy. Jim and I agreed that if she were to meet with the bad weather we encountered in our old ship she would go to the bottom or drive ashore.

We discovered also before long that Captain Gowan was a very different person from our former captain. He had conducted himself pretty well on shore, so that people spoke of him as a very decent man, but when once at sea he threw off all restraint, abused the crew, quarrelled with the mate, and neglected us, who had been placed under his charge.

Jim, who had to work his passage, slept in the fore-peak, but I was berthed aft. I, however, did as much duty as anyone. Jim told me that the men were a rough lot, and that he had never heard worse language in his life. They tried to bully him, but as he was strong enough to hold his own, and never lost his temper, they gave up the attempt. Captain Gowan growled when I came in to dinner the first day, which I knew that I had a right to do, and he asked if every ship-boy was to be turned into a young gentleman because he happened to have saved his life while others lost theirs?

I did not answer him, for I saw an empty bottle on the locker, and another by his side with very little liquor remaining in it. After this I kept out of his way, and got my meals from the cook as best I could.

Jim and I agreed that if the *Nancy* had not been going direct to Portsmouth, we should do well to leave her at Newcastle, and try to make our way south on board some other vessel. Although we went, I believe, much out of our proper course, we at last entered the Tyne. Soon after we brought up, several curiously shaped boats, called kreels, came alongside, containing eight tubs, each holding a chaldron; these tubs being hoisted on board, their bottoms were opened and the coals fell into the hold.

The kreels, which were oval in shape, were propelled by a long oar or pole on each side, worked by a man who walked along the gunwale from the bow to the stern, pressing the upper end with his shoulder while the lower touched the ground. Another man stood in the stern with a similar long oar to steer.

The crews were fine hardy fellows, known as kreelmen. I was astonished to hear them call each other bullies, till I found that the term signified "brothers." So bully Saunders meant brother Saunders.

Jim and I had had the sense to put on our working clothes, which was fortunate, as before long, with the coal-dust flying about, we were as black as negroes; but as everything and all on board were coloured with the same brush, we did not mind that.

With the help of the kreelmen the *Nancy* was soon loaded, and we again sailed for the southward. Matters did not improve. The captain, having abstained from liquor while on shore, recompensed himself by taking a double allowance, and became proportionably morose and ill-tempered, never speaking civilly to me, and often passing a whole day without exchanging a word with his poor mate; and when he did open his mouth it was to abuse. The brig, though tolerably tight when light, now that she had a full cargo, as soon as a sea got up began to leak considerably, so that each watch had to pump for an hour to keep the water under. Jim and I took our turns without being ordered, but though accustomed to the exercise, it was hard work. When we cried "Spell ho!" for others to take our places, the captain shouted, "You began to pump for your own pleasure, now you shall go on for mine, you young rascals!" The men, however, though they at first laughed, having more humanity than the skipper, soon relieved us.

This was the third day after we sailed, when the wind shifting to the south-west, and then to the south, we stood away to the eastward in order to double the North Foreland. After some time it came on to blow harder than ever, but the brig was made snug in time, though the leaks increased, and all hands in a watch were kept, spell and spell, at the pumps. The captain behaved just as before, drinking all day long, though he did not appear to lose his senses altogether. The mate, however, looked very anxious as the vessel pitched into the seas each time more violently than before. I asked him if he thought she would keep afloat.

"That's more than I can promise you, my boy," he answered. "If the wind falls, and the sea goes down, we may perhaps manage to keep the leaks under; but if I were the captain I would run for Harwich or the Thames sooner than attempt to thrash the vessel round the Foreland."

"Why don't you propose that to him, and if he does not agree, just steer as you think best?" I said. "I suspect that he would not find out in what direction we were standing.'

"Wouldn't he, though! Why, Peter, I tell you he would swear there was a mutiny, and knock me overboard," answered the poor mate in a tone of alarm.

He was evidently completely cowed by the captain, and dared not oppose him. The night was just coming on; the seas kept breaking over the bows, washing the deck fore and aft, and the clank of the pumps was heard without cessation. The captain sat in his cabin, either drinking or sleeping, except when occasionally he clambered on deck, took a look around while holding on to the companion hatch, and then, apparently thinking that all was going on well, went below again. When I could pump no longer I turned in, thinking it very probable that I should never see another sunrise. By continually pumping, the brig was kept afloat during the night; but when I came on deck in the morning, the mate, who looked as if he would drop from fatigue, told me that the leaks were gaining on us. We were now far out, I knew, in the German Ocean, and if the brig should go down, there was too much sea running to give us a chance of saving ourselves.

Some time after daylight the captain came on deck, and he had not been there long when there was a lull. "Hands about ship!" he shouted.

The watch below tumbled up, and the brig was got round.

"Will you take charge, sir?" humbly asked the mate. "I have been on deck all night, and can scarcely stand."

The captain raved at him for a lazy hound. "I haven't turned in, either," he said, though he had been asleep in his chair for several hours. "I want my breakfast; when I've had that I'll relieve you."

The mate made no reply, and as soon as the captain went below he hurried forward to bid the cook make haste with the cabin breakfast. It was a difficult matter, however, to

A Disastrous Voyage.

keep the galley fire alight, or the pots on it in their places. The weather seemed to be improving, but the men were well-nigh worn out with pumping. When the captain at last came on deck, in spite of their grumbling, he kept them labouring away as hard as ever, and ordered Jim and me to take our turn with the rest. This we did willingly, as we knew that unless all exerted themselves the brig must founder.

As noon approached, the captain brought up his quadrant, and sent below to summon the mate to take observations, though the clouds hung so densely over the sky that there was but little chance of doing this.

"Might as well try to shoot the sun at midnight as now, with the clouds as dark as pitch," growled the mate. "What was the use of calling me up for such fool's work?"

"What's that you say?" shouted the captain. "Do you call me a fool?"

"Yes, I do, if you expect to take an observation with such a sky as we have got overhead," answered the mate.

"Then take that!" screamed the captain, throwing the quadrant he held in his hand at the mate's head, not, for the moment, probably, recollecting what it was.

It struck the mate on the temple, who, falling, let his own quadrant go, and both were broken to pieces.

"Here's a pretty business," cried one of the men, "I wonder now what will become of us!"

Good reason we had to wonder. The mate, picking himself up, flew at the captain, and a fearful struggle ensued. Both were too excited to know what they were about, and the captain, who was the stronger of the two, would have hove the mate overboard had not the crew rushed aft and separated them.

The mate then went below, and the captain rolled about

the deck, stamping and shouting that he would be revenged on him. At last he also went down into the cabin.

Fearing that he would at once put his fearful threats into execution and attack the mate, I followed, intending to call the crew to my assistance should it be necessary. I saw him, however, take another pull at the rum bottle, and then, growling and muttering, turn into his bed. I waited till I supposed that he was asleep, and then I went to the mate's berth.

"There is no one in charge of the deck, sir," I said. "And if it was to blow harder, as it seems likely to do, I don't know what will happen."

"Nor do I either, Peter, with such a drunken skipper as ours," he answered. "What are the men about?"

"They have knocked off from the pumps, and if you don't come on deck and order them to turn to again they'll let the brig go down without making any further effort to save her," I answered.

My remarks had some effect, for though the mate had himself been drinking, or he would not have spoken as he did to the captain, he yet had some sense left in his head. He at last got up and came on deck. All the hands, except the man at the helm, were crouching down under the weather bulwarks to avoid the showers of spray flying in dense masses over us. The sea had increased, and though we had not much sail set, the brig was heeling over to the furious blasts which every now and then struck her; if she righted it was only to bend lower still before the next.

"Do you want to lose your lives or keep them, lads?" shouted the mate, after sounding the well. "Well then, I can tell you that if you don't turn to at once and work hard, and very hard, too, the brig will be at the bottom before the morning."

Still the men did not move. Jim was holding on near me.

"Come, let you and me try what we can do," I said; "we have pumped to good purpose before now."

Jim needed no second asking. Seizing the brakes, we began, and pumped away with all our might, making the water rush across the deck in a full stream. Before long one man got up and joined, then another, and another. When we got tired and cried, "Spell ho!" the rest took our places.

"I see you want to save your lives, lads," cried the mate, who occasionally took a spell himself. "But you must keep at it, or it will be of no use."

All that day we stood on, the crew pumping without intermission.

"If the wind moderates we'll set more sail," said the mate; "but the brig has as much on her as she can bear. We must be soon looking out for land, though. You, Peter, have a sharp pair of eyes—go aloft, and try if you can see it."

Though the vessel was heeling over terribly at the time, I was about to obey, when Jim said, "No, you stay on deck; let me go, Peter."

To this I would not agree.

"Then I'll go with you," said Jim.

So we both crawled up the weather rigging together. Jim said he thought that he saw land on the starboard bow, but I did not get a glimpse of it, and felt sure that he was mistaken; at all events there was no land visible ahead. We remained aloft till darkness came on, and there was no use remaining longer.

We made our reports to the mate. He said that Jim was right, and that we had probably passed the South Foreland.

This was, however, I suspected, only to encourage the men to keep at the pumps. All night long, spell and spell, we laboured away. When the morning broke no land was in sight. By this time we were all pretty well knocked up, and most of the men declared that they could pump no longer.

The mate now tried to make them keep on, reminding them that if they did not they would lose their lives. Some answered that they would take their chance, but Jim and I and others kept at our duty. Even we, however, began to feel that the struggle would be useless unless we should soon make the land, for the mate could not deny that the water was gaining on us.

The wind, however, began to moderate, and the sun bursting forth from between the clouds cheered us up a little.

At last the captain came on deck. After looking about him for some time he told me to go below and get his quadrant. He was apparently sober, and seemed to have forgotten what had happened.

"Have you a second one, sir?" I asked.

"No; bring the one I always use," he answered.

"You hove it at the mate yesterday, sir," I said. "And he fell and broke his."

"What lies are you telling, youngster?" he exclaimed, uttering a fearful oath. Then he shouted to the mate, who had gone forward to be out of his way,

"Did I heave my quadrant at you?"

"Yes, you did," answered the mate. "You made me break mine, too, and if we lose our lives you'll have them on your head."

The captain made no reply. I think that the occurrence must have flashed on his mind. He looked at the compass, took two or three turns on deck, and then ordered more sail to be set, directly afterwards changing the ship's course to north-west. I therefore supposed that we were steering

A Disastrous Voyage.

for the Downs, or perhaps for St. Helens. The men, though very tired, went on pumping far more willingly than before.

A bright look-out was kept for land, but no land appeared. For some hours the brig made fair progress, but as the evening drew on the wind again got up. The captain had gone below. He could not resist taking a pull at the rum bottle. We were carrying topsails and topgallant-sails.

A sudden squall laid the brig over. The captain sprang on deck and shouted,

"All hands shorten sail! You, Peter and Jim, up aloft with you and hand the maintop-gallant-sail."

The blast had passed over and the brig had righted. Jim and I ran aloft to obey the order.

The rest of the people were still on deck except one man, who had gone up the fore-rigging, about to let fly the sheets and brail up; but, nearly worn out with labouring at the pumps, they must have very slowly obeyed the orders they received, for almost before a sheet was let go, another furious squall struck the brig. Over, over she heeled.

Jim and I slid down into the main-top.

"Hold on, whatever happens," cried Jim.

The warning was given not a moment too soon. There was a fearful cracking sound, the mast quivered, it was almost right over the water, and just as the brig was on her beam-ends it gave way, tearing out the chain plates on the weather side, and Jim and I were hurled with it into the raging sea.

I expected every moment that we should be washed off as the mast was towed along, and so we must have been had not the lee shrouds given way.

To regain the brig was impossible; the next instant the mast was clear and the brig drove on. Before she had got a cable's length from us the foremast also went by the board.

We could see no one on it as it was towed along. A minute or more passed.

The mast to which we clung rose to the top of a sea, we saw the brig plunge into another. Again we looked, for one instant we saw her stern, and the next she was gone.

We were too far off to hear a cry. The foremast must have been drawn down with her. The boats were securely lashed. Nothing that we could see remained floating. We knew that our late shipmates had perished.

Our own condition was fearful in the extreme. At any moment we might be washed from our hold! Now our heads were under water! Now we rose to the top of a sea and looked down into a deep gulf below us.

"Hold on; hold on, Peter," cried Jim, who was clinging on the mast close to me. "Don't give up. Here, I've cut a piece of rope for you. Lash yourself on with it. I'll get a piece for myself presently."

I wanted him to secure himself first, but he insisted that I should take the rope, and I lashed myself with it. He soon afterwards secured himself in the same way. We might thus prolong our lives; but should we be able to hold out till a passing vessel might pick us up? I asked myself.

We were far away from land, and hours, perhaps days, might go by before the mast was seen, and only our dead bodies would be found. We had no food, no fresh water; night was coming on. I did not tell my thoughts to Jim, nor did he say what was passing in his mind; but we tried to cheer each other up. For an instant the clouds broke asunder in the west, and the sun, just as he sank below the horizon, bursting forth, shed a bright glow over the foaming ocean.

"He'll not be long down," cried Jim, "and he'll warm us on t'other side when he rises."

Jim's remark did me good. We had cause to hope for

A Disastrous Voyage.

the best. The squall which had carried away the brig's masts was the last of the gale. The wind rapidly fell, and the sea went down, so that in a short time we could keep ourselves almost entirely out of the water. The mast became more quiet. Had we not lashed ourselves to it when we fell asleep as we both did now and then, we might have dropped off. We talked as much as we could, both to keep up our spirits and to prevent ourselves from dozing.

Thus the night passed. It seemed long enough, but not so long as I expected. I must have closed my eyes when I heard Jim shout, "A sail! a sail!" and opening them I saw a large ship under all sail about a couple of miles away, standing on a course which we hoped would bring her near us.

CHAPTER XIV.

JIM AND I CARRIED OFF AGAINST OUR WILL.

"SHALL we be seen, Jim, think you?" I asked, after we had gazed at the ship some minutes without speaking.

"Ain't quite certain," answered Jim, in a sad voice; "if I thought so, I could sing for joy, that I could, but the ship's a long way off, and maybe she'll haul closer to the wind and pass us by."

"Oh, Jim! let us pray that she'll not do that," I exclaimed. "She's standing, as far as I can make out, directly towards us, and why should we fancy that we are to be deserted? Cheer up, Jim! cheer up!"

"That's what I'm trying to do," said Jim. "Still we must not make too certain. If she doesn't pick us up another vessel may. We are in the track of ships going up and down Channel, and that's one comfort."

Jim did not say this all at once, for he stopped sometimes to take a look at the stranger, and every now and then a sea washed up and made us close our mouths. Still the seas were every instant growing less and less, and we at last unlashed ourselves that we might move about a little and stretch our limbs.

We were on the top, it must be remembered, so that we did not run the same risk of falling off as we should have done if we had had only the mast to support us.

With straining eyes we watched the ship. Still she held

the same course on which she had been steering when we first saw her, and which was bringing her nearer and nearer to us.

"Hurrah, Jim! we shall soon be seen, depend on that," I exclaimed, at last, "and perhaps before to-night we shall be safe on shore. Who can say that we shan't be landed at Portsmouth itself?"

"I wish I could say I was as sure as you are, Peter," observed Jim, in a doleful voice. "If she had seen us it would have been all right; she would pick us up, but she may alter her course. Even now the wind is shifting, and she may have to keep away."

I could not contradict this; still I kept on hoping that we should ere long be seen. I had a white handkerchief in my pocket, although it was rolled into a ball by the wet. I pulled it out, and waved it above my head as high as I could reach. Even now we might have attracted the attention of those on board the stranger, although we could distinguish no signal made to us in return.

"She's a thumping big ship, whatever she is," I remarked.

"She's high out of the water, and that makes her look bigger," observed Jim. "I have seen some like her brought up at Spithead, and to my mind she's a South Sea whaler, outward bound. That's the reason she looks so high. Yes, I am right, for I can make out her boats hoisted up at the davits."

"I think you are right," I said; "but even if she is an outward bound ship, she'll put us on board another vessel homeward bound, or land us on some part of the coast, the back of the Isle of Wight, or Portland."

"First let us get on board her before we talk of where we shall be landed," said Jim. "It seems to me as if she was going about. The head sails are shaking."

"No, no! the man at the wheel was not minding his helm," I answered. "I'll wave again."

"They won't see that little bit of a rag," cried Jim, "I'll try what I can do. Here, Peter, just take hold of my jacket," he continued, as he stripped it off, and then loosening his waistband he pulled his shirt over his head, and began to wave it frantically. I waved my handkerchief, and then in our eagerness we shouted out at the top of our voices, as if the faint sounds could be carried as far as the ship.

Presently our hearts sank, for there was no doubt that the ship was keeping away. Still, should anyone on board be using a spy-glass, and turn it towards us, we should, we hoped, be observed. We waved and shouted even more vehemently than before, but even I was almost in despair.

"She's going to pass us after all," cried Jim, "and there's not another sail in sight."

Just as he spoke there came a puff of smoke with a bright flash, from the ship's bows, followed by a sharp report.

"We are seen! we are seen!" shouted Jim. "That's a signal to us. Hurrah! hurrah!"

The ship now came rapidly on, and we had no longer any doubt about being rescued. This very circumstance caused a reaction in our feelings, and, strange as it may seem, we both burst into tears. We recovered ourselves, however, very soon, and continued waving, still having an idea that the ship might sail away from us, but on and on she came. Presently her courses were brailed up, and she hove to about three cables' lengths from our mast. Almost at the same instant one of her boats was lowered, and came pulling towards us as fast as the men could bend their backs to the oars. In a few minutes kindly hands were stretched out to help us into the boat.

"Are you the only two?" asked the mate, who was steering.

"Yes, sir; all the rest are gone," I answered.

"Well, we'll hear all about it when we get you on board, lads, for you both seem as if you wanted looking after," he said.

The boat leaving the mast, returned rapidly towards the ship.

While most of the crew scrambled up the sides, the tackles were hooked on, and we were hoisted up in the boat, from whence we were speedily handed down on deck. I could not have stood if I had not been supported, and Jim was much in the same condition.

"We were soon surrounded by strange faces, some looking compassionately upon us, others with indifference, as if it was a matter of very little consequence that two boys should have been saved from perishing.

Meantime the yards were swung round and the ship stood on her course.

"We must have the lads below at once," said one of the persons standing round. "They have been many hours wet through and exposed on the mast, and even now, if we don't look out, they may slip through our fingers."

"Very true, Doctor Cockle," said another, who was, I saw by his dress, an officer. "One of them may be put into my cabin, where you can look after him better than for'ard."

"And the other can go into mine," said the doctor, the person who had first spoken.

No one had asked us any questions; probably they saw by our condition that we should have been unable to answer them, for both Jim and I were fast verging towards unconsciousness.

We were at once carried below, when I was put into the mate's cabin, where my clothes were stripped off by the doctor's orders, and, being rubbed dry, I was placed between the blankets. The doctor, who had been looking after Jim, soon came and gave me something out of a glass, which seemed to warm me up wonderfully. But even then I could not have spoken if my life had depended upon it.

"Get some warm broth as quickly as you can," I heard the doctor say to someone, he in the meantime rubbing my feet and hands and chest. It seemed as if scarcely more than two or three minutes had passed when a basin of hot broth was brought me, which I drank without difficulty, and it did me more good than the stuff in the glass.

"You may go to sleep now, my lad," said the doctor, in a kind tone; "you'll do well. You shall tell us by-and-by how you and your companion came to be on the mast."

I obeyed the doctor's orders, and scarcely had the door been closed than I was fast asleep. I was awakened by the doctor coming in, accompanied by a boy who brought some more soup and some bread, and which, being very hungry, I thankfully swallowed.

"You can eat something more substantial now," said the doctor, and he told the boy to bring in some fowl and more bread from the breakfast-table.

By this I guessed that I must have had a long spell of sleep, and that a whole day and a night had passed since we were taken on board. I eagerly ate all that was given me.

"You may get up now, my boy, and dress, and we will find another berth for you; we must not keep Mr. Griffiths out of his bed," said the doctor.

"I would not do that on any account, sir," I said; "I feel quite strong, and am accustomed to live forward."

I soon dressed, and was glad to see that Jim also was up. There were two apprentices on board, who lived on the half deck, and the doctor said that the first mate promised to have some berths knocked up for us with them.

"How did you come to be on board the vessel which went down?" asked the doctor, when I accompanied him on deck.

From the kind way he spoke I was encouraged to give him a full account of myself and Jim, so I told him that he and I belonged to Portsmouth, and had gone in the *Good Intent* to Bergen; and how she had lost her masts, and the crew had been washed overboard. How the captain had died, and we had done our best to keep the brig afloat, and had been driven in close to Shetland, and that I had found a relative there, and was coming south in the *Nancy* to fetch my sister. He then asked me about my father, and I told him that he had been lost at Spithead, and that mother had died, and old Tom had taken care of Mary and me, and how, after he had been blown up in the ship at Spithead, Jim and I had managed to gain our bread and support Mary and Nancy till a claimant appeared for old Tom's property, and our boat had been taken from us, and we had been turned out of the house, and should have been in a bad way if the good Quaker, Mr. Gray, had not come to our assistance.

The doctor listened attentively, and he then asked me what sort of man my father was, and whether I had a brother in the navy.

I described my father, and then said that Jack had gone away on board the *Lapwing* brig of war, but that he was supposed to have been cut off by savages in one of her boats when in the Indian seas. At all events, that we had never since heard of him.

"That's very strange," he observed; "I think, Peter Trawl, that we have met before, when you were a very little chap. Do you remember your father taking off the doctor and the mate of a ship lying at Spithead, when you and your brother Jack were in the boat, and he was to be put on board the brig?"

"Yes, sir," I said, looking up at his face: "I recollect it perfectly, as it was the last time I saw Jack, though I little thought then that I should never see him again."

"I was the doctor, and the first mate of this ship was my companion. When I first heard your name, as it is a peculiar one, I all of a sudden recollected that it was that of the boatman who took Mr. Griffiths and me off on the occasion I speak of. We are now brothers-in law, and have ever since gone to sea together—that is to say, when we have gone to sea, for both of us have taken long spells on shore. If it hadn't been for that, Mr. Griffiths would have been a captain years ago."

"I am very glad to meet you and him again, sir," I said; "and now I look at you I fancy I recollect your countenance, as I did your voice. You were not as well accustomed to the sea then as you are now."

"No," he answered, laughing. "That was my first voyage. I sometimes wish that I had lived comfortably on shore, and made it my last, but I got accustomed to a roving life, and having no regular business or tie, when circumstances compelled Mr. Griffiths—who married my sister—to come to sea again, I agreed to accompany him."

I felt sure from the kind way in which Doctor Cockle spoke that he would wish to serve me.

I asked him if the ship was going to put into St. Helens, or if not, would he get the captain to land Jim and me at Portland?

"We are some way to the westward of Portland, already," he answered. "It is possible that he may land you at Plymouth or Falmouth, or if not put you on board some pilot or fishing boat, or any vessel we may fall in with coming up Channel."

"Surely, sir, he would not carry us away from home? I would give anything to be on shore, where my young sister is expecting me, and it would break her heart to fancy

I was lost, which she would do if I did not appear," I said.

"As Mr. Griffiths and I only joined the ship at Hull, ten days ago, we are not very intimate with the captain: but I hope he would not refuse your request."

The doubtful way in which he spoke made me feel very unhappy. Still, I hoped that when I told the captain the strong reasons I had for wishing to be put on shore as soon as possible, he would not refuse.

The doctor left me to attend to one of the men who was sick forward, and I joined Jim, who had also come on deck. I had a long talk with him about the matter. He fancied we were only then just abreast of the Downs, and that the captain would put in willingly enough for the sake of getting rid of us. It was a great disappointment to find that we were so far down Channel, and that we should thus, at all events, have a long journey back to Portsmouth. Still we neither of us doubted for a moment that we should be put on shore somewhere to the westward, as I saw by a look I had at the compass that we were standing for the land.

While we were talking, the captain, whom we had not yet seen, came on deck. He was a fine, tall, sailor-like looking man, with a handsome countenance and large eyes, which seemed to take in everything at a glance—a person of whom the roughest crew would stand in awe.

His bright eyes fell on Jim and me; he beckoned us to come up, and, looking at me, bade me give him the particulars of the loss of the brig, about which Mr. Griffiths and the doctor had told him.

I gave him the account as he desired, and then thought that I might venture to ask him to put Jim and me on shore, for that, as may be supposed, was the thing uppermost in my mind.

"We will see about that, my lads," he answered. "If

the wind holds as it now does it won't cause us any delay, but I can make no promises. Boys at your age ought to wish to see the world, and we can find employment for you on board. You are sharp fellows, I can see, or you would not have saved your lives. One of the apprentices isn't worth his salt, and the other will slip his cable before long, I suspect. His friends insisted on my taking him, fancying that the voyage would restore him to health."

The captain spoke in so free-and-easy a way that the awe with which I was at first inclined to regard him vanished.

The wind, I should have said, had shifted to the westward of south. We were standing about north-west, a course which would carry us over to the English coast before long. We were obliged to be content with the sort of promise that the captain had made, and I hoped that when the doctor and Mr. Griffiths spoke to him, that he would not refuse to put us on shore.

Though Jim and I were well enough to walk about the deck, we were too weak to venture aloft, or we should have been at the masthead looking out for land. We went forward, however, keeping our eyes over the starboard bow, where we expected every instant to see it.

Several of the men spok: to us good-naturedly, and were as eager as the officers had been to hear what had happened to us. While we were standing there looking out, a lad came up and said, "So I hear you fellows are to be our messmates. What are your names?"

I told him.

"Mine's Ned Horner," he said, "and I hope we shall be friends, for I can't make anything of the fellow who messes with me, George Esdale. There's no fun in him, and he won't talk or do anything when it's his watch below but read and sing psalms."

"I shall be glad to be friends with you," I answered, "but

I don't suppose it will be for long, as I expect we shall leave the ship to-night or to-morrow morning."

"That may or may not be," he remarked, with a laugh. "Have you been long at sea?"

I told him that I had been brought up to it from my boyhood.

"Well, you have the advantage of me, for this is my first voyage; and Esdale didn't know the stem from the stern when he first came on board. Now come along to the half-deck; he and I are going to dinner; I suppose you'll join us?"

Jim and I were beginning to feel hungry, and willingly accepted Horner's invitation.

The savoury whiffs which came out of the caboose as we passed made me feel more eager than ever for something to eat.

Horner took us down to the half-deck, where we found Esdale, of whom he had spoken, seated on a chest reading. He was a pale, sickly-looking youth, taller a good deal than Jim.

He put down his book and held out his hand to shake ours.

"It's your turn to go for the dinner," he said to Horner, "and it must be ready by this time, but I'll go if you wish it."

"Well, you may go," said Horner; "I want to do the honours to these fellows. Take care that you don't capsize with the things as you come along the deck."

Then, without another word, Esdale got up, and putting his book into the chest, went forward.

"I make him do just what I like," said Horner, in a contemptuous tone. "Take care that you don't treat him in the same way, for if he has too many masters he may be inclined to kick."

Before long Esdale returned with a bowl of pea-soup, and

a plate at the top of it containing some potatoes, and a piece of fat boiled pork.

"Now fall to, youngsters," said Horner, in a patronising tone. "I am sorry not to be able to offer you better fare."

While he was speaking he got out of a locker four plates and two metal spoons and two wooden ones.

We did ample justice to the dinner, as we had been accustomed to nothing better while we were on board the *Nancy*. After the meal was finished we returned on deck, though Esdale did not offer to accompany us, as he spent his watch below, as Horner had said, in reading, writing, or singing in a low voice to himself.

We passed the afternoon looking out for the land. At length, when night came on, in spite of my anxiety to see the coast, and the long sleep I had had, I felt scarcely able to keep my eyes open. Still, I should probably have remained on deck after dark had not the doctor come to us and said, "I have spoken to the captain, lads, and he promises to put you on shore to-morrow morning; so now go and turn in, for you require sleep."

We went to the half-deck, where we found that the carpenter had knocked up some rough bunks, in which some mattresses and blankets had been placed. We were both glad enough to turn in. I observed that Esdale, before he did so, knelt down and said his prayers. It was Horner's watch on deck, so that he was not present.

CHAPTER XV.

THE VOYAGE OF THE "INTREPID" BEGUN.

I SLEPT right through the night, and was surprised to find when I opened my eyes that it was daylight. Jim and I at once turned out and went on deck.

There was the land, broad on the starboard bow, still at some distance. When I looked aloft I saw that the yards were square, and studding-sails on either side. A strong north-easterly wind was blowing, and we were running down Channel.

The captain, the first mate, and the doctor were on deck. Jim and I gazed eagerly at the land.

I went up to the doctor.

"Whereabouts are we, sir?" I asked.

"We are off the Start, my lad."

"Off the Start!" I exclaimed. "Oh, sir, won't the captain put into Plymouth to land us as he promised? Do speak to him, sir."

"These lads are very anxious to be landed, Captain Hawkins," he said. "It is of the greatest importance to young Trawl here, and it would not much delay us."

The mate spoke in the same way, and entreated the captain even in stronger language than Dr. Cockle had used.

"No, no," he answered. "Very likely they do wish to be put on shore, but we cannot lose a moment of this fine breeze. The trip won't do them any harm, and they'll thank me for it by-and-by."

Jim, when he heard this, was too angry on my account to speak, but I lifted up my hands and implored the captain to have pity on my young sister, if not on me.

"Very fine, my lad," he answered, with a laugh; "but you are not quite of so much importance as you suppose. It might delay us not only for a few hours, but for days, perhaps, and, doctor, I cannot listen to you. We've got a favourable breeze, and I intend to make the best use of it."

Once more I implored and entreated that the captain would not carry us away from home. All was of no use; he would not listen either to the doctor or the mate, or us. At length, growing angry, he said he would not hear another word on the subject, and Jim and I, by the doctor's advice, went for'ard to be out of his way. There we stood, watching with straining eyes the shore, past which we were running, and at length the Land's End came in sight.

"Cheer up, my lads," said our kind friend, who came for'ard to us. "The wind may change, and we may be driven back, or we may be able to put you on board some homeward-bound ship. Cheer up! cheer up!"

The land, as I stood gazing at it, rapidly sank below the horizon. I strained my eyes—the last faint line had disappeared. I could have cried, but my grief was too bitter for tears. Not that I cared for being carried away on my own account, but I thought of the sorrow my kind relatives in Shetland would feel—Mr. Troil and his daughter, and dear little Maggie, and more than all how Mary would feel as she waited day after day for the arrival of the brig which was never to appear, and then, when all hope was gone, how she would mourn for us, and Nancy also would, I knew, share her feelings.

If I could have sent but a line to my sister to tell her I

was safe, though I might be long absent, it would not have so much mattered. Mr. Gray would take very good care of her, and she would have written to Mr. Troil to explain what had happened; but as it was I could scarcely bear it.

"The doctor told us to cheer up, and that's what I say to you, Peter," cried Jim, trying to console me. "Maybe we shall fall in with a homeward-bound ship after all, though I don't think there's much chance of our seeing the shores of old England again for a long time to come if we don't, as it looks as if the wind would hold in its present quarter till we are well out in the Atlantic."

Jim was right. With yards squared and every stitch of canvas the ship could carry, we bowled along at a rate which soon left our native land far astern.

I had been too long at sea, and knew the duties of a sailor too well, to feel for myself so much as many fellows of my age under similar circumstances would have done. Jim also tried to rouse me up, so instead of moping I determined to exert myself. I still had the hope to support me that before long we might fall in with a homeward-bound ship, and I concluded that the captain would, without hesitation, put Jim and me on board her.

The day after we took our departure from the Land's End he saw us both together on deck.

"What are those youngsters idling there for?" he exclaimed, turning to Mr. Griffiths. "Put them in a watch at once, and let me see that they do their duty. If they don't, let them look out for squalls!"

"Ay, ay, sir!" answered the mate, who, though of a very independent spirit, always spoke respectfully to the captain.

He considerately placed us both in the same watch, knowing that we should like it, as we should be able to talk at night when we were on deck and had no especial duty to perform.

We had no reason to complain of the way the men treated us, rough as some of them were. The doctor and Mr. Griffiths always behaved kindly, but the captain took no further notice of us, except when he ordered Jim or me to do something. To my surprise, I found that the ship was the *Intrepid*—the very one my father and I had put Mr. Griffiths and the doctor on board so many years before. She was then quite a new ship, and, being strongly built, she was as sound as ever. I have spoken of her as a ship, but she was barque-rigged, as almost all whalers are, barques being more easily handled than ship-rigged craft. The *Intrepid* was upwards of three hundred tons burden, with a crew of thirty hands all told, and stored, I found, for a cruise of two years or more. She carried six whale-boats, and materials for building others should any of them be lost. There were three mates, a carpenter and cooper and their mates; an armourer, a steward, and cook; four boat steerers, four able seamen, six ordinary seamen, the doctor, two apprentices, Jim, and me.

I had never before been on board a whaler, and as I listened to the long yarns of the men describing their hair-breadth escapes and the exciting chases after the monsters of the deep, I felt, had I not had such cogent reasons for returning home, that I would very gladly have gone out to the South Seas to witness with my own eyes the scenes the men spoke of. Still I longed as much as ever to get back to England.

Jim and I made it out pretty well with the two apprentices. Horner was inclined to look down upon Jim for his want of education. Esdale treated us both alike with gentleness and consideration, and offered to teach Jim to read and write if he wished to learn. It had never occurred to me to try and do so. Indeed, although we had been so much together, I had not had many opportunities.

The second night we were on board I was awakened by feeling some hairy creature nestling by my side. I sung out, not a little frightened.

"What's up?" cried Horner, who had just come below to rouse Jim and me out to keep our watch.

"A great big brute of some sort has come into my bunk; I wonder it hasn't bitten me," I answered.

"Why, I've got another here!" exclaimed Jim, who just then awoke. "What in the world is it?"

Horner laughed loudly.

"Why, they're our ferrets," he answered. "Didn't you see them before?"

"No, and I never wish to see them again," answered Jim, as he flung the creature down on the deck.

Horner then told us that the captain had taken a couple on board at Hull to kill the rats, and that although a hutch had been made for them the creatures always managed to get out at night for the sake of obtaining a warm berth, and that if we put them into their hutch they would be sure to find their way back again into his or Esdale's bunks before they had been many minutes asleep.

The truth was the ferrets were more afraid of the rats than the rats were of them. We bore the annoyance for three nights more, and then, by the unanimous consent of our mess, we got Horner to carry them down into the hold, from which they never ascended, and we concluded that they either got drowned in the bilge water or were eaten up by the rats.

We had not been long at sea before a heavy gale sprang up, but as the wind was from the westward we were able to lay our course.

To Jim and me it mattered very little, although the waves were much higher than I had seen them in the North Sea, but poor Esdale suffered very much, and Horner's conceit was taken down a good many pegs. Jim and I did our best to look after them, and to try to get them to eat something, but they could only swallow liquids.

"Oh, let me alone! let me alone!" cried Horner.

The doctor came to see Esdale frequently, and advised that he should be taken to a spare berth in the cabin, but the captain would not allow it.

"All lads get sick when they first come to sea if there's a gale of wind, and he'll come round again by-and-by," he remarked in his usual off-hand way.

This was not told to Esdale, who said, indeed, that he preferred remaining where he was.

As the weather was tolerably warm, I believe that he was as well off on the half-deck as he would have been in the cabin.

At last the gale came to an end—or rather we ran out of it. Esdale got somewhat better again, but I observed that he had changed greatly in appearance since we came on board.

I had now to abandon all hopes of the ship putting back, but there was still a possibility of getting on board a homeward-bound vessel.

Two days after the gale had ceased, while I was below, I heard the cry of "Sail, ho!" from the man at the masthead.

I hurried on deck. We had the wind abeam, and so had she—a soldier's wind as it is called. We should meet the approaching vessel before long and pass each other, with not a cable's length between us.

I watched her eagerly. We drew closer and closer to each other. When we got nearly abreast I went up to the first mate and asked him what she was.

"She's from the Brazils, bound for Liverpool," he answered

Just then I saw the captain come on deck. Forgetting what he was I rushed up to him.

"Oh, Captain Hawkins, will you put Jim and me on board her?" I exclaimed. "You don't know how much I want to get home; it won't delay you ten minutes to put us on board."

"Ten minutes of this fine breeze lost for the sake of a boy like you," he answered, with a scornful laugh. "I expended more than ten in heaving to to pick you up, and that was as much as you are worth. Go forward, you young monkey, and give me no more of your impudence."

Undaunted by his heartless answer, I again and again implored that he would put me on board the Liverpool ship, but he stood looking contemptuously at me without uttering a word, till Jim, seeing that I was making no way, coming up, hat in hand, exclaimed,

"If you'll put Peter here on board yonder ship, sir, that he may go home to his young sister and friends, I'll stay here and work for you, and be your slave for as many years as you may want me. Do, sir—do let poor Peter go!"

"Off with you for'ard," thundered the captain, with a fierce oath. "How dare you speak to me? Away, both of you! Somebody has been putting you up to this, I know." And he glanced angrily at Dr. Cockle and the mate.

"If you mean me, Captain Hawkins, I know that the lad has very good reasons for wishing to return home, but I did not advise him or Jim Pulley to speak to you. I certainly wish that you would put Peter Trawl on board that homeward-bound ship."

"You may wish what you like, but I am not going to allow what I choose to do to be found fault with by you or any other man on board this ship!" cried the captain turning on his heel. "So look out for yourself," he added, glancing half over his shoulder.

The ordinary salutes were exchanged, and the two vessels stood on their course.

My heart felt as if it would burst with indignation and sorrow. Had the wind been light, I might, perhaps, have been able to put a letter on board, even although the captain would not have let me go.

Esdale tried to comfort me, and advised me to have one written ready to send should another opportunity occur.

The first land we made soon after this was Madeira. Except the coast of Norway, I had seen no foreign country, and as we passed it within a quarter of a mile, it struck me as very beautiful and fertile.

The wind being light we tarred down the rigging, and a few days afterwards, when we were about eight hundred miles from the land, one morning, on coming on deck, I noticed that the shrouds and every freshly-tarred rope looked as red as if they had been just painted. I asked the doctor, who allowed me to speak to him in a familiar way, what had caused this, and he told me that it was the red sand blown off the coast of Africa, and that it was a common occurrence in these latitudes.

We passed in sight of the Cape de Verde islands, one of which, called Fogo, seemed of a prodigious height. The first place we touched at was the island of Brava, into which the captain put to obtain fresh provisions.

"Now is my time," I thought. "If I can go on shore here, I shall be able to get back by the next homeward-bound vessel which calls at the place."

Jim proposed that we should smuggle ourselves on board some shore-boat, but to this I would not agree.

"We will go with the captain's leave," I answered, "and he surely will not refuse it now that he has no excuse for doing so."

I therefore went up to him as soon as he came on deck.

"Captain Hawkins," I said, in as firm a voice as I could command, "again I ask you will you allow Jim Pulley and me to leave your ship and wait on shore until we can get a passage home?"

"Peter Trawl, if that's your name, I shall do no such thing," he answered. "If I find you attempting to go on shore I shall put you in irons."

I knew from previous experience that there was no use in expostulating. When I told the doctor, he could scarcely conceal his indignation.

"I feel inclined to help you, my lad, at every risk," he said, "but we must be cautious. Wait until the evening, and then we will see what can be done."

I thanked him heartily, and promised to follow his advice. Jim was ready for anything.

The doctor said he would go on shore and then send off a boat which would wait under the starboard bow, and that we must manage to slip into her as soon as it was dark.

The captain in the meantime had landed, but returned very shortly with four tall negroes, whom he had engaged to pull the 'midship oars in the whale-boats. They are, I should say, first-rate oarsmen, and have a gentle disposition, ready to obey, and are happy under all circumstances. Besides the negroes, two boats loaded with fresh provisions came alongside.

These were soon hoisted on board, when the captain ordered a gun to be fired and Blue Peter to be hoisted, a signal to all those on shore to return immediately.

Dr. Cockle and the third mate, with the cooper, whom the captain thought he could trust, had landed.

Presently the captain ordered another and then another gun to be fired to hasten them, and then to my bitter disappointment he directed Mr. Griffiths to loosen sails and heave up the anchor.

According to Esdale's advice I had begun a letter to Mary, but had not had time to finish it. Hoping that I should not be missed by the captain, I ran below to add a few lines and then to close it, under the belief that I should be able to send it off by a shore-boat. I had to get out Esdale's ink-bottle and pen, which he had before lent me; the pen would not write, so I had to search for his penknife, and to try and mend it as well as I could, but having little experience in the art, this took me some time. I at last got the letter closed with a wafer, and directed to the care of Mr. Gray, when I sprang with it on deck. Just then the eye of the captain fell on me.

"Come a't here, youngster," he shouted. "Where have you been away from your duty?"

I had the letter in my hand.

"I wanted to get this ready to send on shore, sir," I answered, holding it up.

"No excuse for leaving your station. Take that!" he cried, as he gave me a blow on the side of the head with his half-clenched fist, which brought me to the deck, and nearly stunned me. When I recovered myself the first person I saw was Dr. Cockle, who, looking at me compassionately, said, "Come below, Peter, and I'll try to put your head to rights, for you seem to be much hurt. How did it happen?"

"I can't tell you now, sir, for I much want to send this letter off by a shore-boat," I answered.

As I spoke I observed that the crew were hoisting away and sheeting home the sails. I ran to the side and jumped on to the main chains. The only remaining boat was just shoving off. I shouted to the people in her to come and take my letter; but they did not understand me, or did not care to remain alongside, as the ship was rapidly gathering way; another stroke of their oars and they were at a distance from the ship. I waved and shouted to them to come back,

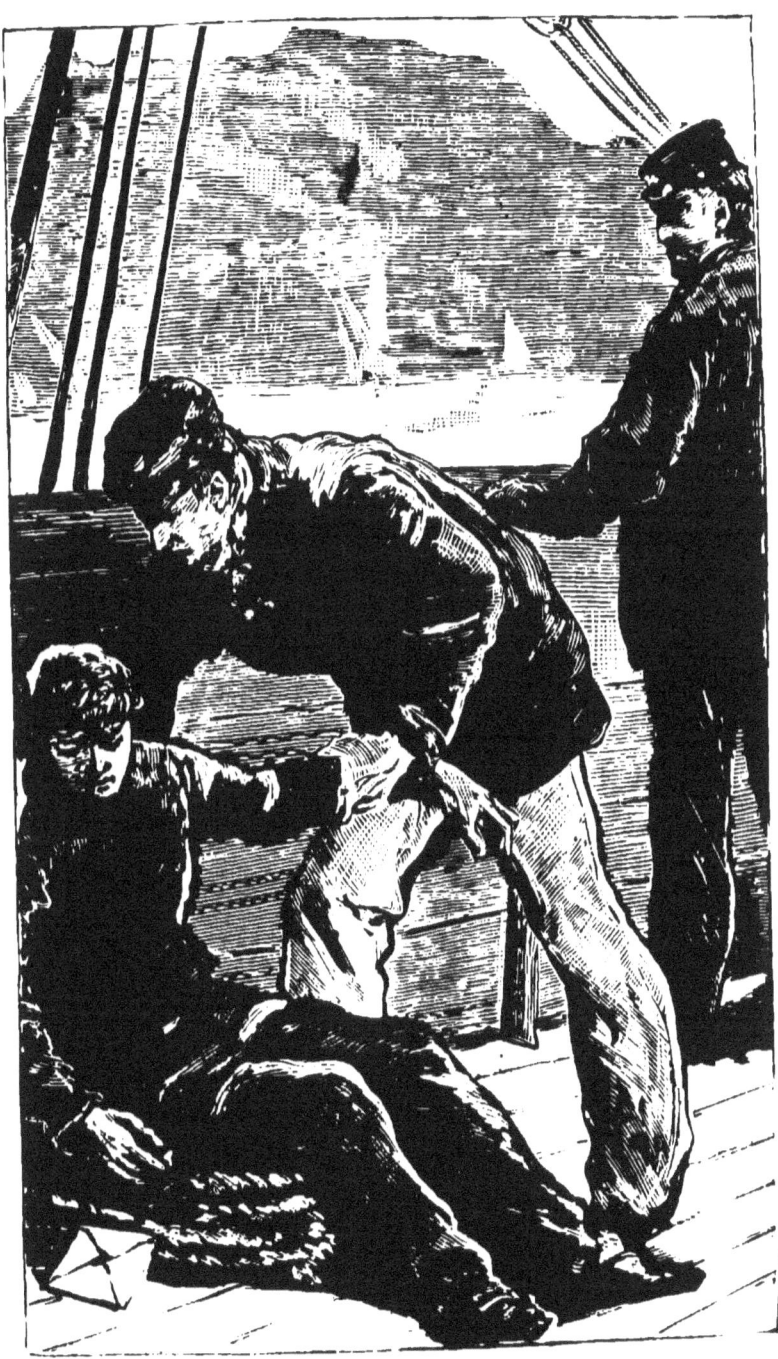

A CRUEL BLOW.

Page 104.

but they did not heed me, and just then I heard the captain calling to me in an angry tone to attend to my duty. I was obliged to obey, expecting another cuff harder than the last; but when he saw me begin to pull and haul with the rest he said no more. Perhaps he observed the blood streaming from my head. The sails were now sheeted home, the yards trimmed, and the *Intrepid* stood away from the land.

Another opportunity of making my escape was lost.

CHAPTER XVI.

WE CROSS THE LINE AND ATTEMPT TO ROUND CAPE HORN.

JIM was always saying, "Cheer up, Peter, cheer up!" but it was a very hard matter to be cheery when I thought of the cruel way in which I had been treated, and the sorrow my sister must be feeling at my supposed loss. I tried, as advised, to keep up my spirits, and did my best to obey the orders I received.

Jim observed that it was all the same to him. His friends would not grieve much over his loss, and, as far as he was concerned, he would as soon be chasing whales in the Pacific as working a wherry in Portsmouth Harbour.

As we approached the line I found that the men were making preparations for going through the ceremony which was performed on board most vessels in those days. One of the boat-steerers, Sam Ringold, who stood six feet four in his shoes, and was proportionably broad, was chosen to act the part of Neptune, and the cooper's mate, who was as wide as he was high, that of his wife. The armourer took the part of the barber, and the carpenter's mate, who was lank and tall, the doctor.

Three of the ordinary seamen, the smallest fellows on board, were their attendants. All the chests were searched for the required dresses, and some curtains belonging to the cabin found their way forward to form a petticoat for Mrs.

Neptune. Some gold paper and pasteboard were manufactured into crowns, and some fishes' tails were ingeniously formed for the attendants. I discovered the preparations going forward, but was charged not to let Horner, or Esdale, or Jim know anything about them. I was more favoured than the rest of my messmates by the men, who seemed to have taken a liking to me; whether it was because they had heard how I had assisted to save the *Good Intent*, or thought that I was ill-treated by the captain, I do not know, but so it was. No one ever abused me, or gave me the taste of a rope's-end.

We had been sailing on with light winds when one morning, after the decks had been washed down and the other duties of the ship performed, having run on for a short distance, we lay almost becalmed with the sea as smooth as a mill-pond. The captain and his mates were seen to be taking an observation, and soon afterwards it became known that we were just crossing the line.

"I've often heard about it, but I can't say I see any line," said Jim.

"Nor can I!" cried Horner, who was looking out eagerly.

Presently a gruff voice was heard, hailing from forward.

"What ship is that, shutting out the light from my palace window?"

"The *Intrepid*," answered Captain Hawkins, who with the mates and doctor were standing aft.

"Then go ahead, will you, or I'll indict you for a nuisance," cried the voice, the remark producing a general laugh.

"I can't think of standing on until I have had the pleasure of a visit from Daddy Neptune," said the captain.

"Ay, ay! glad to hear that. Then I'll come aboard in a jiffy with my royal missus and some of our precious young family; and maybe, captain, you'll have something to give them, for they're very fond of any hot potions which may come in their way."

"Be smart about it, then, Daddy, for I see a breeze springing up, and I may have to run you out of sight before you and your precious family have had time to take a sip apiece," cried the captain, who seemed to be in far better humour than usual.

All this time Jim and Horner were standing with me abaft the main hatchway, with their eyes staring and their mouths agape, wondering what was going to happen.

Presently, over the bows, appeared the strangest group I had ever set eyes on.

First there came Daddy Neptune with a glittering crown, a beard of oakum reaching to his middle, a girdle of rope yarn round his waist, a cloak covered with strange devices, and a huge trident in his hand.

His wife wore a crown like that of her husband, with ringlets of the same material as his beard, a huge sash of some gaily-coloured stuff, and a cloak formed out of a blanket. The barber had in his hand a pot containing lather, a big bowl tucked under one arm, with a razor a yard long and a shaving brush of huge size under the other; while the children or attendant imps—for it was hard to say what they were—waddled about in green clothing, looking like sea monsters, behind them.

"Well, I have heard of strange things, but these chaps are stranger than ever I saw," cried Jim. "Where do they come from?"

"From the bottom of the sea, I suppose," said Horner, who evidently did not admire their looks as they advanced aft.

The captain, after a little palavering, ordered the steward to bring up some grog and serve it out to them. Then retiring a short way forward, Neptune commanded all who had not before visited his dominions to come and pay their respects to him.

We all did so, not feeling very comfortable as to what was to follow, when his attendants got hold of Jim and me. Horner tried to escape, but was quickly captured and brought back.

No one interfered with Esdale, who had, I found, crossed Neptune's hand with a crown-piece; which, of course, none of us were able to do. A huge tub of water had been placed in front of his majesty. The barber now came forward and insisted on shaving all those who were for the first time crossing the line. Three of the ordinary seamen were novices like us.

The barber first lathered our chins with some abominable mixture from his pot, and then, scraping it off with his razor, finally ducked our heads into the tub. Horner, when undergoing the operation, had the brush several times thrust into his mouth, and his whole face and head daubed over. When he opened his mouth to expostulate, in again went the brush. As he kicked and screamed and spluttered, he was treated worse and worse.

Jim, taking a lesson from me, kept his mouth shut. I was let off even more easily than he was. Once Horner got loose, but instead of wisely remaining on deck and holding his tongue, he ran up the rigging and began abusing Daddy Neptune and his gang, whereupon he was again captured and compelled to undergo the same operation as before.

Blacky the cook next brought out his fiddle, and Neptune and his party—indeed, the whole crew—began dancing round and round, singing and shouting every now and then as an interlude, catching hold of the "green hands" and pitching them into the tub, chase being always made after those who attempted to escape.

The grog circulated so rapidly among the crew that they would all soon have been intoxicated had not the captain, in a thundering voice, ordered them to knock off and bring their tomfoolery to an end.

They obeyed. Neptune and his followers dived below, and presently returned like stout seamen as they were.

The order was given to brace the yards sharp up, and, with an easterly wind, we stood on our course.

The next land we made was a solitary islet. Near it stood a remarkable rock called the "Ninepin," detached from the land. The doctor told me that it is eighteen hundred feet in height. It had the appearance of a monument standing out of the ocean. There are no inhabitants on the island, nor any good landing-place, but fresh water is to be obtained there, as well as pigs and vegetables.

We soon after this began to fall in with stormy weather. We found our ship, which had remarkably sharp ends, very wet, and as we were now approaching the land of storms in the dead of winter, with the days scarcely more than seven hours long, the greatest caution was deemed necessary. The royal masts were sent down and replaced by stump top-gallant masts. The flying jib-boom was sent in and the studding-sail booms were also sent down. All the boats except one were got in, the hatches were battened down, and everything was done to make the ship light aloft.

We were nearly off the River Plate when there were indications of an approaching gale. The hitherto blue sky was overcast, and the scud flew rapidly along, as if impelled by a hurricane.

"You youngsters will have to look out for yourselves before long," said Tom Ringold, the boat-steerer, who had acted the part of Neptune. "We shall be having old Harry Cane aboard here, and he's a precious deal more difficult to tackle than Daddy Neptune, who paid us a visit on the line."

"Oh, dear! oh, dear! I wonder what we shall do?" cried Homer, who did not exactly understand what was going to happen.

"Why, hold on to the weather-rigging, if you haven't to be pulling and hauling, and duck your head if you see a sea coming," answered Jim, who understood the joke about Harry Cane.

In a short time the captain ordered the topsails to be reefed and the mainsail to be stowed and all the lighter sails handed. Jim and I were sent aloft to the foretop-gallant sailyard to furl the sail. We were laying out when, to my horror, I saw Jim disappear. I nearly fell from the yard myself, from thinking that he would be dashed to pieces, and that I should lose my staunchest friend.

"Jim! Jim! Oh, save him! save him!" I shouted out, not knowing what I was saying, or considering how useless it was to shout.

"Here I am all right, Peter," cried Jim, and his voice seemed to come not far from me.

What was my joy to discover that he had been caught in the belly of the sail, and there he lay as if he had been in a hammock, the reef tackle having been hauled out just at the time he fell. He quickly scrambled on to the yard again, resuming his duty as if nothing particular had occurred. We having finished our work came down. Scarcely was this done when the gale struck us, taking us right aback. The cabin dead-lights not being properly secured, the cabin was nearly filled with water. The carpenter and his mates hurried aft to close them, and we youngsters were sent below to help him, and put things to rights.

When this was done down came the rain in such torrents that it seemed as if it would swamp the ship, while as she fell off into the trough of the sea, she began to roll in a way which threatened every instant to shake the masts out of her. It seemed wonderful that they stood. Had the rigging not been well set up they must have gone. The only accident I have to mention was that one of our remaining pigs was killed, but this did not grieve the crew, for as we had no salt on board, and the meat would not keep, the portion not required for the cabin was served out to us.

Another, and what might have proved a far more serious matter, occurred. Tom Ringold was steering, when a sea striking the rudder with tremendous force knocked him over the wheel, carrying away several of the brass spokes as it flew round, and sent him against the bulwarks. For a moment everyone thought he was killed, but he picked himself up, and although he could not use his arm for two or three days, at the end of that time he was able to do his duty as well as ever.

That storm soon came to an end, but the old hands told us that we might look out for others, and so the captain seemed to think, for although he was anxious to get round Cape Horn we were always under snug canvas at night, and during the day a bright look-out was kept, lest one of those sudden squalls called Pamperos might come off the land and whip the masts out of the ship, or lay her on her beam-ends, as frequently happens when the hands are not ready to shorten sail. We, however, got to the southward of the Falkland Islands without accident.

My poor friend and messmate Esdale severely felt the cold which we now began to experience. He came on deck to attend to his duty, but a hacking cough and increasing weakness made him very unfit for it. The doctor at last insisted on his remaining below, although Esdale declared that he would rather be on deck and try to do his best.

"But I insist on your remaining in your bunk until we round Cape Horn and reach a warmer latitude," said Dr. Cockle. "I will see the captain, and tell him plainly that he will be answerable for your death, should he insist on your doing duty any longer."

Esdale still pleaded, but the doctor was peremptory.

"It is his only chance," he said to me; "I cannot promise that he will live. He will, however, certainly die if he is exposed to this biting wind and constant rain. I intend to tell the captain, but you, Trawl, go and stay with him whenever you can; it will cheer him up, poor fellow, to have someone to talk to, and that dull Horner cannot speak two words of sense."

Before the doctor had time to do as he proposed, Captain Hawkins, missing Esdale from the deck, ordered me to tell him to come up.

This I determined not to do, for it was blowing hard at the time from the south-west and the wind would have chilled him through in a minute. I, however, went below, and after remaining a little time, I returned, and said,

"Esdale is very ill, sir, and is not fit to come on deck."

"How do you know that, youngster?" asked the captain, in an angry tone.

"Dr. Cockle has seen him and says so," I answered boldly.

"Tell him to come up, or I'll send a couple of hands to bring him neck and crop," thundered the captain.

I was as determined as before not to tell Esdale, knowing that he would come if sent for.

"Go below and bring up that lazy young rascal," shouted the captain to Tom Ringold and another man standing near him.

I immediately dived below to persuade Tom to let Esdale remain in his bunk.

"It will be his death if he is exposed to this weather," I said.

"I am not the fellow to kill a shipmate if I can help it,"

answered Tom. "Tell him to stay and I'll take the consequences."

When Tom returned on deck, the captain enquired in a fierce voice why he had not carried out his orders.

"Because he is too ill to be moved, Captain Hawkins," answered Tom, promptly.

The captain, uttering an oath, and taking a coil of rope in his hand, was just about to go below when Doctor Cockle came on deck, and guessing, from the few words he heard, what was the captain's intention, came up to him and said,

"It would kill the lad to bring him up, and as he is my patient, I have told him to stay below "

"Am I to be thwarted and insulted on board my own ship?" cried the captain. "Whether he is ill or well, up he comes."

And going down to the half deck, he asked Esdale why he had not obeyed his orders.

Esdale, of course, had not received them, and said so, beginning at the same time to dress. Before, however, he could finish putting on his clothes the captain seized him by the arm and dragged him up. Scarcely, however, had he reached the deck when the poor fellow fainted right away. Tom, on seeing this, lifted him in his arms and carried him down again.

"I warn you, Captain Hawkins, that you will cause the death of the lad if you compel him to be on deck in this weather," said the doctor firmly, as he turned to follow Tom and Esdale.

The captain, making no remark, walked aft, and did not again interfere.

Whether that sudden exposure to the cold had any serious effect I do not know, but Esdale after this got worse and worse. Whenever I could I went and sat by his side, when he used to talk to me of the happy land for which he was bound. He did not seem even to wish to live, and yet he was as cheerful as anyone on board. The doctor and first mate used also to come and talk to him, and he spoke to them as he did to me, and urged them to put their trust where he was putting his. I believe that his exhortations had a beneficial influence on them, as they had on me. When I said how I hoped that he would get better after we were round the Cape, he answered,

"I shall never see the Horn, Peter; I am as sure of that as I can be of anything."

Two days after this land was sighted on the starboard bow. It proved to be Staten Island; but scarcely were we to the south of it when we encountered a furious gale blowing from the westward.

For two days, by keeping close hauled, the captain endeavoured to gain ground to the westward, resolved, as he declared, "to thrash the ship round the Cape." On the third day, however, while I was on deck, a tremendous sea came rolling up.

"Look out! Hold on for your lives, lads!" shouted the first mate.

Every one clung to whatever was nearest to him. One poor fellow was to leeward. There was no avoiding the sea, which, like a mountain topped with foam, struck the bows. The ship plunged into it, and for a few seconds I thought would never rise again. On swept the roaring torrent, deluging the deck; and had not the hatches been battened down, would have half filled her.

A loud, crashing sound followed, and when the water had passed over us nearly all the lee bulwarks were gone, and with them our shipmate who had been standing a minute before as full of life as any of us. He was not again seen, and must have gone down at once.

The captain was compelled at last to heave the ship to, and there we lay, now rising to the top of a sea, now sinking into the trough, with walls of water, half as high as the maintop, round us. The seas in the German Ocean and Bay of Biscay were nothing to be compared to those we encountered off the Horn, though, perhaps, equally dangerous.

As soon as I went below, I hurried to the side of Esdale. He asked what had happened. I told him.

"Some one was carried overboard?" he inquired.

"Yes," I said. "Poor Jack Norris," wondering how he knew it.

"And I shall soon follow him," he replied.

His words proved true. That very night, as I came off my watch and was about to turn in, I heard my messmate utter my name in a low voice. I went to him.

"I'm going," he whispered. "Good-bye, Peter; "you'll remember what I have said to you?"

I promised him I would, and told him I must run and call the doctor.

"No, stay," he said. "He can do me no good. Tell him I thank him for his kindness. Good-bye, Peter."

The next instant his hand relaxed its hold of mine, and stooping down over him I found he had ceased to breathe.

So died one of the most amiable and excellent young men I have ever met. The next morning he was sewn up in canvas, with a shot at his feet, and brought on deck. The captain stood aft watching the proceedings. Whether he felt he had hastened Esdale's death I know not; but his countenance was stern and gloomy as night. The boldest seaman on board would not have dared just then to speak to him. Hail and sleet were driving in our faces; a furious gale threatening to carry our only sail out of the bolt-ropes was blowing; the mountain seas raged round us; there was scarce time for a prayer, none for form or ceremony. A foaming billow came thundering against the bows; over the deck it swept. We clung for our lives to ropes, stanchions, and ring-bolts. When it had passed we found that it had borne our young shipmate to his ocean grave.

CHAPTER XVII.

ROUNDING CAPE HORN.

FOR well-nigh six weeks we were endeavouring to get round Cape Horn, when the weather moderated, making way to the westward, but again being driven back often over more ground than we had gained.

The captain was constantly on deck, exhibiting on all occasions his splendid seamanship. He was ever on the look out to take advantage of the least change of wind which would enable us to lay our course. Day and night were alike to him; he seemed indifferent to the piercing wind and tremendous storms of sleet and hail we encountered. Twice we sighted Cape Horn, but each time, before many hours had passed, were again to the eastward of it. The captain thought he could endure anything, and certainly did not expose others more than he did himself. We saw numerous sea birds—albatrosses, Cape pigeons, stormy-petrels (or Mother Carey's chickens, as they are called), and many more. The albatross appeared to me a truly noble bird when on the wing; no matter how rough the weather or how heavy the sea, he sat on the water perfectly at ease, seeming to defy the very elements.

One of the mates having got a strong line with a large hook at the end of it, a piece of meat as bait, and a cork to float it, let it drop astern. In an instant a huge albatross pounced down on the tempting bait, and was hooked. It required two men, however, to draw him on board over the taffrail. Even when brought on deck he attacked everyone who came near him. The doctor advised us to stand clear of his wings and beak, but Horner thoughtlessly held out his hat, when the bird, seizing hold of it, bit the crown clean out in a moment. Not until he had had several blows on the head with a handspike did he drop dead. He measured seventeen feet from tip to tip of the wings. The feathers under his wings and breast were as white as snow, and as they glanced in the sunlight, shone like silver.

In contrast with the albatross was the stormy-petrel, a black bird scarcely larger than a sparrow, and, of course, web-footed. Vast numbers flew about the ship, but they were more difficult to catch than the albatrosses.

Again we sighted Cape Horn, standing out solitary and grand into the Southern Ocean. The wind had moderated and become more in our favour, although the vast billows rolled on like moving mountains of water. Now the ship forced her way to the summit of one, the next instant to glide down rapidly into the vale below, performing the same course again and again.

At length even the billows subsided, and we began to look forward to having fine weather. About noon one day the look-out from the masthead shouted,

"There she spouts! there she spouts!"

A school of whales was in sight.

"Lower two boats," cried the captain.

No sooner was the order given than their crews, hurrying aft, jumped into them, and very few minutes were sufficient to place all their gear in readiness and to lower them into the water.

The captain himself went in one as harpooner, the second mate in the other. I should have liked to go, but I knew that it was useless to ask leave of the captain.

Away the boats pulled at a rapid rate to windward, the direction in which the whales had been seen, and that we might keep as near them as possible the ship was hauled close up. They were soon not discernible from the deck, and on they went increasing their distance till even the look-out from the masthead could no longer distinguish them. Still the first mate had carefully noted the direction they had taken, and seemed to have no doubt about picking them up. The weather, however, which had been fine all day, now gave signs of changing, and in a short time the wind began to blow in strong gusts, creating a nasty sea, but still it was not worse than whale-boats have often to encounter.

Whether or not they had succeeded in striking a fish we could not tell, for the days were very short, and evening drew on.

Fresh look-outs were sent to each of the mastheads, and we waited with anxiety for their reports. They soon hailed that they could see neither of the boats. At length, the darkness increasing, they were called down, and lanterns were got ready to show the position of the ship.

"Shouldn't be surprised if we were to lose our skipper and the boats' crews," said Horner to me. "I've heard that such accidents have happened before now."

"I hope not," I answered, "for although our captain is a severe man, it would be dreadful to have him and the other poor fellows lost out in this stormy ocean, with no land for hundreds of miles where they could find food and shelter, even were they to reach it."

While we were speaking a heavy squall struck the ship, and the remaining hands were ordered aloft to take two reefs in the topsails. Jim and I were on the foreyardarm. We had just finished our task, when Jim declared that he saw a light away to windward.

On coming on deck we told Mr. Griffiths. He at once

ordered a gun to be fired as a signal. A blue light was then burnt, the glare of which, as it fell on our figures, gave us all so ghastly an appearance that Horner, who had never seen one before, cried out, "What has come over you fellows? Is anything dreadful going to happen?"

As the firework died out we looked in the direction Jim had seen the light, and in a little time we caught sight of it from the deck. The men on this gave a hearty cheer to show their satisfaction. Now the light disappeared, now it came in sight again, as the boat rose on the summit of a sea.

The ship was hove to. Presently a faint hail was heard. We answered it with a shout from our united voices. At length one boat could be distinguished. Where was the other?

The captain's voice assured us that he was in the first. He was soon on deck, and the boat was hoisted up. He looked pale and haggard, and much annoyed at not having killed a whale. The other boat he said was not far off.

We kept hove to for her, fearing that if she did not soon appear she might be swamped before she could be hoisted in, for as the wind and sea were now rapidly rising every moment was of importance. At length she came alongside, but it was with the greatest difficulty that the men got out of her. They looked thoroughly worn out with their long pull. We had scarcely made sail again and were standing on our course when the gale came down on us, more furiously than before, blowing right in our teeth. It was now evident that had a whale been killed we should have been compelled to abandon it.

In spite of his fatigue the captain remained on deck, swearing fearfully at his ill-luck. Those who had been away with the boats were allowed to turn in, but the rest of us were kept on deck, for at any moment all our strength might be required.

Suddenly, while I was aft, the captain uttered a loud cry, or shriek it seemed to me.

"What's the matter, sir?" asked the mate.

"I cannot see!" groaned the captain. "Where am I? What has happened?"

The mate went to him and took his arm. "It may be but for a moment," he said.

There had been no lightning; nothing, as far as we could discover, to produce blindness. Still the captain refused to leave the deck, declaring that it would pass over. The doctor, who had turned in, was called up, and came to him.

The increasing gale compelled the mate to attend to the duties of the ship. The doctor summoned me to assist in leading the captain below. I took his arm; he was trembling like an aspen. We led him to his berth, and assisted him to undress.

"Shall I be better in the morning, think you, doctor?" he asked, in an agitated tone.

"I cannot say, Captain Hawkins. I believe that this blindness has come on in consequence of your having overtaxed your physical powers. In course of time, with rest and a warmer climate, I trust that you will recover your sight."

"Oh that it may be so!" cried the captain, as he laid his head on the pillow.

We had a heavier gale that night than we had before encountered. The seas again and again washed over the deck. It seemed wonderful that more of the men did not knock up.

The first mate looked thin and haggard, and so did most of the other officers and men. The bulwarks on both sides had been carried away, two of the boats had been injured, and the ship had suffered various other damages.

Still we kept at it; the wind shifted; Cape Horn was actually weathered, and at length a joyous cheer burst from the throats of the crew as the ship's head was directed to the north-west. It was some days, however, before we felt any sensible change of climate, but after that it grew warmer and warmer, for we were now fairly in the Pacific.

The captain was disappointed in his expectations of recovering his sight. He came daily on deck and stood turning his head round in every direction, and I observed a painful expression on his countenance.

"I'll tell you what, Peter, I've a notion how the captain came to lose his sight," said Horner to me in a confidential tone. "It's a punishment to him for the way he treated Esdale, and you, and Jim."

"We have no right to think that," I answered; "even if he had treated me ten times worse than he has done, I should not wish him to suffer what must be to a man of his nature so terrible a misfortune."

"Well, then, I suppose I must keep my opinion to myself," answered Horner.

In a few days we reached the island of Juan Fernandez, and hove to off it that the boats might go in close to the shore to catch some fish. Mr. Griffiths gave Jim and me leave to go in one of them. We were provided with hooks and lines. The water was so clear that we could see the fish take the bait, which they did so ravenously, that in a short time we had as many rock cod and other fish as we required. We afterwards landed and brought off a quantity of wild mint, which grows in profusion over the island. We made it into tea, which we enjoyed very much after drinking pea-coffee so long.

While we were collecting the mint we saw a number of goats bounding among the rocks, some standing still and looking down on us. They were descendants of those which inhabited the island in the days of Alexander Selkirk, who was taken off by Dampier during his last voyage to the Pacific.

At first we thought that there were no inhabitants, but just as we were shoving off we heard a shout, and a white man and negro were seen rushing down towards us, shouting and gesticulating furiously.

They were both dressed in skins, with high fur caps, and had long sticks in their hands to help themselves as they ran.

"Why, I do believe that must be Robinson Crusoe and his man Friday," cried Horner, at which all hands laughed.

"He got home long ago, or he never could have written his history, stupid," said the mate, "but whoever they are we'll wait for them."

Still Horner had not got his first idea out of his head. He had not read much, but he had read Robinson Crusoe, and believed in it as a veracious history.

The strangers soon reached the boat.

"Now, I say, ain't you Robinson Crusoe?" cried Horner, as the white man got up to the boat.

"No, my name is Miles Soper, and I know nothing of the chap you speak of," answered the stranger.

"I say, mister," he continued, turning to the mate, "will you take us poor fellows off? We were cast ashore some six months ago or more, and are the only people out of our ship, which went down off there, who saved their lives, as far as I can tell. Sam Cole here and I came ashore on a bit of a raft, and we have had a hard time of it since then."

"Why, as to that, my man, if you're willing to enter and serve aboard our ship, I daresay the captain will take you, but he doesn't want idlers."

"Beggars can't be choosers," answered Miles Soper. "If you are willing to take us we shall be glad to go, and both Sam and I are able seamen."

"Well, jump in, my lads," said the mate; "but haven't

you anything at the place where you have lived so long to bring away?"

"No, we've nothing but the clothes we stand up in, except it may be a few wooden bowls and such like things," answered the stranger, who looked hard at the mate as he spoke, probably suspecting that we might pull off, and that he and his chum might be left behind. Both the men seemed in tolerably good condition. They told us that they had had abundance of goat's flesh and vegetables, as well as fruit, but that they had got tired of the life, and had had a quarrel with four mongrel Spaniards, who lived on another part of the island, whom they thought might some day try to murder them.

They both asked to take an oar, and, by the way they pulled, they showed that they were likely to be useful hands. When we got on board the *Intrepid*, Mr. Griffiths spoke very kindly to them, and as they at once said that they would be glad to enter, their names were put down as belonging to the crew.

I took a liking from the first to Miles Soper, though he was perfectly uneducated, and could neither read nor write. Sam also seemed an honest merry fellow. He and the other Africans soon became friends.

The crew had been employed on the passage, whenever the weather permitted, in preparing what is called the "cutting in gear," which consists of the various tackles and ropes for securing the whales alongside when caught and taking off the blubber. Then there was the gear of the various boats, and it would astonish anyone to see the enormous number of articles stowed away in a whale-boat when she starts after a whale.

Everything was now got ready, as we were in expectation every day of falling in with whales, and the men were on the look-out from the mastheads from dawn until dark, in the hopes of seeing them. I longed to see a whale caught, for as yet the voyage had been profitless, and every one was out of spirits. The captain, who still remained perfectly blind, notwithstanding the assurances of Dr. Cockle that he would recover, was so especially. He seemed like a heartbroken man ; his countenance gloomy, as if troubled with melancholy thoughts, and his whole manner and appearance were changed. It was sad to see him come on deck and stand, sometimes for an hour together, turning his face round, as if he were picturing to himself the sparkling ocean, the blue sky overhead, and the busy scene which the deck of his ship presented.

I observed that Mr. Griffiths never gave an order if he could help it while the blind captain was on deck. The health of the latter, however, by degrees improved, the colour returned to his cheeks, and his voice, when he spoke, again had the ring in it which I had from the first remarked.

Day after day, however, we sailed on without seeing a whale. At length one day, soon after noon, the first mate having just taken an observation, and the captain being in his cabin, we were cheered by the cry from the masthead of—

"There she spouts! There she spouts!"

The loud tramping of the men on deck roused those below, who quickly sprang up, eager to engage in the expected chase.

Among the first who appeared was the captain, who ran up the companion-ladder with as much agility as he had ever displayed.

"Where away—where away?" he asked.

The men pointed to windward, and to our surprise the captain turned his eyes in the same direction.

"Lower three boats," he shouted. "I'll go in one of them."

Presently I saw a low, bush-like spout of white mist rise from the surface of the sea, not two miles off.

"There she spouts! There she spouts!" shouted the captain, showing that he saw too.

With wonderful rapidity, as everything was prepared, the boats were lowered. The doctor had come on deck.

"Where are you going, Captain Hawkins?" he asked, in an astonished tone.

"In chase of those whales out there," answered the captain; "for, doctor, I can see them as well as you do."

Of this there could be no doubt. Several at that instant appeared at various distances.

The excitement of the moment had given the required stimulus to the captain's nerves, and he was restored to sight.

I remembered the fruitless chase off Cape Horn, when the captain and those with him so nearly lost their lives, but this promised to be successful. The captain's boat took the lead. His aim was to get up to one of the monsters of the deep just as it returned to the surface for breathing, as it would be some time before it could go down again, and before that interval many a harpoon and lance might be plunged into its body.

The captain soon took the lead; the men pulled as if their lives depended on it. Before they were half a mile away a whale rose just ahead of the captain's boat. Springing into the bows, he stood, harpoon in hand, ready to strike.

Presently he was close up to the monster; the weapon flew from his grasp, followed by three lances hurled in rapid succession. The whale, feeling the pain, darted off. Another boat came up, and a second harpoon was made fast, while several more lances were plunged into its side.

Presently its enormous flukes rose in the air.

"He has sounded! he has sounded!" cried those on board.

The whale had dived, and the lines coiled away in the tubs ran rapidly out. The monster, however, had not finished its breathing, and soon after a second line had been secured to the first it came again to the surface. The boats pulled rapidly towards it, and the harpooners plied it with their lances. Presently we saw them pull away as if for their lives. The whale rose nearly out of the water, and began turning round and lashing the surface with its flukes, each blow being sufficient to destroy any boat and her crew within its reach.

"The monster is in its flurry," I heard the doctor say. "It is ours to a certainty."

He was right. After lashing the water into a mass of blood-tinged foam, it lay perfectly still.

Those on board raised a shout as they saw a little flag fixed on the body.

The boats now made chase after another whale, which gave them more trouble than the first; but they attacked it bravely, now pulling up and hurling harpoons and lances into it, and now pulling away to avoid being attacked in return.

Presently we saw one boat again dash forward, almost the next instant its fragments rose in the air, and the crew were scattered far and wide around. Which boat it was we could not tell. Some fancied it was the captain's, others that it was the second mate's.

"He regained his sight to-day," said an old Orkneyman. "It's a question whether it wasn't that he might have a last look on his fellow-creatures and the mighty sea."

CHAPTER XVIII.

OUR FIRST WHALES CAUGHT—I HEAR NEWS OF JACK.

THE moment the accident was perceived Mr. Griffiths ordered the only remaining boat away, and jumped into her, for the carpenter had not yet finished the two building to replace those lost off Cape Horn. I asked to go.

"No! you stay on board and help to work the ship up to us," he answered.

I accordingly went to the helm, as I steered better than most of those remaining on board, while the doctor and steward lent a hand to the rest in pulling and hauling, as we had continually to go about; but the wind was light, and it was not very hard work. I kept an eye constantly towards the boats, and soon saw a whift planted on the back of the last whale attacked, which showed that it was dead.

Our anxiety was relieved when, instead of returning, they made chase after another whale. It proved that although the boat had been destroyed, the men had escaped with their lives.

"I do believe we shan't have the skipper aboard again," observed Horner.

"I hope so," I said.

"Ahem!" was his answer, as he walked away.

At length, shortening sail, we ran up alongside the first

whale that had been killed. The men descended to its back with ropes round their waists to hook on the tackles to its head and flukes. We had then to wait until the boats towed the other whale up to the opposite side. We eagerly watched their proceedings.

The third whale was attacked. After sounding twice and carrying out, apparently, three, if not four lines, we saw it suddenly come to the surface and leap completely out of the water. This is called breaching. It then began rolling round and round, endeavouring in its agony to get rid of the weapon sticking in it. The boats for some time kept at a distance. Then once more they approached, again to pull off as the whale commenced lashing the water with its huge flukes.

"It's in its flurry," observed the doctor, who was looking through his telescope, which he handed to me.

At last we saw the three boats approaching, towing the whale by the nose. The wind having fallen, and having a whale alongside, we were unable to near them to save them their long pull. On they came, towing the monster at the rate of a mile and a half an hour. It was thus upwards of that period of time before they got alongside.

The first man handed up was Miles Soper—or Robinson Crusoe, as we called him—whose leg had been broken by the second whale attack. He had willingly endured the suffering, lying at the bottom of the boat, rather than give up the chase. No one else had been injured, though all had run a great risk of being drowned; but a whaler's crew know that such may be their fate at any moment.

The doctor at once took the man under his charge.

No time was lost in hooking on the other whale, and commencing the operation of "cutting-in." This I may briefly describe as taking off the blubber with large spades, the handles of which are twenty feet long. The whale is turned round and round by means of tackles brought to the windlass, the blanket-piece, or blubber covering, being thus gradually stripped off till it reaches the tail, which is hove on board with the last piece. The blubber is lowered down the main hatch-way and cut up into small pieces, called "horse pieces." These are afterwards piled up on deck to be minced into thin slices for boiling in the pots. The operation of "cutting-in" is a very dangerous one when there is any sea on to make the ship roll. The first and second mates stand on stages lowered over the side, cutting the blubber from the whale as the crew heave it round with the windlass. The four boat-steerers are on the gang-ways attending to the guys and tackles, the captain superintending the whole process, while the carpenter grinds the spades.

All round the sea swarms with sharks attracted by the oil and blubber. When not otherwise employed, Tom and I and Homer attacked them with the spades and killed great numbers. We worked away until night, but did not finish even then, as it takes twelve hours to strip the blubber off a large whale. We commenced again at daylight, and it was dark before we began to cut into the second whale. We had still a third to operate on, but as each was worth nearly a thousand pounds, no one complained.

Fortunately the weather remained fine, and we got the blubber of the third whale on board by the end of the next day. We had also boiled the spermaceti oil out of the head, with small buckets at the ends of long poles. This is the most valuable production of the whale, and is used for making candles.

For night work the ship's company was divided into two watches, from six to one, and from one to six. The instant the last piece of blubber was on board, the carcasses were cast loose to be devoured by fish and fowl.

We began the operation of trying-out, as boiling the

blubber is called, by first putting some wood under the trypots. As soon as the blubber was boiled, the scraps which rose to the surface were skimmed off with a large ladle, and after being thrown into a pot with holes in the bottom to drain off the oil remaining in them, were used as fuel for boiling the remainder of the blubber.

The appearance our decks presented, with huge fires blazing away under our pots, and the men with the ladles skimming off the scraps, or baling out the oil into the coolers, was strange and weird in the extreme. Had I been suddenly introduced among them, I should not have recognised them as my shipmates, begrimed as they were with smoke and oil. I was, however, much in the same condition. Dr. Cockle had become accustomed to it, but I cannot fancy that it was very pleasant to him.

The doctor told me that he should be glad, whenever I could, if I would go below and talk to poor Miles Soper.

I willingly did so. He was suffering occasionally great pain, but in the intervals it cheered him to have some one to speak to. I found that he was even more ready to talk than listen, and I accordingly got him to tell me about himself. He happened to ask my name. I told him.

"Peter Trawl!" he exclaimed. "Trawl! that's curious. I remember a chap of your name aboard the *Lapwing* brig-of-war."

I at once was deeply interested.

"He must have been my brother Jack," I exclaimed. "Do tell me what has become of him, for I heard he was lost out in the Indian seas."

"That's just where he and I were nearly lost. We were coming home when a boat was sent away, and we, with six more men and an officer, went in her, to visit an island on some business or other, I forget what, and I didn't know it's name."

A SERIOUS AFFRAY WITH PIRATES.

Page 193.

"There are wild sorts of chaps out in those parts, who go pirating in their proas, as they call them. While we were just shoving off, a dozen or more of these proas came round us. We knew if the pirates got hold of us we should all be knocked on the head, so we began blazing away to keep them at a distance. We kept on at it till we hadn't a charge left for our muskets. Two of our men were killed, and our officer badly wounded. The pirates then came nearer and fired their gingalls into us. Just then one of their proas caught fire, and sent up such clouds of smoke that for some time, as we were near her, we could not be seen.

"'Now, lads,' said the officer, 'those among you who are not wounded try and swim to shore. It's your only chance. The rest of us must die like men.'

"Our oars, you see, were shattered, and by this time all hands except Jack and me were more or less hurt. We followed our brave officer's advice, and leaping overboard reached the beach before we were seen by the pirates. Some gingalls were fired at us, but we got away among the bushes, and ran as hard as our legs could carry us in shore. We did not know where we were going, or what sort of people we should meet. Whether the pirates landed or not we did not stop to learn, but as we ran for three or four hours there was not much chance of being overtaken.

"We saw at last a river before us, and as it was too broad to cross, and we were afraid, should we attempt to swim over, that we might be picked off by one of those big scaly beasts they call crocodiles, we kept down along the bank, as we knew that it must lead us to the opposite side of the island to where we had landed.

"'Cheer up,' said Jack to me. 'Maybe our ship will come round there and take us off. Our fellows are sure to be searching round the coast on the chance of finding us.'

"'I hope you're right, Jack,' said I, 'for it will be a bad

job for us if we can't get away, as how we are to find food is more than I can tell, and it's very clear we can't live without it.'

"There were plenty of trees growing on the bank, though not so thickly but that we could manage to make our way between them.

"Says Jack to me, 'If those cut-throat fellows come after us, we must climb up one of these and hide ourselves among the branches.'

"'I don't think they will take the trouble to follow us so far,' I answered. 'But it's a good idea of yours, and it will give us a chance of saving our lives.'

"We of course could not run as fast as we had been going in the open country. Sometimes we came across fallen trees, over which we had to climb, and at others we had to go round thick bushes which we could not get through. Still, what stopped us would stop our enemies. On and on we went, till just as we got out of a wood we saw before us a village of curious-looking houses, built on stout piles, many of them right in the water.

"'Hadn't we better go back?' I said to Jack; 'the people who live there may be the same sort of cut-throats as those we have got away from. They'll be for knocking us on the head when they see us.'

"Jack agreed with me that it would be better to stay in the wood till it was dark, and we might then make our way clear of the village down to the sea. We were just going back, when a woman came out on a sort of verandah in front of the house nearest to us, and we knew by the way she was looking that we were seen. Then she turned round and called to another woman, who also came out.

"'Come,' said Jack, 'we had better go on boldly and ask those dark-skinned ladies to give us their protection. They are sure to do that if we look humble enough, and show them that we want to be friends, for to my mind women are alike all the world over.'

"So we moved on, kissing our hands, and then holding them up clasped before us. The women did not run away, or seem a bit frightened; and as we got nearer one of them came down the ladder and held out both her hands, which we took and put on our heads. She then beckoned us up the steps, and made signs to us to sit down on mats inside the house. As we were both very hungry by this time, we pointed to our mouths to show that we wanted something to eat and drink. The younger girl went to another part of the house and brought back some fish and yams, and a bowl with some liquor in it. There was not much to be said for the taste, but we were too thirsty after our long run to be particular. We tried to make the women understand that there were enemies coming after us, and that we wanted to hide away, so when we had finished our meal they beckoned us to come into another room, and, placing some mats on the ground, they told us that we might sleep there safely—at least, that's what we made out.

"Night came on, and Jack and I, agreeing that we had got into good quarters, went to sleep. There was no bell striking, and no bo'sun's mate to rouse us up, and so we slept on till it was broad daylight. We got up and looked out from the verandah, or platform, which went round the house, when we saw three men talking together. As soon as they caught sight of us they came towards the house, and one of them mounted the ladder. He looked at us with surprise, and seemed to be asking who we were. We told him as well as we could by signs that we had come across from the other side of the island, and wanted to get off to our ship, which would soon be round to take us aboard. This did not seem to satisfy him. Presently in came the women, and they had a talk about the matter, but what they said we could not make out. The first man then called the other two, and after more palavering they began to look savage, and gave us to understand that we were to be their slaves, and work for them.

"'Well,' says Jack to me, 'all we've got to do is to grin and bear it. Maybe, as we are near the sea, we shall have a chance of making our escape.'

"This was one comfort; so we nodded, as much as to say we were ready to do what they bid us, for, you see, we were in their power and couldn't help ourselves. After we had gone into the house and sat down, waiting to see what would next happen, the women—bless them for their kindness!—brought us some more food for breakfast, and a capital one we made. Bad as was our lot, yet it was better than being knocked on the head or having our throats cut. A number of people now came out of their houses, and there was great rejoicing among them to think that they had got two white men as slaves. We found that we had plenty of work to do to cut wood and fetch water, and to hoe in their fields, which were some way from the village, or to go out fishing with them.

"This we liked better than anything else. If it had not been for the women our lot would have been worse, for they took care to give us food every day, which I don't think the men would have troubled themselves about doing, for they were regular savages.

"Day after day went by; we were getting accustomed to our life, and as yet had had no chance of escaping. A precious sharp look-out was at all times kept over us, and I don't think even the women would have wished us to go, for we had to do a good deal of the work which would have otherwise fallen to their lot. Though we were, as I was saying, used to the life we led, we both wanted to get away.

"I've an old father down in Dorsetshire, and there's a bright young girl who lives with him whom I would give something to see again; and Jack sighed to go home, as he said, to see his father and mother, and a young brother and sister. He used to talk much to me about you all, and it seemed to me as if I knew you long before we ever met.

"We found that we were much farther from the sea than we had at first supposed, for although we went a good way down the river we never reached its mouth.

"The people in the village didn't lead quiet lives, for they were always on the watch, fearing that they might be attacked by enemies. At night they made fast their boats under their houses, and had their goods all ready for a start into the woods, while they had men on the look-out night and day to give notice should any strange vessels come up the river.

"Jack and I agreed that if any enemies should come in the night we might have a good chance of escaping, but from what we had seen of the fellows who had attacked our boat we had no wish to fall into the hands of such characters. We thought that we might manage to slip into a boat and pull up the river and hide ourselves until the pirates had gone away.

"You must know that we did not wish any ill to our masters, for though we were their slaves we had taken a liking to them, as they did not ill-treat us, and gave us a good deal of time to ourselves.

"Weeks and months went by. We began to think that no enemy would come, and that we must try to get off by some other means than that we had first thought of. At last we saw the men sharpening their long knives and polishing their spears, and new painting their shields.

"'Depend upon it there's something in the wind,' said Jack to me. 'They are going on a war expedition.'

"'No doubt about the matter,' I said, 'and they'll want us to go with them.'

"'Then we must take care not to go,' said Jack. 'I for one won't be for killing men, women, and children, as these fellows are likely to do. We must pretend to be sick, or that we do not understand what they want of us, and get off somehow or other.'

"Whether or not it was talking about being sick I don't know, but the very next night I was struck down with fever. Our masters saw that I was not shamming. The women also stood our friends, and declared that I was not fit to get up and work, while Jack was allowed to stay at home and nurse me. I was very bad, and I believe he thought that I should die.

"If he had been my own mother's son he couldn't have looked after me better than he did; night and day he was always by my side, ready to give me what I wanted. One day I heard a loud shouting and singing, and Jack, who had gone out, came back and said that the men had all started with their spears and shields. They had wanted to make him go, but the women said he must stop behind, though he had a hard matter to escape from the men. I was already getting better, and this news made me feel better still.

"'It will be a bad return to run off with one of their boats,' said Jack, 'but there seems no help for it, and it may be our only chance, for the men will be back again in a day or two.'

"That very night, while Jack and I were sitting up talking, we heard shrieks and cries in the distance; and presently, looking out, Jack said he saw the houses lower down the river burning.

"'Then depend upon it the pirates have taken the place, I said.

"'No doubt about it,' exclaimed Jack, 'and now is our chance. If we could defend the poor women and children we would, but we cannot do that. They'll know where to fly to, and so, I hope, escape.'

"Suddenly I felt my strength come back, and I was able to follow Jack down the ladder, at the bottom of which the boat was kept moored. To cut the painter by which she was made fast didn't take us a moment, and springing into her we paddled across the stream. As we looked down the river we could see all the houses in a blaze, and here and there people running off into the woods, while we made out half a score or more of the dark proas stealing up along the shore."

Just as Miles Soper had got thus far in his history I was summoned on deck, and eager as I was to hear how he and Jack had fared, I was obliged to attend to my duty.

CHAPTER XIX.

MILES SOPER'S NARRATIVE CONCLUDED.

"I'VE heard news of my brother Jack!" I exclaimed, as I met Jim directly after I sprang on deck.

"What! is he alive?" asked Jim.

"Miles Soper, who was his shipmate, thinks so," I answered. "At all events, he wasn't killed when we thought he was."

"Then, Peter, we'll find him if we search the world round!" cried Jim, giving me a warm grip of the hand. "I am glad; that I am!"

It takes a whole day to "try out"—that is, to boil down the blubber of each whale. I found that the cooper and his mate had just finished filling up the casks from the coolers, and I was wanted, with others, to assist in rolling them aft.

Here they were chocked and lashed and left to cool for several days before they were in a condition to be stowed away in the hold. In the meantime we had to get up all the empty casks on deck so that we might lay the ground-tier with the full casks. As the casks were piled up, one upon another, the ship was in consequence almost topheavy, and I saw the captain and Mr. Griffiths frequently casting glances round the horizon, to watch for an indication of any change in the weather, for should a sudden squall strike the ship she might, while in this condition, be sent over in an instant. Every possible exertion was therefore made to get the task accomplished, and all hands were employed. Anxious as I was to hear what had become of my brother, I consequently had no opportunity for a long time of listening to a continuance of Miles Soper's narrative. I should have said that though the oil casks were stowed away empty and filled by means of the hose from the deck, the greatest care was required in bedding them, as they might have to remain three years or more in the hold. The blubber from the three whales was at length tryed out and secured in the casks, and the decks being washed down, the ship once more resumed her ordinary appearance, we meantime continuing our course northward. The first moment I was at liberty I went down to see Miles Soper. He said that he felt much better, though still unable to do duty.

"And what about Jack?" I asked; "you and he were just pulling away across the river at night to escape from the Dyack pirates."

"Yes; I have been thinking much about it since I told you. I would not have to go through that time again for a good deal if I could help it. We could hear the shrieks and cries of the old men, women, and children as the cruel pirates caught them and cut off their heads, and we could see the flames burst out from the houses all along the banks of the river. We were afraid that the light would be thrown upon our boat, so that we dare not venture down the river, but pulled up along the southern bank close under the bushes. We thought that we were safe, at all events, till daylight, when we caught sight of two boats coming out from among the pirate fleet and steering up stream. I gave up all for lost, as I knew that they would whip our heads off in a moment should they come up with us.

"'Don't give in!' cried Jack; 'perhaps it isn't us that they're after.'

"We ceased pulling lest the light should fall on our oar-blades, for we should have had no chance if they had made chase.

"'Let's paddle in under these bushes,' whispered Jack; 'they're very thick, and we can lie hid here, while maybe they'll pass us.'

"We did as he proposed. As the boughs overhung the water and almost touched it with their ends, we hoped that the pirates would not discover us. We could just look out across the river, and saw the boats still coming towards us. We both lay down in the bottom of our boat and remained as quiet as mice, scarcely daring to look up above the gunwale for fear of being seen. We could hear the voices of the pirates and the splash of their oars as they drew nearer. If they had before seen us they might have observed the spot where we had disappeared, and I expected every moment to have my head whipped off my shoulders. Just putting my eyes above the gunwale, I saw the two boats, broadside on, pulling along. They hadn't found us out. On and on they went, right up the stream. They must have thought that we were still ahead. We, of course, didn't dare to move, hoping that they would give up the chase and go back again.

"'We must not be too sure that they won't look for us when they do come back,' said Jack. 'Howsomdever, there's no use crying out till we're caught. I'll tell you what; the best thing we can do is to get on shore and make our way inland; then, though they may find the boat, they won't catch us.' I agreed; so, shoving the boat farther in till we reached the bank, we sprang on shore, and having secured her by the painter, set off directly away from the river. As it was very dark, we had to grope our way amongst the trees and bushes, though the glare in the sky from the burning houses enabled us to steer a right course. We half expected that a snake or a wild beast might pounce down upon us, and we had no arms to defend ourselves. But anything was better than to be caught by the pirates. At last, when our clothes were torn nearly off our backs, we reached some open ground, and set off running till we got to a wood on the opposite side. 'Now,' says Jack, 'we won't go farther, but hide here till the morning; then maybe, if we can climb to the top of a tree, we shall be able to catch sight of the river and find out what the pirates are doing.' I thought his idea a good one, so we sat down on the ground and waited. We could hear no sounds, so we concluded that all the poor people had been killed. We hoped, however, that the warriors might come back and beat the pirates off. Not that we wished to fall into the power of our old masters again, for they would have kept us prisoners if they didn't take it into their heads to kill us.

"At last the light returned, and seeing a tall tree near, Jack and I climbed up to the top. Jack went first. 'Hurrah!' he shouted; 'there go the pirates down the river, pulling away with all their oars out!' Sure enough I saw them also. 'But I say, Jack, perhaps the warriors have come back and put them to flight; if so, we must take care not to be caught by them.' I said, 'I can see where the village stood, but I don't see any people moving about.' 'It's a long way, to be sure, so we must be careful,' answered Jack. We soon got down the tree and returned to our boat. The pirates hadn't discovered her, so we got on board, and cautiously shoved out to the edge of the bushes, stopping just inside them. We then took a look out, but could discover no one moving on the opposite shore, so we pulled across to the village. It was a fearful sight we saw there. Bodies of old men, women, and children were scattered about, but the heads were gone.

"We were in a hurry, you may be sure, to get away, but,

says Jack, 'It won't do to put to sea without food or water.' So we hunted about, and found in the bushes several baskets which the poor people had been trying to carry off with food of all sorts, and some calabashes, which we quickly filled at the spring where we were accustomed to get water. We hurried with them back to the boat, and once more shoved off. We then paddled away down the river. The current was running out, so that we made good way, and were soon out of sight of the burnt village. Our craft was not very well suited for a voyage, but anything was better than stopping to be killed on shore. We pulled on until nearly noon before we came in sight of the mouth of the river. There was no bar, and the sea was smooth, so we resolved to pull out at once, in the hope of being picked up by some passing vessel. We were still not certain even now that our masters would not make chase after us, so we didn't stop a moment, except just to look round, but pulled right away to sea. Just as we got outside we caught sight of the pirate fleet under sail, standing to the nor'ard. We therefore pulled south, not that there was much chance of their coming back, but we thought that if we went in their wake we should not fall in with any merchant vessel, for at any rate if they should have met one they would to a certainty have robbed and scuttled her.

"We supposed that there were other islands away to the westward, but then they might be inhabited by the same cut-throat sort of fellows as those from whom we had escaped, and we didn't want to fall into their hands. Our chief hope was to be picked up by some passing vessel or other, perhaps by our own ship, but Jack said he thought she would not have remained at the station, and would have long ago given up searching for us. It was hot work paddling away all day, and we would have given much for a sail, but the boat was not fitted for one, and she was not

Miles Soper's Narrative Concluded. 205

fitted either for a heavy sea—not that there was much chance of that getting up at such time of the year. We had plenty of food and water, so we kept up our spirits. Where we were going to neither of us could tell; all we knew was that we were our own masters. We were queer characters to look at, with our clothes all torn to shreds, our hair long, and our faces as brown as berries. No one would have taken us for Englishmen, but we had English tongues and English hearts, and we made up our minds to stick at it and not be downcast. We wanted to get away as far as we could from the shore, for fear any of the natives might come after us—not that there was much chance of that. We paddled and paddled till our arms ached, and we were well-nigh roasted with the hot sun. We were thankful when night came on, and we were able to rest and take some food.

"We had agreed to keep watch and watch, but it was of no use trying to keep awake, so we both lay down in the bottom of the boat and went fast asleep. When we awoke it was broad daylight, and presently up came the sun and beat down on our heads as hot as the day before. There we were floating on the sea with the water calm as a millpond, and not a sail in sight. There was no chance either of a vessel coming near us while the calm continued. We took our breakfasts, however, and talked of what we should do. Far away to the east we could see the blue outline of the island we had left, but what part to steer for we could not make up our minds. There was only one thing we determined—come what might, not to go back and be made slaves of. It seemed useless to be paddling away and yet not to know where we were going to; but we still hoped that we might fall in with some merchant vessel, it mattered not of what country, though we wished she might be English, and so we might find our way home.

"'Come, let's be moving,' said Jack, at last. 'I've heard

say that there are Dutch and Spanish settlements out in these parts, and maybe we shall fall in with one of them, and both the mynheers and dons are good sort of people, and will treat us kindly.'

"So we took to our paddles and made our way to the westward. All day we paddled on, but no land appeared in sight, and now and then we stopped to take some food and a drink of water, but it was tiring work. We were thankful when night came at last. We didn't sleep so long, and were at our paddles before daybreak, for we knew by the stars how to steer.

"Next day we did just the same, and the next after that.

"'I say, Miles,' said Jack, 'we must soon manage to come to land or we shall be starving. We have not got food nor water for more than one day longer, and without them we shall not be able to hold out.'

"That was very true; still neither of us thought of giving in. A light breeze from the eastward had sprung up, so that we made good way, but there was no land to be seen ahead. We didn't talk much, for we had said all we could say about our prospects, and they were bad enough. But they became worse when we had drunk up all the water and eaten every bit of food we had in the boat. I had heard of people going three or four days without eating, but the want of water was the worst. We would have given a heap of gold if we had had it for a cupful. The wind now shifted to the southward, and blew much stronger than before, knocking up a sea which threatened every moment to swamp our boat, which was not fitted for rough water. We now began to think that it was all up with us, and that all we could do was just to keep the boat's head to the seas to prevent her from capsizing.

"At last Jack sang out, 'A sail! a sail to the southward!'

"A STRANGE-LOOKING CRAFT SHE SEEMED AS SHE DREW NEARER."

Page 207.

"There she was, coming up before the wind. A strange-looking, outlandish craft she seemed as she drew nearer.

"'I wonder whether she's one of those Dyack or Malay pirates,' I said. 'If so, we may as well let the boat turn over.'

"'No, no; let us trust God, and hope for the best,' said Jack. 'Cheer up, Miles! she's sent for our relief.'

"I was not so sure of that, for it was easy to see from her outlandish rig that she was one of the craft of those seas. Presently, as she got near us, she lowered her sails and came close up. Ropes were hove to us, and hands were stretched out over the side to haul us on board, for we had scarcely strength enough left to help ourselves. They tried to secure the boat, but she drifted off and was swamped. We just saw that the people were Chinamen, pig-eyed, with turned-up noses and yellow skins. We both fainted away. They brought us some water, and in a short time we got better. They then carried us into a small cabin aft out of the hot sun. Presently they brought us some food—rice, and some stuff minced with it. We were not particular, for we were desperately hungry.

"We now found that the people who had picked us up were honest traders bound northward with a cargo of sea-slugs, birds'-nests, and other things from these seas. We tried to talk to them, but could not manage it, as none of them understood English, and we couldn't speak their lingo. But as soon as we got stronger we made ourselves useful, pulling and hauling, and doing whatever came to hand. Where we were going to we could not make out, but we hoped that it was to some place at which the English ships touched, and that we might get home some day. As Jack said, we had reason to be thankful that we had been picked up, for the weather came on very bad, and our boat could not have lived through it. The Chinamen kept a bright look-out, and seemed terribly afraid of the pirates. We tried to make them understand that we had seen the fleet sail to nor'ard a short time before, and we ourselves didn't like the thoughts of falling in with them. We told them also that we would fight to the death sooner than yield. They understood us, and seemed to think that we were very fine fellows. We had been sailing on for three or four days, and we began to hope that we were free of the pirates, when just as we passed a headland we caught sight of a number of craft coming out from under it. On seeing them the Chinamen looked very much frightened, hoisted all sail, and brought their arms on deck. We watched the strangers, who, it was very clear, were making chase after us. We should have a hard fight for it, even if we should manage to get off. Presently, however, we saw their sails flapping against their masts as they came under the headland, whilst we still had a breeze and went away dancing merrily over the water. I never felt so pleased in my life, and the Chinamen seemed highly delighted, chattering and jabbering away like so many monkeys. It was pleasant to see the pirates' sails sink below the horizon, and pleasanter still to lose sight of them altogether.

"We ran on day after day. The breeze held fair and we by degrees got accustomed to our new friends, and could make ourselves understood in a fashion. We sometimes were sailing between islands, and sometimes on the open sea. Whereabouts we were we had no idea, though we supposed that we were approaching the Chinamen's country.

"We had been a fortnight or more on board when dark clouds rose up from the south-west, and it came on to blow very hard. The sails were lowered and we ran before the gale. I saw by the looks of the crew that they didn't like it, nor did we, for it seemed as if at any moment the clumsy craft might be capsized. We, however, pumped and baled, and tried to keep her clear of water. It all seemed, however, of no use, for the seas washed into her and she was leaking terribly.

"We had been driven a long way out of our course. We did our best to cheer up our shipmates, and set them the example by working harder than any of them.

"At last the gale ceased, and we once more made sail, but, do all we could, the water gained on us and the crew began to heave the cargo overboard to keep the junk afloat. The boats had been washed away, and we knew that if she went down we should all be drowned. Jack and I talked of what we could do to save our lives, but we agreed that we should have to share the fate of the rest. It seemed to us that the craft would not swim another night, when we made out a sail to the westward.

"The Chinamen by this time were so knocked up that they were scarcely able to exert themselves. Jack and I sprang here and there, now pumping, now baling, now trying to make our companions do the same. It seemed to us that they would let the craft go down in sight of help. The stranger we judged by the cut of her sails to be a whaler. The junk was settling lower and lower in the water. Jack found a flag, an odd-looking piece of stuff it was. He ran it up half-mast high as a signal of distress. The stranger came on slowly, for the wind was light. It seemed even now that she would not be in time to save us. At last she got near enough to see our condition, and hove to. Four boats were lowered, which came pulling towards us.

"By this time the water was almost up to the lower deck. Jack and I stood ready to spring on board the first boat which came up. The brave crew came on, and were in time to haul the greater number of the Chinamen on board before the junk sunk beneath their feet. Several went down in her, too much knocked up to exert themselves. With us and those saved, the boats returned on board. We found that we had been picked up by the *Helen*, whaler. She had been cruising off the coast of Japan, and was going to Macao for fresh provisions. As she was short of hands Jack and I at once entered on board her. Having landed the unfortunate Chinamen and taken in the stores we wanted, we stood away into the Pacific. We found ourselves among a somewhat rough lot, but we were better off than we had been as slaves, though Jack and I agreed that we would much rather serve on board a man-o'-war. We had been cruising for some time, and had caught and stowed away about a dozen whales or more, when one night there was a cry of 'Breakers ahead!'

"The captain, who was on deck in a moment, gave the order to put up the helm and veer ship, but before she could be got round she struck heavily. We sounded round her and found the water deep on the starboard side. But all our efforts proving useless, the order was given to lower the boats. We had five fit for service, and they were got safely into the water. Jack went in one of them, I in another. We were ordered to keep off at a safe distance from the ship till daylight. When morning broke we found that the ship was a complete wreck, and that there was no chance of saving her. The captain then ordered the boats to come alongside one at a time and embark the rest of the crew, with such provisions as could be collected. We now saw land away to the nor'ard, and, having left the ship, pulled towards it. Our great want was water, and to obtain it the captain divided us into two parties to look into any bays we might discover and try and find a spring. I was in the second mate's boat. We were just pulling into a bay, when a dozen canoes full of black savages, with bows and spears, darted out and made chase after us, so we pulled away out to sea. What had become of the other boats we could not tell. Your brother Jack had gone in the captain's, and that was the last I saw of him."

"Do you think they could have escaped from the savages?" I asked, anxiously.

"I have no reason to suppose they didn't, just as we managed to escape," answered Miles, "but we didn't catch sight of them again. We had sails in our boat, and plenty of provisions, and the mate told us he intended to steer for the Sandwich Islands, the nearest civilised place he knew of, but that it was a long way off, and we should be a long time about it. He might have been right, but we were still many days' sail from it when we ran short of provisions and drank up all our water. I believe that we should have died if we hadn't fallen in with another whaler, which picked us up. I entered on board her, as did some of the men, but the mate and others preferred landing at Honolulu. I served on board her for some time. We had gone southward, having got a full ship, when we struck on a coral reef. Though we did all we could to keep her afloat, she went down with all hands, except the black and me, and we managed to get ashore on Robinson Crusoe's Island, from which you took us off."

"But can't you give me any idea as to what has become of Jack?" I again asked.

"Not more than I have told you," answered Miles; "but my idea is that some if not all the boats got off, though in what direction they steered I've no notion."

I was prevented from talking more on the subject just then by being summoned on deck, and when I told Jim he repeated what he had before said,

"We'll find him, Peter. We'll find him."

CHAPTER XX.

A MUTINY AND ITS CONSEQUENCES.

I TOLD Dr. Cockle all I had heard about my brother Jack from Miles Soper. He seemed greatly interested, and said that he sincerely hoped we might find Jack or hear of him, though he confessed that it was very much like looking for a needle in a bundle of hay. Jim and I talked of little else. We neither of us any longer thought of going home, but I got a letter ready to send, by the first ship bound for England, to my sister Mary, and another to Mr. Troil, telling them that I had got tidings of Jack, and much as I wished to get back, should stay out in those seas till I found him.

My great wish now was to fall in with other whalers, that I might make inquiries about my brother. The captain—though, I suppose, Dr. Cockle and Mr. Griffiths told him what I had heard—seemed to take no interest in the matter, nor did he show me any more attention than before.

We had left Juan Fernandez more than a month, when a cry came from the masthead of "Land ho!" It proved to be Chatham Island, one of the Galapagos, a group of volcanic islands almost under the line, some hundred miles away from the coast of Peru. We brought up in a fine bay, but the shore as far as we could see looked black and barren. There were, however, thick, low bushes of a peculiar kind, covering the ground at some distance from the beach. As Dr. Cockle was going on shore with one of the mates and a party of the men, he to botanise and they to obtain fresh provisions, I went up to the captain and asked leave to accompany him.

"I understand you have made up your mind not to run away," he observed, in his usual sarcastic tone.

"Yes, sir," I answered; "I'm content to remain on board your ship, though I know that I would until lately have done anything to get back to England."

"Take care you don't change your mind," he said, in the same tone as before. "If the doctor will be answerable for you, you can go."

I told the doctor what the captain said.

"I know that I can trust you, Peter, and I'll tell the captain that I'll undertake to bring you back," he answered.

I was glad to find that Jim was to form one of the party. Horner also got leave to go. Though he and I were on good terms, I can't say I looked upon him as a friend, but I was well pleased that he should have a run on shore, as I hoped that it would put him in good humour, for of late he had become one of the most constant grumblers on board. I even now recollect the pleasure I felt on thus once more treading the firm ground, as, except for the short time I had landed on Juan Fernandez, I hadn't set foot on shore since I left Shetland. The rest of the seamen seemed greatly to enjoy their freedom.

As soon as we had secured the boat we all set off together, running over the rough black ground, startling a number of strange-looking creatures like lizards, some of which slid off into the water, others hid themselves in holes and crevices of the rocks.

Jim and I, however, went back to join the doctor, as we knew that he would want us to carry anything he might chance to pick up. The mate, after the men had had a good run, called them to him, and we proceeded more leisurely. The shrubs we had seen we found to be prickly pears. We had gone some distance when we caught sight of some enormous creatures like tortoises. The doctor called them terrapins. They had been feeding on the prickly pears, and were now leisurely making their way towards the hills which rose in the distance. We were all suffering from thirst, and the sun beat down on our heads with a great heat. We had in vain been looking for water.

"I'd give anything for a mugful!" cried Jim.

"So would I," "And I!" echoed several more of the men.

"You needn't have long to wait if you can catch those creatures," said the doctor. "They'll yield as much cool water as we want."

We all set off running after the terrapins, which, as they didn't move fast, we soon overtook. As we got close to them they drew their heads into their shells, and remained quiet.

Horner had become unusually lively, and on seeing the creatures stop jumped on the back of one of them, when immediately on it went carrying him along with it. At first he thought it very good fun, and began snapping his fingers and pretending to dance, but whilst he was looking round at us the terrapin carried him against a prickly pear-bush, and over he went sprawling on the ground, to the great amusement of the men.

"Oh, save me! save me!" he shouted out, scarcely knowing what had happened, and believing that the creatures were going to turn upon him and run their bills into his body.

Jim and I helped him up, and found that he was bleeding from a cut hand and a wound inflicted in his side by the point of one of the leaves. The doctor, however, on arriving at the spot, examined his hurts and comforted him by the assurance that there was not much the matter, and that if he didn't think about it he could go on as well as the rest of us.

We soon again overtook the terrapins, when the men who were armed with spears ran them in under the creatures' necks and quickly killed them. We turned them over, and under the doctor's directions, found, as he said we should, plenty of perfectly cool water in their insides. It was fresh as if just out of the spring. Leaving the terrapins to carry back with us on our return, we pushed on in the hope of falling in with some more. We were not disappointed. We in a short time killed four, as many as we could manage to carry on board the boat, and sufficient to give us fresh meat for several days. I was in hopes of meeting with inhabitants, as I wanted, wherever I went, to make inquiries for Jack, not knowing where I might find him. As Miles had come to the east, I thought he might have found his way in the same direction. None of the islands are, however, inhabited, and only one of them, Charles Island, has a spring of water, though people might otherwise exist in them for years. We saw a vast number of birds, which were very tame, but not a single four-legged creature besides the terrapins and lizards. We had to make several trips to carry the meat to the boat. As we shoved off we saw the sea literally swarming with fish, and the next morning the captain sent in two boats, which, in a short time, caught as many as we could eat.

In the evening we sailed and cruised in the neighbourhood of the islands, during which time we added the oil of four whales to our cargo. We also met several other whalers, from all of whom I made inquiries for Jack, but none of the people I spoke to had even heard of the wreck of the *Helen*, and could give me no information. At length the crew began to grumble at being kept so long at sea, and we sailed for Tumbez, on the mainland, where we took in wood and water.

When this task was accomplished the captain gave leave to half of the crew to go ashore, and to remain away three days. On their return the other half had liberty granted them for the same time.

I accompanied the doctor. We went up the river some distance, and then landing walked to a town surrounded by sand, far from having a pleasant look. With the assistance of the doctor, I made inquiries for Jack, thinking that if he belonged to a whaler he might have visited the place; but I could gain no intelligence of him. The night before we sailed it was my middle watch, and when it was over I tumbled into my bunk.

I had been asleep for some time when I was awakened by hearing Horner's voice, exclaiming, "You are here, then? Rouse up and come on deck. The captain is in a great taking. He has found that a boat is missing and some of the hands, and he declares that you have gone with them."

Slipping into my clothes, I hurried on deck. It was just daylight; the captain was standing aft, looking in a fearful rage, while the second mate was forward, shouting to the men to come up and show themselves.

"Do you want me, sir?" I asked.

"So you and Jim Pulley have not taken yourselves off?" he exclaimed.

"No, sir; we never thought of doing so, and I gave you my word that I wouldn't desert."

He made no reply, but ordered Mr. Griffiths to call over the names of the men. Four were found missing.

"Take a boat and six men, well armed, and see you bring the rascals back, alive or dead!" he exclaimed, turning to the mate.

A Mutiny and its Consequences. 217

In a couple of minutes the boat was in the water and the men were ready, and Mr. Griffiths pulled away.

He was absent for some hours. At last we saw his boat coming back, but without the runaways. On reaching the deck Mr. Griffiths reported that he had gone up the river and examined the coast on either side of it, but could find no traces of the boat or men.

As soon as Captain Hawkins had abandoned all hopes of recovering the runaways he ordered Mr. Griffiths to go again on shore to try and pick up some fresh hands in their place, and I was sent to look after the boat. On either side of the river as we pulled up it we saw numbers of alligators sunning themselves on the sandy banks. As we got near them they plunged into the water, and at first I thought they were about to attack the boat.

As we got higher up, the river narrowed and the trees bent over our heads. In the branches we could see numbers of monkeys leaping from bough to bough and chattering at us. At last, after going six miles, we reached a landing-place, near which was an orange-grove coming close down to the water. Mr. Griffiths, taking two men with him, ordered the rest of us to remain in the boat, and on no account to quit her. Scarcely, however, was he out of sight than the men declared that they must have some oranges. When I reminded them of the orders I had received they laughed at me, and one of them, springing ashore, ran off to the grove. He soon again appeared, with a handkerchief in his hands full of oranges, and sucking one as he came along. He was followed by an old gentleman, whom I at once guessed to be the owner of the orange-grove, and who came on till he reached the boat. He then stopped and said something in his native language, which none of us understood. When he found this he made signs to us that we had no business to take his oranges without leave. I tried to explain by pointing to the men's mouths that they were very thirsty, and that I couldn't prevent the sailor from taking the fruit. Whether it was from my manner or looks I can't say, but the old gentleman appeared to be pleased, and going back to an orange-tree picked off a quantity of the fruit, which he brought to me in his own handkerchief, patting me on the back at the same time, as if he was satisfied with my explanations.

While sucking away at the oranges the men were kept quiet. All the time the monkeys chattered away at us from the neighbouring trees, and an ugly alligator would now and then poke his snout out of the water to have a look at us, but the shouts we raised made him swim off. At last Mr. Griffiths appeared with four fresh hands, each man carrying a bundle containing all his worldly possessions. As soon as they stepped into the boat we shoved off, and gave way down the river. I was surprised to find all the men talk in a way far superior to that of common sailors, and soon found that they had deserted from American whalers, and had been, before they came to sea, in good positions, which they had lost by misconduct. The moment we got on board, though it was now late in the evening, the captain ordered the anchor to be hove up, and as the wind was off shore, we stood out to sea.

We proceeded at once to our old cruising ground in the neighbourhood of the Galapagos. While we were on our way the new hands seemed perfectly contented, having little or nothing to do. I, of course, inquired of them if they had heard of anyone who had escaped from the *Helen*, but they could give me no information. To my surprise, I found that, though they had entered in different names, three of them were brothers, and the fourth an old friend. One of the brothers appeared to be a quiet, well-disposed man.

As far as I could make out, he had come to sea to look

after the others, and to try and keep them out of mischief, though he didn't appear to have been very successful, as time after time they had got into all sorts of scrapes, and it was a wonder that they had escaped with their lives. On reaching the old ground we fell in with a number of whales, and had very hard work, for scarcely had we stowed away the oil of one than we were in chase of another. The new hands grumbled, and so did some of the others. Of course they couldn't complain of our success in catching whales, that brought them the work to do. The mates knew of their grumbling, but took no notice of it. At last, one morning, when I came on deck, I found a letter lying on the companion-hatch, addressed to Captain Hawkins. I, of course, took it to him.

"Who sent this?" he asked, in an angry tone.

I told him where I had found it, and that I knew nothing more about the matter.

Tearing it open, as he read it a frown gathered on his brow. "The mutinous rascals! I'll not yield to them," he exclaimed. "Say nothing about this till I come on deck," he said to me. "Send Mr. Griffiths here."

When the mate came the captain read the letter to him. They then armed themselves and went on deck, when the second mate was ordered to muster all hands aft.

"Who wrote this letter?" asked the captain, in a firm tone.

No one answered, and there was silence for some time, until the captain repeated the question.

"It was Muggins," at last said one of the men.

Muggins was one of the last hands shipped, and though a man of some education, he always seemed to me utterly worthless. He was a friend of the three brothers, who went by the names of Washington, Crampton, and Clifford.

"But in this precious letter I have the names of all the crew," exclaimed the captain.

Several of the men on this protested that they knew nothing about the letter, and had not put their names to any paper.

"Well, then, let those who have agreed to it walk over to the port side, and those who wish to stick to their duty and remain in the ship go to the starboard side."

Eight only walked over, including those I have mentioned.

On this Miles Soper, stepping aft and touching his hat, said, "I never like to peach on shipmates, but, as an honest man, I can't hold my tongue. On two different nights I saw Muggins get up and change the meat and throw dirt in among the bread. One night he carried up some of the best pieces and hove them overboard.

"It's clear to me that he did it to make the rest of us discontented with our victuals. I had made up my mind to speak about it, but I couldn't catch him at it again, though I'm certain he played the same trick more than once afterwards."

"I believe you, Soper," said the captain, and at a signal from him the mates rushed forward and seized Muggins, whom they dragged aft, none of the others interfering. The captain then produced a pair of handcuffs which he had got ready, and fixed them on the wrists of the man. He then called to Horner, Jim, and me to assist the mates, and together we carried the man down below and shut him up in the cabin store-room, the captain meantime remaining by himself on deck. When we returned we found that the crew hadn't moved.

"Now, lads!" he said; "you who have made up your minds to remain in the ship return to your duty."

On this the men on the starboard side went forward, but

the remaining seven mutineers stood where they were with their arms folded. I was in hopes that, as they were no longer under the influence of Muggins, they would yield, but they would make no promises. At length, tired of standing where they were, they moved lazily along forward. Dr. Cockle told me that the captain intended to put into the Marquesas, where he could get rid of the men and obtain others.

I found the next day that we were steering in that direction. After this not one of them would do any work, though they were allowed to remain at liberty. I fully expected that they would try to rescue their companion, but the captain and mates kept an eye on them, as did Jim and I.

It was tantalising to us to see whales every day and yet not to go in chase of them, but the captain wouldn't send any boats away with the good men in them for fear of what the others might do in their absence.

At length we reached Witahoo, one of the Marquesas, and brought up in a beautifully sheltered bay. Had there been any English authorities in the place the men would have been imprisoned, but as it was all the captain could do was to release Muggins from his handcuffs, and to send him and the other men ashore. The second mate went in one boat, and I had command of the other. The mutineers were ordered to get into them, and we pulled for the beach. Though they had only their clothes and a few articles put up in bundles, they stepped on shore with as jaunty an air as if they were going among friends, and having walked a little distance they turned round and jeered and laughed at us.

"I pity you poor fellows who have to toil away on board that filthy whaler," cried Muggins. "It's a shame that you haven't spirit enough to lead the happy easy lives we are going to enjoy."

Before we shoved off several natives came down to the beach, with whom the mutineers shook hands, as if they were old friends. Presently a huge fellow appeared, who, judging from the way the rest treated him, we supposed to be a chief. Though the others were of a gigantic size and magnificent proportions, he was taller than any of them. Every part of his body that we could see was tattooed over a deep blue colour, from the crown of his head to his feet. His head was shaven, and every hair, even to the eyelashes, was plucked out.

He introduced himself to the mate, who was standing up in the boat, as Duntee, the chief of the island. He spoke a little English, and from him we made out that a missionary resided a short distance off up the bay. In a short time a number of other people came down, with several women and children. Nearly all the latter appeared to me to be very handsome, their good looks not being spoilt by tattooing. I have never seen so many fine-looking people together in any part of the world. The chief told us that we should be welcome to as much wood and water as we required, and offered to supply us with fresh provisions at a cheap rate.

Next day the missionary came on board, and warned us to beware of the people. He had made but little progress with them, owing very much to the misconduct of the runaway sailors who lived on shore and set them a bad example. Still he had some converts, and he hoped, in time, to make more. I told him about my brother Jack, and how anxious I was to find him. I got Miles Soper to describe him minutely, and the missionary kindly promised to make inquiries for him.

The captain returned with him on shore to look for men, and came back in the evening with eight he had picked up. One of them was a runaway sailor, who had been living on the island several years (such being termed a beach-comber), a Portuguese, and six Kanakas, as the natives are called.

Meantime the blacks and the Sandwich Islanders, with a few of the white men, were employed in bringing off the fresh provisions we required. As Dr. Cockle wished to visit a part of the bay a little distance off, he borrowed one of the boats manned with two natives, Jim Homer, and me. We visited two or three spots, where the doctor collected some plants and some shells from the shore. We were about to return when he proposed that we should look into a little bay a short distance further on. The natives seemed disinclined to go there, and as far as we could make out advised us to return to the shore, saying that there were bad people in that neighbourhood.

The doctor, however, who supposed that they only wished to save themselves from the longer pull, persisted in going on. As we got up towards the head of the bay we saw several natives, who ran off as we approached, and hid themselves behind the trees.

"We must be cautious, for perhaps our men here didn't warn us without reason," observed the doctor as we pulled slowly in. Directly after he exclaimed, "There are two men lying on the beach. Who can they be? We must, at all events, go in and ascertain."

He had brought his fowling-piece, and we had besides two muskets. He told Jim and me to stand up, with the muskets in our hands, for he didn't like to trust Homer, while he stepped on shore. Just as the boat reached the beach, and Jim, who was in the bows, was about to jump out, he exclaimed, "Why, I do believe those two fellows are Muggins and Jones."

The doctor leaped on shore, looking carefully round to ascertain that no natives were near. A cry of horror escaped him. The two men were dead, with their skulls fractured, the brains lying about.

Their "free and happy" life on shore had come speedily to an end. Why they had been killed it was difficult to say. The doctor, stooping down, felt the bodies.

"They are perfectly cold, and must have been dead some time," he observed. "They probably had a quarrel with some of the natives, and were trying to escape to the beach to cry for help, when they were overtaken."

As we could do nothing we returned to the ship, thankful that we had escaped the treachery of the natives, though, as the doctor observed, the men who had suffered had evidently brought it all upon themselves.

CHAPTER XXI.

A CRUISE ACROSS THE PACIFIC AND THE ADVENTURES I MET WITH.

ON reaching the ship we found that the captain, the English missionary, and the big old chief, Utatee, had arrived on board just before us. The doctor at once told them what had occurred.

"The fellows probably brought their fate upon themselves," said the captain. "They must have provoked the savages and got killed in consequence."

"I'm afraid that such was the case," observed the missionary; "but I will ask the chief to inquire into the matter."

Utatee said he would do so, but if the white men were guilty he could not undertake to punish their murderers.

While we were talking some of the crew cried out, "A shark! a shark!" and sure enough there was a huge creature swimming up close under the counter, with his fin just above the water, his wicked eye glancing up at the ship. The chief said something to one of the natives who had come aboard with him, a fine athletic fellow, who, like the chief, appeared to be fully dressed in a tightly-fitting dark blue silk dress, but who, in reality, had only a loincloth round his waist, fastened by a girdle, in which were stuck a couple of knives, the rest of his body being perfectly tattooed from head to foot.

The man looked at the shark, and waiting until it had

gone a little ahead, overboard he went, and swam rapidly up after it. Presently he dived, and we saw the shark floundering in the water. I thought that he had turned to seize the man, and that the blood which tinged the waves was issuing from his body; but no, it was the shark which was wounded. The man rose, and again plunged his knife into the monster's side. He did the same several times, and then towing it up by the tail to the ship, made signs for the bight of a rope to be hove to him. He passed it over the shark's head, and another rope being secured near the tail, the monster was hoisted up, while the native, with wonderful agility, climbed on deck, apparently not in the slightest degree exhausted by his exertions.

Immediately after this we saw a prodigious commotion near the entrance of the bay, while a loud sound like that of stones knocked together reached our ears. We soon made out a number of people, men, women, and children, who had come off from the extreme point forming one side of the entrance of the bay, and were swimming across it, shouting and striking together a couple of big stones, which they held in their hands. Having formed in a line across the bay, they turned and swam up it, and we saw that they were driving before them a shoal of porpoises. On they kept in perfect order, till the porpoises were driven right ashore at the head of the bay. Here a number of other natives met them. Together they attacked the creatures, which they quickly killed. The missionary told us that their object was to extract the teeth, through which they make holes for the purpose of forming necklaces.

"You'll not forget, sir, I hope, to look out for my brother Jack," I said, as the missionary was going.

"You may trust me for that, my young friend," he answered, kindly; "but I shall not be long on these islands, I fear, as the French are coming to take possession of them, and they'll allow no Protestant missionaries to live here."

The captain had no wish to remain for the purpose of inquiring into the death of the two seamen, as they didn't belong to his ship, and we therefore sailed at daybreak the next morning for Dominica, the largest island of the group, where we understood that we could obtain a larger supply of pork than we had obtained at Witatoo.

We quickly came off that island, but could discover only one bay into which we could safely enter.

As soon as we brought up, two of the boats were sent ashore under charge of Mr. Griffiths, he going in one, and I, with Jim and Horner, in another.

As we got near the beach we saw that a heavy surf was breaking on it. Mr. Griffiths, however, thought that we could land safely, and waiting till the wave had burst, we dashed on.

Though we shipped a good deal of water, the boats got in safely. The natives being accustomed to supply whalers, guessing what we wanted, had come down with a number of hogs to sell. The price for one was a bottle of powder, and five could be purchased for an old musket.

We had brought a number of these articles for barter. Mr. Griffiths ordered me to stand by the boats while he carried on the trade.

As was my custom, I looked about in the hopes of seeing some English sailor of whom I might make inquiries about my brother Jack.

When we had purchased as many pigs as the boats would carry, we prepared to shove off.

The natives made signs to us that we had better be careful, but we didn't understand them, and the pigs being put on board, we shoved off.

"I'll lead," said Mr. Griffiths. "When you see me safe outside you can follow," and away he went.

He got through one breaker, but what was my horror to see the next catch the boat and roll her completely over! We knew that the place abounded with ground-sharks, and we expected to see either him or some of the other men carried off by the savage creatures.

He was not a bad swimmer, but, at the same time, was unaccustomed to make his way through a heavy surf.

The rest of the men clung to the boat, but he attempted to gain the shore by himself. I was about to tumble the pigs out of my boat, and to go off in her to his assistance, when three of the natives darted out through the foaming seas towards where he was struggling. Every instant I expected he would disappear, but they quickly reached him, and supporting him in their arms, brought him back safe to the beach, where the rest of the men arrived, without hurt, on the bottom of the boat.

"We must not be defeated, lads," cried out Mr. Griffiths, as soon as he had recovered. "We shall have better fortune next time."

The boat was baled out and put to rights, and the pigs, which had swum ashore, being again put in her, away we pulled, but just as she had got to the middle of the roller she broached to and over she went.

This time I, not without reason, feared that some of my shipmates would be lost, as I saw the boat tossing helplessly in the breakers, but presently she came driving, with all hands and the pigs, at a rapid rate towards the beach, where the natives received them, looking as if nothing unusual had occurred.

Still undaunted, Mr. Griffiths determined once more to make the attempt, and the next time succeeded. I waited until the largest roller, which I had carefully noted, had passed, and my men giving way, we got through, although the boat was nearly half full of water.

We carried the pigs on board, but after this, at the suggestion of one of the natives, we anchored the boats a short distance from the shore by letting him dive down and make fast a cable to the coral at the bottom.

The natives then swam off to us with the pigs and the cocoa-nuts which we bought of them, without making any additional charge for their trouble; indeed, to them it seemed a matter of course. We could obtain no yams, but we got instead some enormous plantains, which served us instead of potatoes. As we could bring off but a few pigs at a time it was rather a long business, and we had then to skin and salt them down.

The wind changing, and the surf no longer breaking at the end of the bay, we were able to land without difficulty. I had one day accompanied the doctor, who took only three other men to pull the boat. As he wished to botanise and obtain some shells and other productions of the island, the men went with him to carry what could be got, while I remained by the boat to prevent the natives from stealing the lead and gear belonging to her.

Before long two or three old women came down to the beach and began talking to me by signs, for words were of no use. Then others joined them. They took hold of my hands and seemed to be admiring my complexion and examining my clothes. As far as I could make out they wanted me to accompany them to their village. When I refused, for of course I was not going to neglect my duty and leave the boat, they grew angry, and at last several of them seized me by the arms and were attempting to drag me off. I struggled violently, and shouted out at the top of my voice, but they didn't seem to mind that.

As they were very strong I was completely in their power, and I fully believed that I should be carried off, when I caught sight of a man running towards the boat. He proved to be one of our crew who had been sent back by the doctor for something he had left. When he saw what was taking place, holding his musket in his hand, he rushed towards the old women, who let me go and scampered off.

"It's lucky for you, Peter, that they didn't succeed in getting you away," he said. "They would have tattooed you all over and turned you into a nigger and made you marry one of their girls. I'll stay by you, for the chances are they may come back and try again to make you a prisoner. The doctor must manage to do without his spud."

When Dr. Cockle returned, though at first he began to scold the man, when he heard why he remained he told him he was right. At all events, had the natives carried me off it might have caused a deal of trouble to recover me.

Sailing from the Marquesas we gradually worked our way westward towards the Society Islands, catching a few whales, till we arrived at Totillah, one of the Samoa group.

The scenery was magnificent, while everywhere the country was covered with beautiful trees, among them the pandamus palm, the tree-fern, the banyan, the bread-fruit tree, wild nutmeg, and superb bamboos. The natives also were very well-behaved and quiet, and were always inclined to treat us hospitably. Indeed, we might have travelled without the slightest risk from one end of the island to the other. The good behaviour of the inhabitants was the result of their having become Christians owing to the indefatigable exertions of missionaries. It was here that John Williams, the great apostle to the Pacific heathen, spent several years. Not far off from where we lay at anchor was Leoni Bay, the scene of the massacre of the French navigator Perouse and his companions. While we were here two of the men we had obtained ran off. Two others were shipped in their stead. One of them, who called himself John Brown, as he stepped on deck seemed to me a remarkably fine fellow. He had belonged to a whaler which had been wrecked some time before, and he had remained behind while the rest of the crew went on to Sydney.

I immediately asked him the question which I put to everybody. "Do you know anything of a young fellow named Jack Trawl?"

"It seems to me that I have heard of the name," he said, "but when or where I can't say. When did you last get news of him?"

"He was wrecked in the *Helen*, and was last seen in one of her boats when the crews were making their escape from the savages," I answered.

"Then perhaps I may help you a little," he said. "Some time ago we fell in with a whaler and we were talking to her crew. At last, as we were going to shove off, one of the men said that he had been on board the *Helen*, and he knew for certain two of her boats had got safely to Timor, but what became of the others he couldn't tell."

I naturally asked which of the boats had reached Timor, and whether the captain's was one of them, but he could not say, and I was obliged to rest satisfied with this information. It gave me fresh hopes that Jack was alive.

I have not described the bay in which we lay. It was very deep and narrow, and might rather have been called a gulf. Just as we got under way the wind came right in, and we had either to anchor again or work out. The captain decided to do the latter. Two boats were sent ahead to tow the ship round, the rest of the crew were at their stations. Not a word was spoken, for we all saw that we had no easy task to perform. As we went about, first on one tack then on the other, we each time gained but little ground.

At last, as we were just again going about, a puff of wind drove her right ashore on a coral reef. In vain the men in the two boats endeavoured to pull her round. The captain and both the mates gave her up for lost, and the crew seemed to think the same, but Brown, who was looking round everywhere, called me, and we hauled away at the fore brace. The foretopsail filled with a flaw of wind which came off the shore, and away the ship went, the wind favouring us till we were clear out of the bay. It was one of the narrowest escapes from shipwreck I ever had.

The next land we made was "Boscawen" and "Keppel" Islands, the former being a high peak, the latter a low, level island. We here landed to obtain provisions, among which we got some of the finest yams I ever saw. The natives were good-looking, friendly people.

We continued on to the north-west, and made the "Duke of Clarence" Island, which has no land within four hundred miles of it. The captain said that he had touched there years before, but that it was uninhabited. As we were nearing it, however, a number of natives came off in large canoes loaded with cocoa-nuts and fruits, so that they or their fathers must have made a long voyage to reach it in their frail-looking vessels.

Thence we proceeded to the Kingsmill group, of which Byron's Island is the largest. The men, who were heathens, were quite naked, but the women wore small aprons of seaweed. They didn't tattoo themselves, but many of them had their skins rough and hanging in flakes, which gave them a most repulsive appearance. This was in consequence of their spending much of their time in the water.

They were savage not only in their appearance but in their customs, for we heard that to prevent overcrowding, as they cannot provide sufficient food for a large population, they kill their infant children.

A Cruise across the Pacific. 233

Such were the people of all these islands, however handsome in appearance, before the missionaries went among them. Many of them had terrible wounds, produced in their battles with each other, either by their spears or clubs, which are covered with sharks' teeth.

We didn't see the land till we were within about ten miles of it, as it is very low, being of coral formation. Its only vegetable production is the cocoa-nut tree, which is of the greatest value to the natives. They build their huts of the trunks and roof them with the leaves. Their canoes are composed of numerous pieces of the wood sewn together with cocoa nut fibre. The form of these canoes, which are from eighteen to twenty feet long, is curious; the shape is that of a whale boat cut in two lengthways; one side is round, and the other perfectly flat, and they are kept upright by having an outrigger to windward which extends about ten feet from the hull. The sail is triangular and made of matting, and in fine weather they can beat to windward with the fastest ship.

We here spent several months, occasionally touching at Byron's Island for fresh cocoa-nuts and water. We had caught nineteen whales, when towards the evening of one day a twentieth was seen at a considerable distance.

"We must have that fellow," said the captain.

The boats were lowered; he went in one, Mr. Griffiths in another, and Mr. Harvey, the second mate, in a third. Another whale appeared much nearer, but in a somewhat different direction. While Mr. Griffiths pulled for the first, the captain and the second mate made for the second. Both were to windward. We had a light breeze, and at once began to beat up after them.

Just before sundown we found that the captain and the second mate had made fast. It took some time before the whale was killed, and we could scarcely perceive the whitt planted on its back before darkness came on. We had, in the meantime, lost sight of Mr. Griffiths's boat, but we hoped that he would be equally successful. We made tack after tack till we got up to the whale, which two boats were towing towards us. We burned a blue light to show the first mate our position, but looked in vain for an answering signal. At last the captain, being anxious at his non appearance, and fearing that some accident must have happened, ordered the second mate to hang on to the whale while he beat the ship up in the direction Mr. Griffiths's boat had taken. The hours went by and the wind increased and the sea got up.

"Never mind," said the captain; "Harvey will hang on under the lee of the whale even if it does come on to blow harder, and he'll be safe enough."

At last, at about half-an-hour to midnight, we made out a faint light dead to windward. It took us some time to get up to it, for, though we were sure it must come from the mate's boat, it didn't approach us.

As we got near we could distinguish the people hanging to the bottom of the boat, one of them sitting astride of her and holding up a lantern. We immediately hove to, and lowered a boat to take them on board. It then appeared that the boat had been stove in by a whale, when the mate and his men clung on to her, the whale fortunately not molesting them.

The boat's lantern is always headed up tight in a keg, together with a tinder-box and candles, and having providentially secured the keg, they managed to open it, get out the lantern, and strike a light. We might otherwise have passed them in the dark, and they would all probably have perished, as we should have run back to pick up Mr. Harvey's boat and the whale we had killed. We now did so at once, and a hard night's work we had of it, as we had to secure the whale alongside, and get ready for cutting in as soon as it was day.

Soon after this, while I was aloft, I saw Jim, who had just been relieved at the wheel, go to the side, and, throwing off his clothes, jump overboard. It was what we often did, always taking care to leave a rope overboard to get up by, to get rid of the soot and grease, besides which, as we were close under the line, the weather was very hot, and a bath refreshing.

Jim swam some way ahead of the ship, when the cook, to play him a trick, hauled up his rope, which I didn't perceive, as I was looking at Jim. Just then I caught sight of the fin of a shark at no great distance off. I shouted to Jim to come back, and he, knowing that I should not give a false alarm, struck out lustily for the ship. Mr. Griffiths, who was on deck, seeing his danger, at once hove him another rope, and shouted at the top of his voice to keep the shark off. Still the monster came nearer and nearer. I saw Jim, to my great relief, get up to the side, but as he took hold of the rope, from its being covered with grease, it slipped through his fingers. The mate shouted to the other men on deck to come and assist him in hauling Jim up. I slid down on deck as fast as I could. On came the shark. Jim was still in the water, and I expected to see my old friend caught.

With all our strength we hauled at the rope, but still Jim couldn't hold on by it, and I feared that it would slip through his fingers altogether, when, as it turned out, there was a knot at the end. This enabled him to hold on, and we hauled him up, more dead than alive from fright, just as the shark, showing the white of its belly, shoved its snout out of the water and made a snap at his feet, not six inches from them.

Jim was saved, and I never in my life felt more inclined

to cry for joy than when I saw him out of danger. While the shark was still alongside looking for its prey, one of the Marquesas islanders who came on deck, taking a knife in his hand, leapt right down, feet first, on the monster's back, which so scared it that away it went like a flash of lightning.

I have mentioned these circumstances just as they occurred to show the sort of life led by the crew of a whaler. I have more interesting events to narrate in the following chapters.

CHAPTER XXII.

A TYPHOON, AND HOW WE GOT THROUGH IT.

THE crew of a whaler had need to exercise much patience. Sometimes they watch for weeks and weeks together, but watch in vain, for fish. At others so many are caught that they have not a moment to rest between the time that one is tryed out and another is brought alongside.

We had at first been very successful, but a week or more having passed without a whale being seen, Captain Hawkins ordered a course to be steered for the Japan whaling ground. The very first day that we arrived in the latitude of these islands, which were, however, far out of sight, we caught two whales.

We had tryed out the first and had the other alongside when another whaler made her appearance. As she got within half a mile of us it feel calm. Soon afterwards a boat was lowered from her, which came pulling towards us. When she came alongside a fine, hale-looking old man stepped on board and introduced himself as Captain Barnett, of the *Eleanor*. He spoke in a hearty, cheery tone, which contrasted greatly with the rough and unpleasant way in which Captain Hawkins generally expressed himself.

Captain Barnett dined on board, and then invited Captain Hawkins and Dr. Cockle to come and sup with him. I managed to address the old gentleman, and told him about Jack.

"Should I ever fall in with your brother I'll say that I met you, and that you were inquiring for him," he answered, kindly.

When the two captains came on deck they took a look round the horizon.

"You must excuse me from accompanying you," said Captain Hawkins, "for I tell you what, I don't like the look of the weather. There's something brewing somewhere. I'd advise you to get on board as soon as you can."

The ocean had hitherto been perfectly calm, but there now came from the north-east a slowly-heaving swell, which every minute increased, and the whole atmosphere in a short time assumed a sombre, melancholy appearance, while a peculiar light tinged the two ships and sea around, owing to the sun's rays passing through clouds of a dull yellowish-red colour. Before this, numbers of birds had been flying about the ship, but they now winged their way to distant lands. As soon as our visitor had pulled away, our captain ordered the hands aloft to shorten sail, although at the time there was not a breath of wind.

Everything was taken in with the exception of a main topsail and storm trysail.

As the swell increased, the ship began to roll in a most frightful manner, her chain-plates striking the water every time she heeled over, while the water as it rose beat against the stern with a force so violent that we were almost thrown off our legs.

We had to cast adrift the last whale caught before the whole blubber was cut in, as it was impossible, without the greatest risk, to keep it alongside.

I asked Brown, who was the most intelligent seaman on board, what he thought was going to happen.

"We shall have a typhoon—a precious hard one too, I suspect," he answered.

A Typhoon, and how We got through It. 239

All night long the swell went on increasing, when suddenly the wind sprang up and broke the hitherto calm swells into foaming seas, which furiously dashed round the ship though they did us no damage.

Just as daylight came on the wind again dropped; but though the wind had fallen, the sea, instead of going down, raged more fiercely than ever, making the ship roll so violently that we feared that at any moment the masts might be carried away. Yet all this time there was scarcely a breath of wind. This state of things continued till about three o'clock, when suddenly, as Brown had foretold, the gale again broke upon us, and continued to blow with increasing violence until about two o'clock on the following morning, when a more furious blast than ever struck the ship.

"Hold on for your lives!" shouted Mr. Griffiths, who was on deck.

The captain, followed by Dr. Cockle, hurried from below. There was little need to give the warning; we all clung to the weather-bulwarks. Over went the ship right on her beam-ends, and away flew the storm trysail, while every article not securely lashed was carried away. Fearful indeed was the uproar. The wind howled savagely, the sea dashed with thundering roars against the sides of the ship, the masts groaned, the bulkheads creaked, the ropes and blocks clashed together and rattled in a way I had never before heard. Indeed, I believed that our last moments had come, for it seemed impossible unless the masts went that the ship would right. Jim and I and Horner crouched down close to each other, sheltering ourselves as we could under the bulwarks. Not far off were Miles Soper, Sam Coal, and Brown.

"Is there any chance for us?" asked Horner, his teeth chattering and his voice showing his terror.

"Chance!" answered Brown; "the chance that many a

stout ship has braved as bad a hurricane, and yet come out of it not much the worse."

We looked out for the *Eleanor*, but she was nowhere to be seen. Some of the men declared that she must have gone down.

"We're afloat and why shouldn't she be?" said Brown, who was ready to cheer every one up.

Some of the hands stole below, and I believe if they could have got into the spirit-room they would have made themselves drunk in order to forget their fears. Most of us, however, preferred remaining on deck and watching what would happen.

Suddenly, during a momentary cessation of the wind, the ship righted, and we flew on before it, though matters in other respects seemed but little mended. As the sea beat against the ship it seemed like a huge battering-ram trying to knock her to pieces, every blow making each plank shake though none gave way. Now she plunged her head into an immense hollow, now she rose rapidly to the top of a foaming sea, while the next instant another rolling on threatened to overwhelm us.

Daylight came, but it brought no cessation of the hurricane. The hours went by; not one of us thought of breakfast. Indeed, it was impossible to cook anything. We watched the masts quivering as the ship plunged into the seas, and we expected every moment to see them go by the board. The carpenter and the first mate had got their axes ready to cut them away, should such occur. At length a tremendous sea came roaring towards our weather bow. The ship struggled as if to avoid it, but she pitched headlong into the deep hollow just before her, and a monstrous sea, lifting its head half way up to the foretop, came right down on our deck, sweeping up to the main hatchway. Horner and several of the men shrieked out with terror, believing that their last moments were come. I scarcely supposed that the ship would recover herself, but suddenly she came up with a jerk, the bowsprit carried away, and the next moment it came right across our forecast'e.

"Rouse up, lads, and secure the foremast," shouted the captain.

Led by the mates, with Brown, Ringold, Soper, Jim, and me, the crew rushed forward to secure the fore-topmast stay. We then got the bowsprit inboard. After this the ship began to ride more easily, though the hurricane continued until near sunset, when it began to abate. The watch below turned in, eager to get some rest. I never slept more soundly in my life. Next morning the sun rose from a cloudless sky. A gentle breeze was blowing. The sea had already gone down, and in a few hours sparkling wavelets alone played over the surface of the deep

Two days afterwards we brought up under the lee of South Island to repair damages. After this we again sailed to resume our search for whales.

I was forward, when I saw a dark object floating some distance on the weather bow. On my reporting it to the captain, he ordered a boat to be lowered to ascertain what it was. Mr. Griffiths went in her with the doctor, Jim and I forming part of the crew. As we got near we saw that it was a creature of some sort, but it made no effort to avoid us, and seemed to be fast asleep. With his harpoon Mr. Griffiths went forward. As we got closer it seemed to be an enormous turtle; the doctor said of the "trunk" species.

We paddled as noiselessly as we could for fear of waking it, and on getting close Mr. Griffiths plunged his harpoon deep into its body through its shell. The creature in a moment was lively enough, and, after swimming away a short distance, turned and made a snap at the rope, which it nearly bit in two. We were up to it again, however, and two or three plunges of a lance quickly finished it. We then secured a rope to it and towed it to the ship. By means of the windlass it was hoisted on board. When lying on deck it was found to measure seventeen feet in length, to be seven feet wide, and four feet six inches in depth. All on board declared that they had never seen a creature of that species of the same size. We boiled it down as we would the blubber of a whale, and it yielded nearly a barrelful. Fish in these seas are very numerous. Sometimes from the masthead I could see the whole ocean alive with them.

Before leaving for the Sandwich Islands, for which we were next bound, we had a day's fishing, and in a few hours caught as many as we wanted. I here also saw numbers of the paper nautilus floating on the calm surface of the water. I managed, with a small net at the end of a long pole, to catch several for my friend the doctor.

I'll not describe our voyage back to Honolulu, the capital of the Society Islands. There were two or three merchantmen and about forty whalers at anchor. The entrance to the harbour is surrounded by coral reefs, and is very intricate. The chief pilot came out in his whale-boat, manned by natives, and as he passed each ship he hailed to have a boat sent him to assist in towing us in. In a short time we had nearly fifty whale-boats, twenty-five on each bow, in two long lines. It was one of the prettiest sights I ever witnessed, towing on the big ship at the rate of about three knots an hour between the coral reefs, making what would otherwise have been a difficult business perfectly easy. Here we exchanged the fish we had salted down for fifty barrels of potatoes and twenty of onions. Among the ships was the *Eleanor*, from which we had parted off Japan. As the old captain had greatly taken Dr. Cockle's fancy, he wished to pay him a visit, and invited me to accompany him.

On getting on board the mate said that he was below, and considering all things, doing wonderfully well.

"What do you mean?" asked Dr. Cockle.

"Why, sir, I'll tell you," answered the mate. "If I ever saw a wonderful thing done, our captain did it. While the typhoon which caught you as well as us was at its height our rudder broke adrift, and on getting it on board to repair, it came right down on his leg, crushing it fearfully. We all thought he must have died, for you see our doctor had left the ship some time before, and there was no one who knew what was to be done. So our skipper sat down on the deck and ordered the carpenter to bring him the surgical instruments. Our carpenter is a wonderfully clever fellow, and between them they managed to saw off the leg below the knee, to take up the arteries and stop the bleeding.* We then got the old man, who is sixty years of age, into bed. Would you believe it? In a few weeks after the accident he had a turning-lathe brought to the side of his bed, and if he didn't turn out a first-rate wooden leg for himself."

On going below the doctor found the old captain doing wonderfully well and not requiring any further aid. Before we left he was stumping about on deck as hearty and cheery as ever. Indeed, through his courage and coolness he had undoubtedly saved his own life.

The old captain probably is dead, but Mr. Rosden, the mate, who is the son of an old Downs pilot, will confirm the account I have given.

The captain was constantly on shore, and Mr. Griffiths kindly let me take one of the boats, with Jim, and Soper, and Coal as a crew, and we visited every ship in the harbour, that I might make inquiries for Jack. As we pulled about,

---

* This account is true in every respect. My friend, Mr. Henry Foster, Trinity pilot, vouches for it.

though disappointed at one ship, we half hoped to find him on board another. My heart grew sick as I approached the last.

"Do you think he's aboard her, Miles?" I asked.

"If he isn't don't lose heart," was the answer.

"No, no, don't lose heart, Peter," echoed Jim. "He'll turn up some time or other. It mayn't be to day or it mayn't be to-morrow, but if he's alive—and there's no reason why he should have lost his life—he'll be somewhere no doubt, and you'll be led to him, that's my opinion."

We got on board the ship. She was an American whaler, the *William and Eliza*. We found the crew in a great state of commotion, and they would scarcely listen to what I had to say. Their commander, Captain Rogers, who seemed to be a great favourite with them, had been wrongly accused of infringing the revenue laws, and had been imprisoned in a mud fort which guarded the landing-place, and they were determined to rescue him.

Most of their boats were away visiting the other ships to obtain recruits, and they declared that if he was not let out that evening they would liberate him before morning.

I, of course, could not join them, but Soper and Coal were very eager to lend a hand. I persuaded them, however, to come back with me to our ship after I had made all the inquiries I could for Jack without success.

Miles and Coal brought the news, and what was to be done on board, and several of our men declared that they would join, as much for the sake of the spree as influenced by a regard for Captain Rogers.

As evening drew in, a number of boats put off from all the American ships, and from several of the English, for the imprisoned skipper was much liked, not only by his own men, but by the captains and mates of nearly all the whaling ships. He was a great friend, too, I found, of Captain

A Typhoon, and how We got through It. 245

Hawkins. When the captain came on board again, he gave any of us leave to go that chose. I don't say we were right, but when I found the second mate about to lead a party of our men, Jim and I offered to go with them, and away we pulled for the *William and Eliza*.

We found her surrounded by boats, carrying well-nigh two hundred men, the whole being under the command of an American captain.

We waited till nearly midnight, when the order was given to shove off. We could not tell whether the authorities on shore knew anything of what was about to take place.

We carried a number of scaling ladders, with stout ropes and hooks. The first who got up with the ladders were to fix on the hooks, so that the others might swarm up, and we might all mount the walls together.

We had no firearms, only axes, blubber-spades, and spears. We pulled in, forming a long line abreast, as silently as possible. On reaching the shore, two hands were left in each boat, and the rest of us rushed up to the fort to fix the ladders.

It took but a few seconds before we were all at the top, and down we leaped into the fort.

Nearly the whole of the garrison were asleep. When they found the place full of men some of them ran away and hid themselves, and others dashed out at the gate. We soon found the room in which Captain Rogers was shut up. The door was broken open and he was set free. Not wishing to have a disturbance with the natives, we hurried back with him the way we came, and before long were on board again. The captain made us a speech, and thanked us for setting him free, and we returned to our respective ships. I don't know that any notice was taken of the affair by the authorities, but of course Captain Rogers was unable to go on shore again while he remained in the harbour.

Having repaired our ship and taken on board several fresh hands, who wished to return home to England, we sailed again for the Marquesas, in order to land the natives whom we had taken from those islands.

The passage lasted five weeks, during which time we didn't see a single ship. We proceeded at once to Resolution Bay. On entering we found a French man of-war, which immediately sent a boat on board us.

The officer in command informed the captain that the islands now belonged to France, and that we must not land anything in the shape of firearms or ammunition.

While he was still on board a boat pulled off from the shore, bringing a dozen soldiers, who, without asking leave, came up the side.

"Why do these men come on board my ship?" asked the captain.

"To see that you comply with the orders you receive," answered the officer, who spoke very good English.

"I have no intention of breaking the laws you impose," exclaimed the captain, who was not the man to stand that sort of thing, "but I'll not submit to have foreign soldiers placed on board my ship."

The French officer shrugged his shoulders, and said that he was but carrying out the orders of his superiors.

On this the captain ordered his boat to be lowered, and pulled away on board the French man-of-war. He there threatened to throw the ship on the hands of the French if the soldiers were not immediately withdrawn.

After a little time the captain returned, accompanied by a French lieutenant, who brought an order for the soldiers to return on shore. Our stay here was rendered very unpleasant by the French. As soon as we got our fresh provisions on board we sailed again for the westward, proceeding as before among the coral reefs, which lie to the

OVER THE CORAL REEF.

Page 247.

north of the Society Islands. The navigation is exceedingly dangerous, as many of them are so low that they cannot be seen till the ship is close to them, and we had to keep a very sharp look-out as we sailed on. The most dangerous of all those we sighted was the Sidney group, which consist of bare sandbanks, without the least vegetation, and are nearly level with the surface of the sea. We landed on some of them to obtain birds' eggs and fish, which are very plentiful, but they are uninhabited, as there is no fresh water.

Still sailing west we touched at the Kingsmills, passing also several other islands, till we came off Strong's Island. Here is a magnificent harbour, surrounded by coral reefs, but the mouth is so narrow that we could not have attempted to enter had not the boats of three vessels lying there come out to assist in towing us in. On bringing up, a number of natives came off, who talked capital English, and seemed very intelligent fellows. We found that the chief of the island was named King George.

In a short time another canoe came off with a fine-looking fellow on board, who seemed as eager to trade and obtain anything he could as the rest of the natives.

At last Captain Hawkins, turning to him, said, rather roughly, "You and the other chaps must be off now."

"You know who I am?" asked the native. "I King George, chief of all these islands."

"I beg your majesty's pardon, but you don't look much like a king," said the captain, laughing.

The chief, however, didn't appear to be angry, and shook hands with the captain and officers, and stepping into the canoe paddled away for the shore.

"We must take care these fellows don't play us any trick," observed the captain to Mr. Griffiths. "We'll give them a salute to show them that we're wide-awake."

We carried four nine-pounders, which we forthwith fired. It was the first time we had to use them during the voyage. It was hoped that this would awe the natives, and that we should not be molested during the night. The sound of the last gun had scarcely died away, when a Captain Rounds, commanding one of the whalers, whose boats had assisted to tow us in, came on board. After he had shaken hands and the usual civilities had passed, he said,

"You are wise to show that you are wide-awake, and when you hear the account I have to give you of the fearful work which took place here not long ago, you will judge whether it will be prudent to put yourself or any of your people in the power of the natives."

CHAPTER XXIII.

A FEARFUL NARRATIVE—DOINGS AT STRONG'S ISLAND.

AS it was very hot below, the captain had ordered chairs and a small table to be brought on deck, and he, with Captain Rounds, Dr. Cockle, and Mr. Griffiths, took their seats, while Mr. Harvey, Horner, and I stood within earshot to hear the account our visitor had promised to give.

" I came in here about two months ago for the first time this voyage to obtain provisions and water," began Captain Rounds, "and as none of us understood the language of the people, I shipped a couple of natives who spoke English very fairly to act as interpreters. Besides having been to sea on board other whalers, they were, I thought, likely to prove useful hands. Everything went on in a satisfactory way while I lay here. The natives who came on board behaved themselves well, and King George, their chief, seemed a very decent sort of fellow, and was as honest in his dealings as I could expect. I had made it a rule when I came out to these parts never to trust many of my people ashore at a time among the heathen natives without having some of the principal natives on board as hostages, or so well-behaved and friendly did these appear that I should otherwise not have hesitated to let half my crew land at a time, feeling confident that they would be well treated. Thus it was that I every evening at sundown fired off my guns, and kept a strict watch during the night. I did this, not from any fear of being attacked, but that I considered it prudent to keep to the rule I had laid down, and to maintain discipline on board. You'll see that I was fortunate in doing so. I parted on good terms with King George and his people without having any reason to alter the favourable opinion I had formed of them, taking the two native interpreters with me. From the way I treated them they became very friendly and much attached to me. We had been at sea for some time, and had caught three or four whales, each of which cost us, perhaps, more than the usual trouble to take. The two natives, who go by the names of Jackey and Tubbs, seemed very much struck by the exertions we had to make to secure the whales, and one day they came to me and said that they could put me up to the means of filling the ship with perfect ease if I would follow their advice. I asked them what they meant. They then told me that a ship lay sunk in their harbour loaded with casks of oil, and that they knew the exact spot where she went down. I then learnt from them the following particulars.

"You, Hawkins, well knew Barber, who commanded the *Harriet*, of London, as you sailed together as mates with old Captain Newton in the *Felicity*. I met Barber when I first came out to the Pacific, and was wondering that I had never since heard of him or the *Harriet*. The natives now told me that about a year ago she had put into this harbour, there being no other vessels here at the time. You remember what a good-natured, yet somewhat careless fellow he was. The natives came in numbers on board his ship, and appeared to be on the most friendly terms with him and his crew. They at length, one day, invited his men to go ashore, and he consequently allowed the greater number of them to land. This sort of thing continued while he lay in the harbour. King George and most of his chiefs, though they came down to visit the ship when she first arrived, were, at that time, living in another part of the island, and the people just here did pretty much as they liked.

"Barber, with a boat's crew, only remained on board, when, on going on deck in the morning, he caught sight of three of his men running down towards the beach as fast as they could go, with a posse of natives after them. Presently they were overtaken. First one was struck down by the club of a savage, and directly afterwards the other two shared the same fate. The natives, on reaching the shore, jumped into their canoes, a whole fleet of which came paddling off towards the ship. The crew, on seeing this, I suspect, took fright, thinking that they should all be murdered, as their mates on shore had been. Captain Barber himself would, I am certain, have stopped to defend his ship, but probably fearing that it would be of no use to make the attempt while his crew were so faint-hearted, he ordered the boat to be lowered with such provisions and water as could be hastily thrown into her. They had scarcely left the side of the ship before the savages were up to her. They pursued the boat for some distance, but at length gave up the chase, eager to get back and secure their prize. They then set to work to plunder the vessel of everything they considered of value. They stripped her of her sails and rigging, and all the iron-work they could get at, managing even to carry away her topmasts, jibboom, and yards. Having done this, they towed the vessel higher up the harbour and scuttled her.

"When King George, who had known Captain Barber and some of his people—for he had been down at the harbour when the ship first arrived—heard of the massacre he was very indignant, and Jackey and Tubbs told me that he killed no less than thirty of those who had taken part in it with his own hand. Whether this was actually the case or not I could not make out; but, after cross-questioning the two natives, I came to the conclusion that he himself had no hand in the massacre, and was entirely ignorant of it till afterwards. What has become of poor Barber and his boat's crew I am anxious to ascertain; but he would have had a fearfully long passage to make to any other island, and I'm afraid that he and his companions must have perished from hunger and thirst before they could have reached any friendly shore.

"Having fallen in shortly after I heard this with the *Lydia* and *Pearl*, I communicated the intelligence to them, and we determined to put in here to ascertain the truth of the story.

"Now you have come we shall be sufficiently strong-handed both to defend ourselves from the natives, and to recover the *Harriet's* cargo if we cannot raise her."

Captain Hawkins at once entered into Captain Rounds' views, and they agreed the next morning with their brother captains to set to work. Captain Rounds, who was a very ingenious man, had a diving-bell constructed out of a cask, with pipes to lead the air into it.

Proceeding with the boats, we found the ship sunk in six fathoms of water at a spot Jackey and Tubbs pointed out. They willingly agreed to descend in the diving-bell, and Brown and another man also went down in it. It was then found that the ship had been set on fire, but she had sunk before the flames had reached the cargo. It was calculated that there were one thousand six hundred barrels of oil in her.

Her figure-head and other articles were got up, thus clearly identifying her as the unfortunate *Harriet*.

The captains proposed raising her, and dividing the oil between them; but after a great deal of consultation it was considered that they had better give up the plan, as it would have occupied a long time, and caused a difficulty on their arrival at home as to whether they had a right to possess themselves of it. Thus the results of many a hard month's labour were lost.

King George watched our proceedings with much interest, generally hovering about the boats in his canoe while we were at work. Perhaps he thought from the first that we should not succeed, though I think we should have done so had it been desirable to make the attempt. As soon as the undertaking was abandoned, the other vessels, which had only come in for water and provisions, sailed, and we were left alone in the harbour. The king, who did not appear to be at all offended by the way Captain Hawkins had treated him on his first visit, at once came on board, and appeared to be excessively friendly. He spoke English remarkably well, having learned it on board a whaler in his youth, and kept it up by frequently talking to runaway sailors who had remained at the island. He invited the captain to go ashore and visit him in his palace, the name we gave to the great hut in which he lived.

"With great pleasure, king," answered the captain: "but fair play's a jewel, you know. If I go to visit you, your brother here will remain on board to keep my mates company till I return."

The captain told Mr. Griffiths to keep a strict watch on the king's brother, and not to allow him to leave the cabin, lest he might slip overboard and swim on shore.

We called the young savage Charlie, though that was not his real name. Charlie, who spoke a little English, seemed perfectly content; and when the king and the captain went on shore, descended to the cabin without the slightest hesitation. As the stern-windows, through which Charlie might have squeezed himself if he had had a mind, were let open for the sake of the air, Mr. Griffiths told me to remain in the cabin whenever he was on deck. At night he was locked up in the state room. I don't know that the captain was very well pleased at having the savage sleeping in his bed.

Next morning the captain came back, saying that he had been hospitably treated. In the afternoon, as Charlie wished to return, and as the doctor and several men were on shore, the captain sent me, with Miles Soper and Brown, to bring the king off, that he might take his brother's place.

We pulled up a long narrow creek for several miles, till we arrived at the royal residence, which was a large hut with a framework of poles and roofed over with matting. Near it were other huts, and a number of natives were employed in different ways, some pounding kava between two large stones, when the root, thus thoroughly bruised, was thrown into water. This is a much pleasanter way of preparing the beverage than by employing the women to chew it, as is done in Samoa.

The king was away when we arrived, and we had thus plenty of time to walk about the village and look around us. Some natives were engaged in cooking fish and yams. This was done by putting them into a hole on the top of some hot stones and leaves, and then covering them up with more hot stones, leaves, and earth at the top of all. We soon had an opportunity of tasting them, and I can answer for their being most delicious.

As the king didn't appear we walked some little distance into the country, for we knew that we were perfectly safe while the king's brother remained as a hostage. Going into a hut we found a young woman about to light a fire. I watched the process. She first took half of the log that had been split in two and laid it down with the split side upwards; then taking a small piece of hard wood about a foot long and pointed at one end, she sat down astride of the log and commenced rubbing the sharp point of the stick up and down the grain of the large piece, thus making a groove, and shoving the shavings which she worked out to the farther end, till at length they ignited, when immediately catching up some dry leaves which lay handy, and blowing gently, she soon obtained a blaze. I tried the experiment under her directions and succeeded very well. Though simple and easy as is this method of obtaining fire, I have never seen it tried in any other place.

On our return to the village we found the king, who invited us to feast on the fish and yams which I had seen cooking. We were now joined by the captain and Dr. Cockle, with the second mate and several men, and I was directed to go back with the king, who had to take his brother's place on board.

His majesty preferred going alone in his own canoe. I sat in the bows with a long pole to keep the bow off the rocks as we went down the creek, and he placed himself astern with a paddle in his hand. He giving the canoe a shove from the bank, away we went. I was highly amused at the thought of carrying off the king as a prisoner. He, however, seemed to take it as a matter of course, and chatted and laughed as we glided along. Presently he asked,

"You young Englishman ever been here before? I think I know your face."

"When was it your majesty fancied that you saw me?" I inquired.

"Let me see," he said, holding his paddle in the air for a moment; "were you ever aboard the ship that my rascally people sent to the bottom out there?" and he pointed to where the *Harriet* lay.

"No," I answered, a dreadful thought coming into my

mind. " Was the person you fancy I am killed with the rest of the crew ? "

" I think not. If I think so, I no ask you," he answered. " I see him with the captain when he visit the shore, and each time I go on board the ship. When I come down to the harbour I took great fancy to him, and asked captain to let him stay with me, but he and captain say no. He want to go home to see father and mother, brother and sister. When I found the men killed I remembered him, but no find him 'mong them. Dat all I know, but me think that he was with captain when they got away in the boat."

At first, on hearing what the king said, I was almost in despair, for I was very sure that he was speaking of my brother Jack, as I thought that by this time I should have grown very like him, as I often heard my mother say that I was so when I was at the age at which he went to sea. How he had got on board the *Harriet* I could not tell, any more than I could what had become of her boat. Still there was a possibility of his having escaped. I had no wish to return on shore with "Prince Charlie" after I had handed the king over to the care of Mr. Griffiths, as I wanted to talk about the matter to Jim. As may be supposed, we did talk about it for many an hour. I was now eager to be out of the harbour, in the hopes that we might visit some other islands at which Jack might be found. Jim was as sanguine as ever that he would be found. When I told Mr. Griffiths he looked very grave.

" It is possible, my lad," he said, " and nothing would give me greater pleasure than to find him at last ; but you know what is likely to have been the fate of the poor fellows in a boat, with a scanty supply of provisions and a long voyage to the nearest land. Just look at the chart. We are away from all civilized countries, with the wildest savages on each side of us."

Next day, when the captain and the rest of the party came on board, and as soon as our royal visitor had taken his departure, I was very glad to hear the order given to get under way. The breeze being fair we stood out of the harbour.

We were soon at our old work again. My patience was sorely tried. If I had not been actively engaged I don't know what I should have done.

My idea was that the captain would at once sail in search of the missing boat, but he had no idea of the sort in his head. He either was convinced that she was lost, or considered that it was his business to fill up his ship as soon as possible, and not to waste time in looking for those who might never be found.

We had caught several whales, when the time came for returning to the Japan fishing ground, as it's called, some distance off the east coast of those islands. My hope of finding Jack decreased, but didn't die away altogether.

Jim kept me up. "We don't know in what direction the boat went," he observed. "She may have steered to the northward, and we are as likely to fall in with him the way we're going as anywhere else."

I often consulted the chart. To the northward of Strong's Island I saw the Caroline group, consisting of a vast number of coral islands, and north-west of them, again, the Ladrone Islands, the principal of which, Guam, is inhabited by Spaniards. Knowing this, Captain Barber may have attempted to reach it, and one day, to my satisfaction, I heard from the doctor that Captain Hawkins intended to call there before returning home.

We were now leaving those islands I have mentioned to the southward. We were very successful on the Japan ground, and nearly completed our cargo, at least the lower hold was full.

At length, one calm day, a large whale was seen spouting at some distance from the ship. Four boats were lowered. The captain, the two mates, and Brown went in them, Miles Soper going as the chief mate's boat-steerer. His boat was the first up, and in a short time Soper put two irons into the whale, which almost instantly turned over on its back, threw its lower jaw open, and nipped her clean in two.

Wonderful to relate, the men all got clear, and Mr. Griffiths, standing up on half of the boat, plunged his lance right down the whale's throat, and then jumped off and swam with the other men to the next boat coming up. The captain's boat now fastened to the whale, which, turning as before on its back, treated her in the way it had the first. When we who were on board saw this, we began to lower the spare boats as fast as we could. While we were thus employed, the doctor, who was looking on, exclaimed,

"There's a third boat caught!"

And we saw that the second mate's boat, which had got up, had been nipped by the whale. Brown's boat, the fourth, now pulled gallantly up, watching every movement of the monster, if necessary to get out of its way; but the wound it had received had already weakened it, and though it made at his boat he escaped, and succeeded in plunging several harpoons and lances into its body.

Meanwhile the crews of the other boats which had been destroyed had been hanging on to them, and though the sea was swarming with sharks it was a remarkable fact that not one of the men was lost. Sharks rarely bite people when a whale is bleeding, but keep following the track of the blood. Brown took some of the men on board, and we in the spare boats, leaving only the doctor and two hands to take care of the ship, pulled quickly up and rescued the remainder.

We soon had the whale alongside; it was the largest we

had caught—nearly a hundred feet in length; but we got very little oil out of it, for, having been fastened to previously, there was a huge swelling on its back as big as a tun butt, which was, no doubt, the cause of the blubber being so thin. We had still some spare space, and the crew were eager to catch the additional whales required to complete our cargo, that we might at length direct our course homeward. Although I should have before been the most eager of any to return to England, yet now, with the idea that had taken hold of me that Jack was somewhere in the neighbourhood, I was anxious to remain until I had found him. Jim shared my feelings, but I didn't suppose anybody else did.

We remained a week or more, however, after killing the last huge whale which had cost us so much trouble, without seeing another, when the captain determined to steer for the Ladrone Islands. As we had now been some months without obtaining fresh provisions, we first directed our course for the Bonins, some degrees to the eastward of the coast of Japan. We understood that there were wild pigs, if not goats and sheep, on them. At all events, that fish could be caught in abundance off the shore. In a few days we sighted them, and ran under the lee of one of the group called South Island. Here the ship was hove to, and a boat lowered, in which Mr. Griffiths, the doctor, Horner, Jim and I, Brown and Miles Soper and Coal, with two other men, went. We took with us besides fishing-lines the whaling gear and a couple of muskets, three or four casks to fill with water, and provisions for the day, for we didn't intend to get back to the ship till evening.

Mr. Griffiths, who had been there before, took the boat inside a high reef of rocks, where he had, he said, caught a number of fish.

Our first object was to obtain bait. Miles Soper and

Coal undertook to swim on shore with baskets and catch some crabs, for which the fish in these seas seem to have a special fondness. We pulled in as close as we could to land them, and in a short time they filled their baskets, and shouted to us to return and take them off. We now dropped our kedge anchor just inside the surf, in between two and three fathoms of water, which was so clear that we could see the fish as they swam about, darted at the bait, and swallowed the hooks.

We quickly hauled in a number of magnificent fish. We were so eager at the sport that we didn't consider how rapidly the time passed, while the doctor was more occupied with admiring the variously-coloured coral, the richly-tinted seaweeds, and the curiously-shaped fish of all the hues of the rainbow, swimming in and out among the trees of their marine gardens.

At last Mr. Griffiths, pulling out his watch, exclaimed, "Hulloa! How time has gone by! Get up the anchor, lads. We ought to be off."

The order was more easily given than obeyed. We hauled and hauled, but the anchor had got foul of the coral, and we ran a risk of losing it. Soper offered to go down and clear it, but just then a huge shark showed his ugly throat alongside, and Mr. Griffiths would not let him go. At last, just as it was dark, Brown managed to get the anchor up.

When we pulled outside the reef we found that the weather had changed. It was blowing very hard, though, sheltered as we had been, we had not discovered this. We looked eagerly out for the ship, but she was nowhere to be seen.

CHAPTER XXIV.

OUR LIFE ON AN UNINHABITED ISLAND.

WE were still in smooth water, but the sea was breaking in the offing, the white caps rising against the dark sky. Mr. Griffiths thought that the ship might have stood to the eastward and be concealed by the point of land which ran out in that direction. We eagerly gave way and pulled off from the shore. Several times he stood up to look about him. At length he cried out,

"There she is! there she is! she's burning a blue light."

We all looked in the direction he pointed, which was almost abeam, and there we saw a light, appearing, however, just above the horizon. He at once steered the boat towards it, but as we pulled on the seas increased and frequently broke aboard us; the wind was rising rapidly, and in a short time blew a heavy gale. In vain we again looked out for the light; none could be seen, and there was a great risk, should we continue to pull on, of the boat being swamped.

The doctor and Mr. Griffiths talked together earnestly; the latter then said,

"Lads, there's no help for it, we must try and get on shore for the night, and in the morning, if the wind goes down, the captain will stand in to look for us."

We all knew the danger we were in, for in pulling round the boat might be caught on her broadside and turned over; but it had to be done, and we trusted to Mr. Griffiths' steering. We gave way as he told us, though for a moment I thought all was over as a sea struck the boat abeam and half swamped her.

We got round, however, and while Horner and I baled her out, the men pulled in towards the shore. It was now very dark. All we could see ahead was an irregular line of black, but whether rocks or hills rising near the beach we could not tell. As we neared the shore Mr. Griffiths stood up looking out for a landing-place, but no opening could he discover in the rocks, against which the surf was now breaking furiously; should we get within its power the boat, we knew, would be dashed to pieces in a moment. The wind went on increasing till it blew almost a hurricane. At last Dr. Cockle exclaimed,

"There is an opening. We passed it this morning. I remember it by the clump of trees on the top of a rounded hill, and I can now make them out against the sky."

Mr. Griffiths hesitated. Should the doctor be wrong in another minute we should be hurled to destruction against the rugged rocks. Just then the moon rising on the other side of the island broke through the clouds and showed us clearly the outline of the trees and the hill.

The mate hesitated no longer, but telling us to give way steered in for the opening. The surf broke wildly on either side of us, flying up above our heads; the seas came roaring on astern, threatening to engulf us. We all gave way steadily together. Now the boat rose on the top of a foaming sea, and then down she glided into comparatively smooth water inside the reef, and we were safe.

Pulling on, we saw ahead a small bay with the trees coming down to the water's edge. Their tops were waving wildly, but we felt but little wind where we were, and we were able to run the boat's head on to the beach and land without difficulty. We at once drew her up and looked out for a sheltered spot under some rocks to camp. Here we got a fire lighted, as there were plenty of broken branches and leaves lying about, and soon had some of the fish we had caught cooking before it.

Outside the tempest was howling furiously, and we had reason to be thankful that we had gained the shore, as no boat could have lived in the sea which was by this time running.

After supper was over, and we had dried our clothes, wet through and through by the spray, we lay down to sleep under the rock. Mr. Griffiths assured us that there were no wild beasts or natives to molest us in the island, though we were not altogether free from danger, as the trees which grew on the top of the rock above our heads might be blown down, or the upper part of the rock itself might give way and crush us.

That we might have some chance in being awakened so as to enable us to attempt to escape, as also to prevent the fire going out, Mr. Griffiths arranged that one of the party should keep watch. The doctor offered to keep the first watch. Mr. Griffiths and the rest of the men then stowed themselves away close under the cliff. I, feeling no inclination to sleep, joined the doctor, who was sitting by the fire on one of the water-casks, every now and then throwing on a few sticks and making it blaze up cheerfully. I asked him if the ship were likely to return soon to take us off.

"Not till the hurricane is over," he said; "the captain will not like to come near the coast for fear of being driven on it."

"Then you think, sir, that we shall remain here long enough to explore the island?" I said.

"Why do you wish to explore the island?" he asked.

"Because I have a notion that my brother Jack is upon it,' I replied. "They say there are pigs here, and there are, no doubt, plenty of birds, and he would be able to live as well as Miles Soper and Coal did on Juan Fernandez."

"But it's a hundred to one—I may say a thousand to one—that the boat was driven here; besides which, so many whalers pass by this island that he would have been seen and taken off even if he had come here. You only raise up such ideas to disappoint yourself. Don't think about it; lie down and go to sleep."

Notwithstanding what the doctor had said, I could not get the idea out of my head, and longed for morning, that I might set off and make a tour round the island with Jim, who, I knew, would be ready to come with me, as would Miles Soper and some of the others.

Notwithstanding the howling of the wind above our heads, and the wild roar of the breakers on the rocky coast, contrary to my expectation I fell fast asleep, and didn't wake till the mate roused up all hands at daylight. The storm was raging as wildly as ever. Furious torrents of rain had come down, but the watch had managed to keep in the fire, and we all gathered round it to cook some more fish and dry our damp clothes. We were in good spirits, for we knew that the gale would blow itself out in a short time, and we expected that the ship would then come and take us off.

As soon as I proposed to Jim to explore the island, he at once agreed to accompany me. The doctor and Miles Soper also said that they would go. The latter carried one of the muskets, which the mate said we might take, and the rest of us armed ourselves with long pointed sticks. The mate thought we might as well go armed, for though the island had hitherto been uninhabited, it was possible that some savages might have been driven as far north in their double canoes, and might attack us if they found we were unable to defend ourselves.

We took some cooked fish for provisions, and we hoped to find water as we proceeded. We had first to make our way through a thick forest, of what the doctor called tamana-trees—some of them being of gigantic size. It was often so dark beneath their thick boughs that we could with difficulty see our way; but we went on, guided by the doctor's pocket-compass, in a straight line, until we at length got out of the forest into more open country. He proposed going on till we reached a hill which we saw some way off, and there to light a fire, that the smoke might attract the attention of any one living on the island. He carried out his plan, and collecting sticks as we neared the spot, having brought tinder and matches, we quickly had a fire blazing. We looked in vain, however, all round the island for an an wering signal.

"Perhaps, if there is any one, he is down by the shore, and has no means of s riking a light," said the doctor; "or maybe he is still sheltering himself from the storm."

As this seemed very likely, leaving the fire burning, we made our way down to the beach on the farther side of the island.

The view from the hill on the north side showed us only rugged and broken ground, and we therefore proceeded along the shore as close as we could get towards the southern end. We saw plenty of birds, which would have afforded us food if we had had time to stop and shoot them. It was somewhat rough work, especially in the more exposed places against the wind. At last we got back to the part we had started from, just as night was falling. From every height we kept a look-out for the ship, but she did not appear.

"You're convinced now, Peter, that your brother is not on this island," said the doctor. "I should have rejoiced if we had found him, but I did not think it at all likely that he is here. However, that is no reason why he should not be somewhere else."

We had found water on our way, and the mate had discovered a spring not far from our camp. The hurricane, which had abated somewhat during the day, came on again as night approached, and we were thankful to obtain the shelter of our rock. The wind blew more furiously than ever, the lightning flashed and ran along the ground—now and again crashes were heard as some tall tree was struck and rent in two, while the rain at times came down in torrents, and nearly put out the fire. We, however, got shelter from the overhanging rock.

We had just done supper, when Mr. Griffiths observed,

"I'm afraid something may happen to our boat. The breakers sound so loud that they perhaps are dashing over the reef, and the sea may sweep up and carry her off."

We hurried down to where we had left the boat. A bright flash of lightning revealed her to us, with the seething water rushing up under her keel. Dashing forward, we seized her just as a second wave was lifting her, and in a few seconds would have carried her off. We dragged her up the beach till we had placed her, as we hoped, out of the reach of the water.

While we were thus employed we heard a loud crash coming from the direction of our camp. On returning, we discovered our fire nearly out, but it blazed sufficiently to show us a mass of earth and rock, and two tall trees, which had fallen on the very spot where a few minutes before we had all been collected.

We were thankful for our preservation, though we had lost the only shelter we knew of. The mate suggested that we should go back to the boat, turn her over, and creep under her for shelter. As no trees were near where she lay, we hoped that we might thus rest in perfect safety. Having taken the things out of her, we did as he proposed, and one by one crept in, and stretched ourselves upon the damp ground. After the exertions I had made during the day I felt very sleepy, and though I remained awake for some time thinking of Jack, my eyes at length closed.

I was awakened by hearing three distinct loud raps on the bottom of the boat. I fancied that I must be dreaming, but I found that Jim and Horner, who were sleeping next to me, were awake, and had heard the sounds.

"What are you lads making that noise for?" asked Mr. Griffiths.

I told him of the raps which had awakened me.

"I thought it was one of you that made them," he said.

"I heard them also," remarked the doctor, from his end of the boat.

The rest of the men were asleep; all of us were inside, and the sound certainly came from the outside. On this I crawled out from under the boat, half expecting to see some one standing there, but neither human being nor animal was visible. The rain had ceased, but the night was very dark, and there was time for a person after the knocks had been given to retreat into the woods. Still, I didn't think that it could have been Jack. I returned to the boat, supposing that whoever had knocked would knock again. The expectation of this kept me awake, and I determined that I would try to spring out and catch the person, whoever he was. I waited, however, in vain, and in less than two hours saw the daylight coming in under the gunwale.

The surf was still breaking with a loud roar on the rocks, but the wind had ceased to howl through the trees, and I hoped that the hurricane was nearly over. The noise I made in getting out from under the boat awakened those sleeping near me, and the rest of the party were soon on foot.

The first thing we did was to go back to our camp and see the effect of the landslip. The spot where we had been sitting was covered with a large mass of earth, rocks, and trees. We found a hollow in the rock near the spot, which appeared safe, and here we determined to light a fire and cook some more of our fish. While most of the people were thus employed, Mr. Griffiths, the doctor, and I climbed to the highest rock in the neighbourhood, that we might take a look-out for the ship. The sun was just rising, and cast a ruddy glow over the still heaving ocean covered with foam-crested seas, which, rolling in towards the shore, broke into masses of spray as they reached the surrounding reefs. In vain we looked round for the ship; not the slightest speck of white appeared above the horizon.

"Can anything have happened to her?" said the doctor, in an anxious tone.

"She has weathered out many a worse gale than we have just had," observed the mate. "My only fear is that in attempting to make the land she may have been driven on one of the hidden reefs which abound everywhere hereabouts."

"And if so, what are we to do?" inquired the doctor.

"We must try to reach the nearest islands inhabited by civilised people. We have casks sufficient to hold water for the voyage."

"I still hope she will come," said the doctor; "but we must not lose heart whatever happens."

Taking another look round, we returned to the camp, where we found a blazing fire and the fish cooked. We remained all that day and the next, unable to get out and catch any more fish. By this time our stock was completely exhausted—indeed, for the last day it had been scarcely eatable. While two of the men remained on shore to collect salt from the rocks, the rest of us went off, and with the crab-bait soon caught a large quantity of fish. In two days we got as many as we could well carry. Some of these were salted, others were smoked over the fire. We didn't fail, as may be supposed, to pay frequent visits to our look-out place on the rock. Day after day went by and no sail appeared.

"She's not coming back," said Mr. Griffiths, at length; "something must have happened to her; and I put it to you whether we remain here or try to reach either Japan or the Ladrones. Though Guam, which is the chief island of the Ladrones, is much farther off than Japan, we are likely to receive better treatment from the Spaniards than we are from the Japanese, who may either send us off again or put us to death. The passage there is also likely to prove more boisterous than to Guam."

The mate, having concluded his remarks, put the matter to the vote. Two of the men said they would rather remain on the island. No one proposed going to Japan, and the doctor and Miles Soper wished to steer for Guam. The rest of us voted with them. The mate considered that the sooner we were off the better. He said that the island was not a bad residence, but that when the winter came on we should have rains and storms, and might be unable to catch any fish or find other means of supporting life.

We therefore at once set to work to prepare for the voyage.

We first put off and caught a supply of fish, which we cured as before. We might have killed some birds, but we were unwilling to expend our small stock of powder, which we might require to defend ourselves against any natives who might prove hostile.

Led by the doctor, Brown, Jim, and I started to explore the neighbourhood, to collect scurvy grass or roots of any sort which might serve as vegetables. The natural productions of the country appeared to be very limited, but we dug up some roots which the doctor pronounced wholesome.

We were about returning in despair of obtaining what we wanted, when we came, near the shore on the other side of the bay, on a small open space overgrown with what at first looked like weeds, but I saw the doctor's eye brighten as he espied them. Hurrying on he pulled away eagerly at the seeming weeds.

"Here are onions," he cried, "of more value to us than gold; and see, here are potatoes, and these are cabbages, though somewhat overgrown, but there are leaves enough to supply us for a month."

We set to work to dig up the onions and potatoes with our pointed sticks, and to pull away at the cabbage leaves.

"Some beneficent person must have planted a garden here not long ago," said the doctor, as we were labouring with might and main. "These vegetables may be the means of preserving our lives, for without them we should have run a great risk of suffering from scurvy."

We each of us loaded ourselves with as many of the roots as we could carry, and staggered back with them to camp. We were received with a loud shout by our companions, who knew the value of what we had brought.

We quickly had some of the potatoes roasting in the ashes, on which, with some onions and fish, we made a more hearty meal than we had taken since we landed. We had fortunately an iron pot, in which we were able to boil a quantity of the potatoes, and afterwards the greens and some of the roots, which, being well-seasoned with salt, the doctor hoped would keep for some time.

All our preparations being made, one morning, having breakfasted at daylight, the doctor and I went up to the top of the rock to take a last look-out for the ship. On coming down we saw the boat in the water loaded, when, all hands getting aboard, we shoved off and stood out through the reef with a fair breeze from the north-west and

HOW WE LIVED ON THE ISLAND.

Page 270.

a smooth sea. The wind would have been directly against us had we been bound for Japan, so we were glad that we had decided to sail to the southward.

Our boat was somewhat deeply laden with provisions and water, but our cargo would be rapidly lightened, and Mr. Griffiths told us we must be prepared to heave some of it overboard should bad weather come on. We were all in health and good spirits, our chief anxiety being about the fate of the ship.

I must pass rapidly over the first part of our voyage. We had the boat's compass to steer by, but having no quadrant to take an observation or log-line to mark accurately the distance run, we could only guess at the rate we made. Mr. Griffiths, however, was a good navigator, and was pretty certain that he was correct. We had, we fancied, plenty of food, but from the first he put us all on an allowance of water.

While the sea remained smooth he also made us change our places constantly, and by the doctor's advice he ordered one at a time to stand up and move his arms and legs about to prevent them from becoming stiff. He also encouraged us to spin yarns and sing songs; indeed, he did everything in his power to keep us in good spirits.

After the first day of our landing we had not touched any of the biscuits we had brought with us. These we now husbanded with great care in case our other provisions should run short or spoil, which the doctor feared might be the case. We were much indebted to him for the precautions taken, as Mr. Griffiths carried out all his suggestions.

We had a whole week of fine weather, and we could favourably compare our lot with that of many poor fellows who had to voyage in open boats in the Pacific, exposed to storms, and often with a scant allowance of food and water.

The wind was generally from the northward, and when it fell calm we took to our oars. Mr. Griffiths told us that we had a distance of between seven and eight hundred miles to run, as far as he could calculate, and that if the fine weather continued we might hope to reach Guam in ten days or a fortnight.

We had got on so well that we began to fancy that we should have no difficulties to encounter. We were, of course, constantly on the look-out for vessels. At length we sighted a sail, but she was standing away from us. We steered after her for some distance, but before nightfall her topgallant sails sank beneath the horizon, and we again kept on our course.

"I wonder whether that craft out there is the *Intrepid?*" said Jim to me.

"Little chance of that," I remarked. "If she escaped shipwreck, or has not been severely damaged, she would have come to look for us long before we left the island."

"Perhaps the skipper fancied that we were lost, and didn't think it worth while to come and look for us," said Jim.

Four days after this, according to Mr. Griffiths's calculations, we were in the latitude of Guam, but to the eastward of the island. Brown, however, was of opinion that we had run farther to the south, and that if we stood east we should see it on our port bow. We accordingly hauled up on the port tack. Scarcely had we done so when the weather, which had lately looked threatening, completely changed, A strong wind began to blow from the north-west; it rapidly increased, and the sea got up and began to break over the bows in a way which threatened to swamp the boat. Three hands baled away together, but even thus we could scarcely keep the boat free of water.

"We must form a raft to serve as a breakwater," said Mr. Griffiths.

We lashed three oars together, the sail was lowered, the boat rounded to, and the raft, with a stout rope to it, was hove overboard, the rope being secured to the bows. At the same time the steering-oar was peaked and fixed into the after-thwart, with the flat of the blade facing the bows. This served as a sail, and kept the boat's head to the sea.

Thus, with the seas roaring and hissing round us, driving at the rate of two miles an hour to the southward and west, we prepared to pass the night, all of us feeling that we might never see another sun rise.

CHAPTER XXV.

A PERILOUS VOYAGE IN THE WHALEBOAT.

THE night was very dark, the sea rose fearfully high. Now the water broke over the starboard, now over the port bow, nearly swamping the boat, and all hands were employed in baling it out. We worked for our lives, for should another sea come before the boat was clear she might be swamped. Some of the men cried out that we should not live through the night.

Mr. Griffiths and the doctor cheered them up, but if it hadn't been for the raft ahead, which broke the seas, I believe that we must have gone down. I had heard of boats being saved by hanging on under the lee of a dead whale, but I had not supposed that a few oars lashed together would have served as an effectual breakwater.

The peaked oar played a most important part by keeping the boat's head to the wind, and at a sufficient distance from the raft. She must otherwise have broached to, and it must have been driven against her and stove in the side.

As soon as the boat was clear of water, Brown sang out, "Now let's have a stave, lads," and he began to sing, but few were able to join in with him.

Jim and I tried, knowing Brown's object, but we had scarcely got through a verse when another sea came roaring on board, nearly carrying over the men in the bows, and washing away some of our provisions. We all had immediately to turn to again and bale out the boat. No one thought of singing after this, for directly we were free of one sea another broke aboard us. It was a mercy that they didn't come together.

"We must pray to God, lads," cried Mr. Griffiths. "He who rules the seas and winds, if we ask Him, can save us if He thinks fit. Don't cease baling. He likes people to work and pray, but not to fall down on their knees while there's work to be done and leave it undone."

He and the doctor set the example by baling away as hard as any of us. We had the boat's regular balers, our iron pot, and a couple of small buckets; the rest of us used our hats and caps. Still, do all we could, it was a difficult matter to keep the boat free from water. We were wet through, as was everything in the boat, and we were afraid that our provisions would be spoilt, except perhaps the onions and potatoes.

Hour after hour went slowly by, for we had no time for talking to make it appear shorter. Still the night did come to an end at last, but there were no signs of the gale abating. As soon as the sun rose we looked out eagerly on all sides for land. Nothing broke the uniform line of the horizon except the foam-topped seas, which rose up tumultuously between us and it. We were driving all this time, it must be remembered, to the southward at the rate, the mate said, of two knots an hour, so that if we had been near Guam when the gale came on we were being driven farther and farther from it, and it would be a hard matter to regain the island.

We had taken nothing during the night, and we now all cried out for food. The store of salt fish we had remaining was scarcely eatable, for the salt had been washed out of it, and it was becoming bad. What we had smoked was a little better, but that also was almost spoilt, yet such as it was we were glad to have a portion with an onion apiece, and a small mug half full of water. The mate would give us no more.

"What I do is for the good of all of us, lads," he said. "I can't tell when we may make the land, or what provisions we may find when we get there."

Horner sang out, "We had some biscuit. What has become of that? Why don't you let us have a piece for our breakfasts?"

"Because the biscuits will keep longer than anything else, and are all we may have to depend upon," answered the doctor, who had got them under him in the stern-sheets, and had been trying from the first to keep them as free from water as possible.

We had till now fancied that we had an abundance of food, but some had been washed overboard and some had been completely spoilt, so we found to our dismay that we had a very small quantity remaining. Horner now began to complain bitterly of hunger and thirst, declaring that if he didn't get some food he must die.

Jim and I endeavoured to cheer him up. It was not a matter to joke about; indeed I was myself feeling the pangs of hunger and getting weaker and less able to work, though I did my best. Jim kept up better than I did. We had not much time to be thinking, however, for we were compelled to be constantly baling the greater part of the day.

Towards evening the sun broke through the western clouds, sending his rays athwart the troubled ocean, and tinging the seas with a ruddy hue, while his heat dried our wet clothes.

Soon afterwards the wind began to drop, but the seas still ran so high that the mate thought it prudent to hang on some time longer to our raft. However, they no longer broke on board as they had been doing, and we had better hopes than on the previous night that we should see another sun rise. We had been awake so long that none of us were able to keep our eyes open, and I suspect that at times every person in the boat was fast asleep. I know for my part that I must have dozed through the greater part of the night, for I was awakened by hearing the mate's voice saying,

"Now, lads, we will get the raft on board and make sail."

I jumped up to lend a hand. We got the oars out and put the boat before the seas while we set up the mast and hoisted the sail.

The wind was still in the same quarter, blowing directly from where we supposed Guam to be, and as there were no hopes of making it the mate determined to run for some island to the southward, where, though it might be uninhabited, we should probably find cocoa-nuts and water, and might catch some fish.

As none of the islands are very close together we ran a great risk of passing between them without seeing land, but then again he argued that we might be days or weeks beating up to Guam, and as he could not tell its exact position, we might even pass it after all, while by keeping to the south we might have a better prospect of having fine weather, and finding food on any shore at which we might touch. On the other hand again there was the risk of falling among savages, for the natives of these latitudes were known to be fierce, treacherous, and inhospitable to strangers.

We might, however, possibly meet with some ship, as we should cross the course pursued by Spanish vessels sailing from America to the Philippines. Should we pass through the Caroline group we should have another long channel to sail over, and must then reach the coast of New Guinea.

If driven thus far south our prospect of escape was small indeed; though we might obtain food, the people were supposed to be extremely savage and cruel.

The doctor, to cheer us, said that he had some doubts about that, for although such was the character of the natives of some parts, there were others who might treat us kindly should we fall among them, provided we behaved well and showed that we wished to be friendly.

As we sailed on the sea gradually went down, and at length we were running with a light breeze over the smooth ocean. Though at first the warm sun was pleasant it soon became very hot, and while it dried our clothes increased our thirst.

At the same time the heat destroyed the remaining portion of our fish, which became so bad that we were obliged to throw it overboard. We had now only a few raw potatoes and onions, and the little store of biscuits which the doctor had so wisely husbanded.

The mate told us that we must make up our minds to live on very short allowance, and be content with a quarter of a biscuit, an onion, and a small piece of raw potato. To make the latter more wholesome he cut them and hung them up to dry in the sun. Our food was served out about noon, and each day we sat eagerly waiting for the hour. Horner would turn his eyes up and watch the sun till he fancied that it had gained its greatest altitude, and then cry out to the mate,

"It must be twelve o'clock, now, sir. Won't Dr. Cockle look at his watch and see?"

The doctor was the only person who kept his watch wound up. The mate had collected all the provisions and placed them in the stern-sheets, and he didn't think fit to tell us how rapidly they were going. The quantity he served out was scarcely sufficient to keep body and soul

A Perilous Voyage in the Whaleboat. 279

together, but he acted for the best; there was no doubt about that. We were all becoming rapidly weaker, and longing for some substantial fare. Homer at last cried out that if he didn't get it he must die. Two or three of the other men said much the same thing. As I looked at their faces I felt afraid that they spoke the truth. Our limbs were swollen, and we felt so stiff that we were scarcely able to move.

"Trust in God, lads," said the mate, to try and cheer us up.

We were no longer inclined to spin yarns or sing songs, and only now and then exchanged a few words with each other. Not long after this, as I was gazing over the side, I saw a movement in the water, and presently a score or flying-fish rose from the sea, their wings glittering in the sunlight, and about a dozen pitched into the boat. Oh, how eagerly we all stooped down to seize them! Just then, as I was looking out, expecting some more to come, I saw several dolphins, which had no doubt been pursuing the flying-fish, and now came close up to the boat, looking out for them.

Notwithstanding our hunger the doctor advised that we should split the fish and hang them up in the sun to dry. We were, however, too hungry to do this, but the mate insisted that all should be handed to him. He then served out to each of us half a fish, which we eagerly devoured. This meal, scanty as it was, somewhat restored our strength.

"I told you to trust in God, lads," said the mate. "See He has sent us these fish, and He'll send us more, never fear."

Before long I saw, a hundred yards off, another flight of flying-fish rise from the sea, and come darting through the air like masses of silver, when, to our joy, a number struck the sail and dropped into the bottom of the boat. The mate immediately served out the remainder of those which had at first been sent to us. This made the men cheer up more than ever, as we expected that, now we had got into the tropics, we should have an ample supply every day.

We saw large quantities of dolphins, bonitos, and albicores, which pursue the flying-fish, and induce them to seek for safety in flight; but none of the larger fish came near enough to enable us to catch them, though Brown, harpoon in hand, stood up as long as he could keep his feet, in the expectation of striking one. It was very tantalising to see them sporting round us, and yet not to be able to get one on board. We had, however, a sufficient number of flying-fish to give us a good meal each for that and the next day. The mate proposed drying some in the sun and reserving them in case no more should come aboard, but nearly all hands cried out that we were certain to have some more sent us, and begged so hard to have the fish while they were good that the mate yielded to their wishes.

During the night we steered south-east, with the wind on our port quarter. It was in that direction Mr. Griffiths said he knew the islands lay thickest. We had a regular watch set, and a bright look-out kept ahead, for we could not tell when we might come upon reefs, and the boat might be knocked to pieces on some uninhabited spot where neither food nor water was to be procured. The next day was passed much as the previous one had been, but no flying-fish came on board, though we saw them glittering in the air in the distance. It was drawing towards evening when I saw a black triangular fin, which I knew to be that of a shark, coming up astern.

"What are you looking at?" asked the doctor

I told him. Presently we caught sight of the monster's cruel eyes and back a couple of fathoms from the boat. I saw by their looks that the men did not like its appearance.

"We hab him," cried Sam Coal. "We eat him if he no eat us."

Brown, on hearing this remark, stood up, with his harpoon in hand, but the savage brute seemed to know its danger, and kept just beyond his reach, eyeing us, we thought, as if he expected to make a feast of the whole party.

The men made their remarks on the shark, for having had sufficient food they had somewhat recovered their spirits. Still I wished that the shark would take its departure, but it kept on swimming alongside the boat, and as the breeze freshened it made faster way to keep up with us. Brown at last proposed shooting it, for our powder, being in a metal flask, had kept dry, but Mr. Griffiths objected to any being expended for the purpose. It was a hundred to one that the shark would be killed, he said, and every charge might be of value. Still, as no flying-fish had been caught, the men cried out that they must have the shark, and Mr. Griffiths at length allowed Brown, who was a good shot, to try and hit it in a vital part. Just, however, as he stood up with the musket in his hands the shark dived and disappeared.

"Ah, ha, Jack Shark know what you going to do. Him know eberyting," said Sam Coal.

Shortly after this the sun sank amid a bank of black clouds, and darkness came down on the world of waters, the weather again looking very threatening. I was awakened by a splash of water in my face. On sitting up, though a heavy sea was running, I found that the boat was still keeping on her course. The sail had been reefed, but it was as much as we could carry. Again and again the sea broke on board. The sleepers were all aroused, and we had to bale as fast as we could.

Presently the mate said, "We must heave her to, lads. Get the raft rigged."

We soon had this done, but as we were rounding to a heavy sea came rolling up, and breaking on board, nearly carried Sam Coal over the side. The raft was hove into the water, and we lay head to wind as before, with the oar apeak. This did not prevent the seas from occasionally breaking on board, though they came with less violence than they would otherwise have done; but the boat was severely strained and shattered as they beat against her, and she now began to leak in a way which gave us just cause for alarm.

We spent the night baling as hard as we could, all striving to save our lives; but we hoped almost against hope that we should succeed.

At last some of the men, as before, began to despair, saying that it was as well to die now as a few hours later, and that it would be better to give in and let the boat sink, but seeing the mate and doctor calm and composed as ever, I tried to imitate their example.

"God wants us to labour on, lads," cried Mr. Griffiths. "He'll help us if we do. Gales in these latitudes never last long. Perhaps to-morrow we shall have a fine day and catch some more flying-fish, or maybe we are not far off from an island, and we shall be able to stretch our legs and find plenty of cocoa-nuts, and perhaps yams and pigs. We shall soon have a fire alight and something cooking before it, and then won't we eat, boys!"

This sort of talk had a good effect upon the men, and they no longer had any thought of giving in. Still, the night went by very slowly. Sleeping, even if we had had time, with the water washing into the boat, was next to impossible.

Daylight came back at last, and as the sun rose the clouds dispersed, the wind rapidly dropped, and the sea went down. In a short time the mate ordered the raft to be got on board, and we ran on as before. We were very nearly starving, for we had had nothing to eat since we had devoured the raw flying-fish on the previous day.

"The doctor's got some biscuit," said one of the men, and they at once all cried out, begging that they might have it. The mate, however, would only give us a quarter of a biscuit each, with a little water. It just served to stay the gnawings of hunger, but as the day grew on we wanted food as much as ever, and our spirits again sank.

For the first time I began to think that I should not survive, even if the mate and Dr. Cockle did. Though they had eaten no more than any of us, they endured their sufferings better. By this time we were a scarecrow crew, our hair long, our faces wan, our bodies shrunk, and our skin tanned to a yellow by the hot sun. At last the men entreated that they might have the remainder of the biscuit, declaring that they were ready to die after they had had one good meal if we could not catch any more flying-fish.

"No, lads," said Mr Griffiths; "I know what is best for you. Your lives are committed to my charge, and I'll not yield to your wishes. See, while you have been talking the water has been coming into the boat. Turn to and bale away."

They obeyed, though with scowling countenances. The mate had both the guns in the stern-sheets, and he and the doctor looked as if they were prepared to resist violence. The men knew also that Jim and I would have sided with the officers. The wind had dropped, and with a gentle breeze we were gliding on, when suddenly, not ten yards off, a number of flying-fish rose out of the water and came towards the boat. Some struck the sail, and others we beat back with our hands.

"I told you not to despair, lads," said Mr. Griffiths. "Thank God for what He has sent us!"

I believe we all did so most heartily. The mate allowed all the fish we had caught to be eaten. I heard the doctor ask him why he did so, as we might catch no more till the next day.

"I'll tell you presently," he answered.

We had finished our meal, with just a small piece of biscuit apiece and a quarter of a pint of water, when the mate stood up, and, shading his eyes, gazed ahead.

"I would not say so before, lads, for fear of disappointing you, but I now tell you that we're in sight of land. It is not very large, and may not be inhabited; it may have no cocoa-nuts or other vegetables on it, but it will give us room to stretch our legs, and we may be able to catch as many fish as we want off it."

"Thank God!" burst from the lips of most of the crew, and I and some others knelt down to return thanks to Him who had thus far preserved us, while we prayed that we might be brought in time to a place of safety.

We all now wanted to stand up and see the land. The mate told us to sit quiet, but he allowed each one of us at a time to rise to our feet and take a look ahead. A blue irregular line could just be distinguished above the horizon, clear and defined. That it was land none of us had any doubt. A fair breeze carried us along at the rate of four or five knots an hour. In less than a couple of hours we might hope to be on shore, but the sun was sinking, and it would be dark, unless the breeze freshened, before we could reach it.

In a short time the wind fell, on which our hopes of landing before night were disappointed. We got out the oars, however, and pulled on.

"We must be careful, lads," said the mate, after we had rowed some distance.

"Most of these islands are surrounded by coral reefs, and

we may run upon one of them in the dark and knock the boat to pieces. We must heave to, shortly, and wait for daylight."

Some of the men grumbled at this, and asserted that the noise of the surf upon the reefs would give us sufficient notice when we were approaching them, but the mate was firm.

"I will not risk the safety of the boat for the sake of getting on shore a few hours earlier," he said.

We all, however, had the satisfaction of taking another look at the land and assuring ourselves that it was land before darkness came on. Mr. Griffiths then ordered us to lay in our oars, and except two who were to keep watch and bale out the water which leaked into the boat, to lie down and go to sleep.

I don't think many of us did sleep. We were all thinking too much about getting on shore in the morning to care for rest. We forgot that before that time another gale might spring up and drive us off the land, or dash the boat a hopeless wreck upon the coral reef.

CHAPTER XXVI.

MORE STARTLING ADVENTURES.

THE night passed by, and as dawn at length broke, the mate rousing up all hands, we hoisted the sail, and again stood towards the land. The sea was smooth, and the wind light and fair.

As we glided on, the mate told Brown to stand up in the bows and keep a look-out for reefs. As we approached the land we could see trees on the shore and some on the hill, so that we had no doubt that we should find fresh water. It was a question, however, whether or not it was inhabited, and, if so, whether the natives would prove friendly or hostile. The mate told the doctor that he believed it was one of the most north-western of the Caroline group, the natives of which are generally more friendly to strangers than the inhabitants of the islands farther south; still, they are perfect savages, and it would be dangerous to trust them. We could, however, see no smoke or other signs of the country being inhabited.

We had not gone far, when Brown sang out, "Starboard! hard a-starboard! A reef ahead!"

On this the mate, luffing up, ordered us to lower the sail. It was done in an instant, and not a moment too soon, for we saw close abeam a coral reef not two feet under the surface.

"We may be thankful that we didn't stand on during the night," said Mr. Griffiths to the doctor.

We now got out the oars and pulled cautiously on. We soon found ourselves in a channel, with coral reefs on either side, all of them just below the surface; and as the passage twisted and turned in all directions, it required the greatest possible caution to thread our way through it.

We might well be thankful not only that we did not stand on during the night, but that we had not driven farther south during the gale while we rode to the raft. Nothing could have preserved the boat from being dashed to pieces. At length we got clear of the encircling reef, and found ourselves in a broad expanse of perfectly smooth water. The rocks rising directly out of it formed the shore. We had to pull along them some distance to find a convenient landing-place. At last a beautiful bay opened out, with a sandy beach, the ground rising gradually from it, covered with cocoanut-trees.

On seeing it, led by Brown, we uttered a cheer, and giving way with a will ran the boat's keel on the beach. He jumped out first, and we all followed, without thinking of savages, and only very grateful to find ourselves once more on firm ground. Led by the mate and the doctor, we fell on our knees, and I believe with grateful hearts returned thanks to God for our safety.

We were hurrying up to the trees with our eyes fixed on the cocoanuts which hung temptingly from them, when the mate called to us to be cautious, for though we had seen no natives, there might be some in the neighbourhood, who might come suddenly down and attack us while we were engaged in obtaining the cocoanuts.

He and the doctor then proceeded with their muskets in their hands a little way in advance, while under Brown's directions we prepared to get down the nuts. Miles Soper, Sam Coal, and Jim were the best climbers, but without assistance, weak as we all were, they found that they could not swarm up the trees. We therefore got some ropes from the boat, and Soper soon twisted one of them into a grummet, or hoop, round the tree, with sufficient space for his body inside it; then shoving the opposite side of the grummet above him, and holding on with his knees, he worked his way up the smooth trunk. Coal did the same on another tree, but Jim, after making the attempt, had to give up.

"I never tried that sort of thing before, and can't manage it," he said, coming down and ready to cry for weakness.

"Look out there!" shouted Sam Coal, who was the first to reach the top of his tree; and he threw down a cocoanut, and then another, and another, but they all broke as they touched the ground.

"I say, that'll never do!" cried Brown, as he picked up one of them, while Horner and I got hold of the other two. "You must hang them round your neck somehow. We want the juice, which is the best part."

Coal, on this, fastened three or four together in a handkerchief; Soper had in the meantime done the same, and they descended with four cocoanuts apiece. Horner and I had run with those we had picked up to Mr. Griffiths and the doctor, munching a portion as we went, while Brown divided his among the other men, who were as eager to eat them as we were. So we found were the mate and the doctor. They tasted delicious to us, so long accustomed to salt or raw fish; but still more refreshing was the milk, which we got on tearing off the outer rind by cutting holes in the eyes with our knives. The cocoanuts, indeed, served us as meat and drink.

All this time the doctor and mate had seen no signs of inhabitants, and as we were all far too weak to think of exploring the country, we sat down in the shade of the cocoanut-trees to rest. We talked a little to each other for a short time, and first one dropped off to sleep, then another. Mr. Griffiths himself didn't long keep his eyes open, though I fancy I heard him tell Brown that we must set a watch, lest any natives should come suddenly down upon us. The mate and the doctor had both been awake during the whole of the last night in the boat—no wonder that they went to sleep.

At last I opened my eyes, and sitting up, looked about me, trying to recollect where I was, and what had happened. This I soon did. My companions lay scattered around me on the ground. In front was the sea, and the two sides of the bay were formed by moderately high cliffs. Behind us was a grove of cocoanut-trees, extending along the shore to the cliffs, and beyond them I could see a hill, which formed the farther end of the valley, opening out on the bay. Every one was asleep, and I was thankful that while in that condition we had not been discovered by savages, who might have been tempted to massacre the whole of us. I was glad that I at all events was now awake. I didn't, however, like to arouse my companions, so I got up noiselessly, and to stretch my legs walked through the palm grove. On my way I found a cocoanut fallen to the ground, and as I felt hungry, having taken off the rind, I sucked the milk, and then breaking the shell, ate as much of the fruit as I felt inclined to take. This restored my strength, and I went on till I got beyond the trees, which extended to no great distance up the valley. Farther on the ground was tolerably open, with here and there a few trees and bushes growing by the side of a stream which ran through the valley, and formed a small lake, without any outlet that I could discover.

A number of birds, some of which I took to be pigeons, were flying about, but I saw no four-legged creatures of any sort. The birds were so tame that they came flying about me, and perched on the boughs without showing any signs of fear.

"This is a beautiful spot," I thought to myself. "How thankful I am that we reached it! We shall have plenty of food, and if there are no natives we can remain as long as we like till we are all strong again, and Mr. Griffiths determines to pursue the voyage."

I was stopping, looking about, when I saw something move on the top of the hill at the farther end of the valley. The object stopped, and then I made out distinctly against the sky the figure of a man. He was too far off to enable me to make out how he was dressed, or whether he was a native or a white man. He stopped for some time, as if he was looking down into the valley, and I fancied that he might have seen me, for I was in an open spot, away from any trees or shrubs. At last I beckoned to him, to show that my companions and I wished to be friends with the natives.

He took no notice of my signals, but stood looking down into the valley as before.

At first I thought of going towards him, but then it struck me that others might appear, and that I might be taken prisoner, or perhaps killed, and that I ought to go back and tell Mr. Griffiths what I had seen. I found him and the doctor awake.

"I'm sorry to hear that," said the former. "I had hoped that there were no natives on the island. If the person you saw had been a white man he would have come down to us immediately. I suspect that he must be a native. We must look out for a visit from others, and keep a more careful watch than heretofore."

He and the doctor agreed to return with me, and if the person was still where I had seen him, to try and open up a friendly communication with him and any others who might appear.

Rousing up Brown and the rest of the people, and telling them where we were going, we set off. On our getting to the spot where I had been when I saw the man, he had disappeared. We, however, went on past a little lake, and along the bank of a stream, looking out very carefully on either side lest the natives might come down from the cliffs and cut us off. No one appeared; and as it was getting late, Mr. Griffiths thought it wise to return.

It was almost dark by the time we reached the palm grove. We found that Soper and Coal had in the meantime collected some more cocoanuts; and that Brown, with the rest of the men, had obtained some large clams and other shell-fish from the rocks. They were now lighting a fire to cook them, while Jim had brought a kettle of water from the lake. We had thus materials for a hearty meal, of which we all partook with good appetites. We had been unable to do anything to the boat during the day, but Mr. Griffiths remarked that our first care must be to put her to rights, that we might go out fishing in her, and afterwards make a voyage to some place where we might find a vessel to take us home. The mate said that we might either sail northward again to Guam, or westward to the Pellew Islands, the inhabitants of which were said to be friendly, and thence on to the Poilippines. Various opinions were expressed, but nothing was decided.

We had now to prepare for the night. Notwithstanding the sleep we had had during the day, we all felt that a longer rest was necessary to restore our strength. Mr. Griffiths, however, insisted that a watch should be kept, as now that we had discovered the island to be inhabited, it would be folly to allow ourselves to be caught unawares at night. Though the weather was warm, as we had had no time to put up a shelter of any sort, the fire was found pleasant; we therefore agreed not to let it go out during the night. It was settled that the doctor should keep the first watch, Mr. Griffiths the middle and I was to have the third with Jim. Brown kept it with the doctor, and Soper with the mate. Our arrangements being made, we lay down to pass the night.

It appeared to me that I had been asleep only a few minutes, when Mr. Griffiths called me up, and Jim and I, taking the muskets, began our watch. The mate told me that the doctor's and his watches had passed quietly away, and they had not heard any sounds to indicate that any natives were near. As we were not obliged to keep close to the fire, and as there was a bright moon in the sky to enable us to see our way, I proposed to Jim that we should go through the grove, where, should any natives approach in the morning, we should discover them sooner on that side than we should by remaining at the camp. He agreed, and without difficulty we made our way through the trees, which stood apart, with little or no undergrowth. The scene which presented itself to us as we got out of the grove was very beautiful. The silver moon and the surrounding trees were reflected in the calm waters of the lake, while the outline of the hills on either side appeared sharp and distinct against the sky. Finding a clear piece of ground not far from the shore of the lake, Jim and I walked up and down, keeping a look-out now to one side, now to the other, as also up the valley.

We had taken several turns, when Jim exclaimed, " Hillo! Look there ! "

Gazing up in the direction to which he pointed, I saw distinctly against the sky the figure of a man. How he was dressed it was impossible to say; still, he had on clothes of some sort.

" He's not a native savage, at all events," said Jim. ' We'll hail him, and if he's an Englishman he'll answer."

We shouted at the top of our voices, but no reply came, and the figure disappeared.

"That's strange," said Jim; "I thought he would have come down and had a talk with us, whoever he is.· Can't we try and find him?"

"We mustn't both leave our post," I answered; "but if you stop here I'll try and get up to where he was standing, and unless he has run away he can't be far off."

Jim didn't like my going, but I persuaded him to stop, and hurried across the valley. When I got to the foot of the cliff I could find no way up it, and, after searching about, had to abandon the attempt.

I returned to where I had left Jim, and we resumed our walk, thinking that perhaps the figure would again appear.

"Perhaps if he sees us he won't show himself," said Jim. "Wouldn't it be better to go and stay under the trees? and then perhaps he'll come back."

We did as Jim proposed, keeping our eyes in the direction of the cliff, but we looked in vain for the reappearance of the s'ranger.

"He guesses that we are watching for him," said Jim. ' Perhaps if we were to shout again he would come back. If he's a white man he'll understand us, and know that we are friends"

"There can be no harm in shouting," I answered, "though he may be a native and there may be others with him; they would have come down before this and attacked us, had they had a mind to do so."

We accordingly went from under the trees, and standing in the open ground, I shouted out,

"Hillo, stranger, we're friends, and want to have a talk with you. We have just come here for a day or two, and intend to be off again on our voyage."

Jim then said much the same sort of thing, and as his

voice was even louder than mine, we made sure that the stranger must have heard us. He didn't, however, show himself, though we sometimes shouted together, sometimes singly. At last we heard voices in the cocoanut grove.

"I hope that no enemies have got down between us and the sea," I said. "We had no business to come so far away from the camp."

We stood with our muskets ready, watching the wood. In a short time our anxiety was relieved by the appearance of the doctor and Mr. Griffiths.

"Why, lads, what made you shout out in that fashion?" asked the mate. "We fancied you wanted help."

We told him of the man we had seen on the cliffs.

"It's very extraordinary," said the doctor; "I don't think he can be a native, or he would not have shown himself in that way. He must be some white man who has been left by himself on the island, and has lost his wits, as often happens under such circumstances. He's been accustomed to see savages visit the island, and has kept out of their way to save himself from being killed or made a slave of. He had not the sense to distinguish between us and them."

"I believe you are right," said Mr. Griffiths. "We must take means to get hold of him, both for his own sake and ours. He'll soon come round, supposing he's an Englishman, when he finds himself among countrymen, and he'll be able to show us where to get provisions if the island produces any. He can't have lived always on cocoanuts and shell-fish."

By this time the dawn began to appear, and after waiting a little longer we all returned to camp, and roused up the men to prepare for breakfast. Miles Soper and Sam Coal again climbed the trees to get some cocoanuts. Some of the men went down to the shore to collect shell-fish.

Others made up the fire, while the mate and the doctor examined the boat to ascertain the damage she had received, and to see how she could best be repaired.

"We have a few nails, and we must try to find some substance which will answer the purpose of pitch," observed the mate. "Doctor, I dare say you'll help us. We will strengthen her with additional planks, and get a strake put on above her gunwale. It will be a work of toil to cut the planks, but it must be done, and she will then be fit to go anywhere."

At breakfast the mate told the men of his intentions. They all agreed to do their best to carry them out.

We had first, however, to search for provisions. Not knowing whether there might be savages on the island, even supposing that the man we had seen was not one, the mate did not like to leave the boat unprotected. He therefore ordered Brown and one of the men to remain by her while the rest of us proceeded together to explore the island.

The mate would not allow us to separate until we had ascertained whether or not there were inhabitants besides the man we had seen on the island.

One musket was left with Brown, the mate carried the other, and we set off, keeping up the stream I have before described towards the end of the valley. We looked out on either side for the stranger, but he didn't appear. Some of the men declared that we had not really seen any one, and that we had mistaken a small tree or shrub for a man; but Jim and I were positive, and the doctor, at all events, believed us.

On reaching the top of the hill, we looked down into a large hollow, with water at the bottom, dark rocks forming its sides, grown over with creepers, huge ferns, and various other plants. The doctor said that it was the crater of a long extinct volcano, and that the whole island was volcanic. There were many other hills out of which smoke was rising. The doctor said that this was an active volcano; indeed, the country in that direction presented a very different aspect from the part where we had landed. It was black and barren, with only here and there a few green spots. We therefore turned to the east, the direction which promised us a better chance of finding roots or fruits, or vegetable productions of some sort.

The strange thing was, that though the island appeared fertile, not a single habitation or hut could we discover. The doctor supposed that this was on account of the occasional outbreak of the volcano, and that the people from the neighbouring islands were afraid to take up their residence on it.

We now descended the hill, and went along another valley, of course looking out all the time for the stranger.

We were passing a small grove near a hollow in the side of a hill, which was partly concealed by trees, when we heard a cock crow just as an English cock would do. At once that sound made my thoughts, as it did those of the others, probably, rush back to our far-distant homes.

"If there's a cock, there must be hens and a hen-roost hereabouts," observed Miles Soper, hurrying in the direction whence the sounds proceeded.

We followed; there, sure enough, sheltered by the hill, and under the shade of the trees, was not only a hen-house of good size, but a hut scarcely bigger than it was neatly built and thatched with palm-leaves.

"It must be the residence of the stranger. He himself can't be far off," said the doctor.

The hut was just large enough to hold one man. It had a door formed of thin poles lashed together with sinnit. At the farther end was a bedstead covered with rough matting, and in the centre a small table, with a three-legged stool.

No one had any longer any doubt that we had seen a man, or that this must be his abode, and that he must be a white man, but whether English or not was doubtful. Miles Soper examined the matting, and as he was looking about he found a knife on a shelf close to the bed. Taking it up, he examined it with a curious eye, opening and shutting it, and turning it round and round.

"Well, that's queer, but I think I've seen this knife before," he said. "If the owner is the man I guess he is I am glad."

"Who do you suppose he is?" I inquired, eagerly.

"Well, Peter, that's what I don't want to say just yet. I must make sure first," he answered.

"Can he be my brother Jack?" I exclaimed, my breath coming and going fast in my anxiety.

"Well then, Peter, I'll tell you. Jack knew how to make matting just like this, because he learnt the way on board the *Harriet*, and so did I. He had a knife which, if this isn't it, is the fellow to it, so you see that I have some reason to think hat the man who built this hut, and lives in it, is he. But then again, you know, I may be mistaken.

"Why, if he is Jack, he should run away from us puzzles me. If he couldn't see our faces he must have known by our dress that we were English or American, and that there was no reason for him to hide himself. There are many men who know how to make this sort of matting, and there are many knives just like this, and that's the reason why I can't tell you whether he's Jack or not. But if Mr. Griffiths will let me I'll go on alone and look for him, and when he sees who I am he'll come fast enough to me, and you may depend on it, Peter, if it's he I'll bring him back with a lighter heart than I've had for many a day."

CHAPTER XXVII.

THE LOST ONE FOUND AT LAST.

I WANTED to accompany Soper in his search for the stranger.

"No, no, Peter," he answered; "if he is Jack he'll know me; but he won't know you; and if he's grown queer by living all alone on an island, as has happened to some poor fellows, he'll get out of our way if he sees two together."

The doctor assented to the wisdom of this, and advised me to be contented and remain by while Soper set off himself. The rest of the party were meanwhile examining the hen-roost.

The fowls were mostly of the English breed, which made us suppose that they had been landed from some English vessel. We were confirmed in this belief by discovering an old hen-coop, in which they had probably been washed ashore. There were other pieces of wreckage scattered about, but the hut itself was composed entirely of the products of the island.

At last the doctor proposed that we should proceed onwards, as the stranger, whoever he was, would not be likely to come back if he saw us near his hut. I, however, believed that it must be Jack, and, notwithstanding the doubts that Soper had expressed, begged that I might be allowed to remain behind that I might the sooner meet him. Mr. Griffiths gave me leave to stay if I wished it. I thought that Soper was more likely to bring him back to the hut than to follow the rest of the party.

As soon as they had gone I closed the door and sat down on the three-legged stool. I should have been glad if I had had a book to read to employ my thoughts, but the hut contained only some cocoanuts cut in two for holding water, some long skewers, which had apparently been used for roasting birds, a small nut fixed in a stand to serve as an egg-cup, and a little wooden spoon. There were also shells, some clams, and others of different shapes. Two or three of these would serve as cups and plates. I could judge from this what had been the food of the solitary inhabitant of the hut. This didn't look as if he were out of his mind.

The time appeared to go by very slowly. I remembered my disappointment at South's Island when I heard the mysterious knocks on the bottom of the boat, and I began to fear that after all the stranger might not prove to be Jack.

I was now sorry that I had not accompanied the rest of the party—at all events the time would not have appeared so long if I had been walking and looking out for Jack. At length I determined to get up and to go out and try and find my companions—perhaps Soper and the stranger were all this time with them, though I knew they would come back and look for me. I rose and went to the window, which had a view right down the valley, probably that the inmate might watch anybody coming in that direction.

I couldn't see any object moving, and I turned towards the door, intending to go out, when the sound of voices reached my ears. I listened. One of the speakers was Miles Soper, the other spoke so indistinctly that I could not make out what he said.

I opened the door and saw two persons coming through

the grove. One was, as I expected, Soper; the other a strange-looking being with long hair, his skin tanned of a deep brown, his dress composed of an old jacket and trousers, patched or rather covered over with leaves, while his feet and head were destitute of covering.

I stood gazing at him for a few seconds, unable to trace in his countenance any of the features of my brother Jack, which I fancied I recollected.

"What, don't you know one another?" exclaimed Soper. "This is Jack Trawl and no o her—the only Jack Trawl I ever knew. Come, Jack, rouse up, that's your brother Peter Trawl. Give him your fist, man. He's been talking about you, and looking for you everywhere we've been."

The stranger stopped and gazed eagerly in my face.

"What, are you my little brother Peter?" he exclaimed. "How are Mary, and father, and mother, and Nancy?"

I knew from this that he was Jack, and springing forward, took both his hands, and looked earnestly in his face.

"Yes, I am Peter, and I know you are Jack. Mary was well when I left home long ago, though you wouldn't know her now, and Nancy is with her."

I didn't like at first to tell Jack that father and mother were dead, but it had to come out at last, and it seemed for a time to do away with the happiness he and I felt at meeting; for he was happy, though he looked so strange and talked so curiously. He couldn't get out his words at first, but we sat down, he on the bed, I on the stool, and Miles Soper on the table, Miles drawing him out better than I could, and he telling us how he had come upon the island.

He had been on board the *Harriet*, as I had believed, from what King George had told me, and had escaped from her with Captain Barber in the boat. They had had a long voyage, and suffered dreadfully. missing Guam, for which they had steered, just as we had done, and been driven south. The other men died, one and then another, till at last only Captain Barber and he had been left.

The captain was in a dying state when the boat was driven on the reef, and Jack could not tell how he had managed to reach the shore. He found himself at last in the very bay where we had landed. He had just strength enough to crawl up to the palm-grove, where he found some cocoanuts on the ground, and managing to eat one of them, he regained his strength.

He looked about for the old captain, but could nowhere find him, and supposed that he was drowned when the boat went to pieces. He didn't want to die, he said, so he got some shell-fish and cocoanuts, and now and then caught some birds, which were very tame. He had learnt how to get a light from King George's people on "Strong's" Island, and after a few days he managed to make a fire and cooked the shell-fish. He found some roots, but was afraid to eat them for fear they might be poisonous.

It was very melancholy work living thus alone, and sometimes for days together he scarcely knew what he was about. At last, however, came a furious storm, and as he went down to the beach he saw a ship driving towards the island. He knew that there were reefs all around it, so he feared that she would be knocked to pieces and bring no help to him.

His fears proved true; the ship struck at a distance from where he was. He made his way down to the nearest point to where she was, hoping that some of the crew might reach the shore alive, but the only thing of any size which had come ashore was a hen-coop and some fowls lashed to some gratings and some spars. His idea was that the people had been trying to make a raft, but that the ship had gone to pieces before they could finish it, and the raft had been driven on shore by itself. He secured the hen-coop and fowls, most of which were alive, and carried them up to where he had built a hut for himself. Shortly afterwards, seeing three canoes full of wild-looking natives coming near the shore, he collected all his fowls and carried them away right up to the spot where he had built his present hut. He there lay concealed, as he was afraid of falling into the hands of the natives after the way in which he had seen his shipmates murdered at "Strong's" Island, as he thought the savages would treat him in the same way. This idea seemed to have upset his mind. He was nearly starved, for he would not kill any of his fowls because they were the only living beings that seemed to care for him.

At last he ventured out from his hiding-place, and, creeping cautiously on, saw the savages sailing away in their canoes. They had nearly stripped the trees of cocoanuts, and found his hut and pulled it to pieces. Why they had gone so suddenly he could not tell, but on looking towards the burning mountain it was spurting out fire and smoke, and he concluded that they had gone away from being frightened at it. His mind was now more at rest. He employed himself in building his hut and the hen-roosts, where his fowls might be safe from hawks or such-like birds, or any animals which might be in the island. He had seen wild cats at some of those he had touched at, and knew that if they found out his fowl they would soon put an end to them. He had plenty to do to find food for his poultry. He got shell-fish and berries, roots and cocoanuts, and watched what they seemed to like best. They soon became so tame that they would come and sit on his shoulders and knees and run about between his feet. What seemed to have upset him was another visit from the savages some months afterwards, when he was nearly caught. Though they pursued him they didn't discover his hen-roost or hut, but after that he was always fancying they would come and kill him. When he saw our boat he thought we must be some savages, and yet he said he couldn't help coming down to have a look at us, though it was so long since he had heard a word of English spoken he didn't understand what was said. Fortunately, Miles Soper had passed close to the place where he was hiding. At length, when he heard his own name shouted in a voice which he recollected, he came out, and at once knew his old messmate. He could not at first understand that I had grown into a big fellow, and had come to look for him, though he told Miles Soper that he should know me at once if I were like what I had been when he went to sea. When Miles told him that Mr. Griffiths and Dr. Cockle were with me—the gentlemen father had put on board their ship at the time he had joined the *Lapwing*—he seemed to have no doubt on the matter, and by degrees, with Miles speaking soothingly to him, the balance of his mind seemed gradually to be restored. He still found, however, a great difficulty in speaking; he had been so long without uttering a word except when he talked to his poultry. He was almost all to rights when Mr. Griffiths and the doctor and the other men came back. They seemed very much pleased at seeing Jack, and all shook him warmly by the hand. The doctor and Mr. Griffiths told him that they remembered him well when he was a young lad, first going to sea, little thinking that from that day to this he should be knocking about the world far away from home. He looked very shy and reserved, and seemed inclined to keep close to Miles Soper and me, but in other respects he was as much in his senses as any of us. The doctor had found several roots and fruits, which he said were wholesome, and would serve us as food, and Jack offered to catch as many birds as we wanted, begging that we wouldn't touch his poultry. The doctor promised that they should not be molested while we remained on the island, but said to me,

"You must persuade your brother to let us have them for sea-stock when we go away; they will afford us sufficient provisions to enable us to reach the 'Pellew' Islands or Manilla, with the help of the birds and fish we may salt."

When Mr. Griffiths was about to go away, Jack asked that Miles Soper and I might stay to keep him company, promising to go down to the boat the next morning. To this Mr. Griffiths agreed, and Soper and I remained behind with Jack. When they had gone Jack said,

"I haven't food for all the party, but I can give you a good supper," and he showed us his store-room at the back of the hut, in which he had several cocoanuts, some birds dried in the sun, and a dozen eggs.

He showed us a sort of trap he used for catching the birds without frightening the rest. He quickly got a fire from a split log in the way I have before described, and with the help of some fresh water and the milk of the cocoanuts we had a very good meal. He had a supply of mats like those on his bed, and with these he rigged us up a place for sleeping in when it was time to lie down.

I felt happier than I had been for a long time. My hope of finding Brother Jack was realized, and now my great wish was to return home with him to Mary. I forgot for the moment that we were on a remote island, and that we had only a small boat to carry us to civilised lands.

When we got up the next morning Jack seemed more refreshed and better able to talk than on the previous evening. As soon as we had had breakfast, which was very much like supper, we set off to join the rest of the party at the bay. We found them all busily employed, some in caulking the boat, others in splitting a tree to form planks.

We fortunately had a couple of axes with us, which were

of great service, and while Soper and I lent a hand Jack went down to collect shell-fish, which he did much more rapidly than we could, being well accustomed to it.

The weather was so fine that we required only a very slight hut, which we formed partly of the boat's sails and partly of the boughs and stems of small trees.

Jack showed us a way up to the top of the cliff, and here Mr. Griffiths erected a flagstaff with a whift, which we had in the boat, increased in size by a couple of handkerchiefs. This was large enough to attract the attention of any vessel passing near the island, but Mr. Griffiths said that he believed, owing to the surrounding reefs, none would intentionally approach.

We were all anxious to get the boat finished as soon as possible and commence our voyage. We had many reasons for being in a hurry, though we might have lived very well on the island for months together, but the burning mountain might again burst forth and overwhelm us, and the savages might return in large numbers and either kill us or make us prisoners, for as we had only two muskets and a scanty supply of ammunition, we could scarcely hope to beat them off should they prove hostile. Mr. Griffiths and the doctor talked the matter over.

"One thing is certain," observed the mate, "the sooner we're away while the fine weather lasts the better, but at the same time it won't do to start until we have fitted the boat thoroughly for sea. We have a long trip before us, and if we're caught in a gale we shall have reason to regret it if we don't take the trouble to fit our boat in the best way we can."

It took a long time, first with our axes to split up the planks, and then to smooth them with our knives. We had next to shape out additional timbers to strengthen the boat, as to which also to fix the planks to. We likewise decked over the fore and aft parts, both to keep out the sea and to prevent our provisions from getting wet. The doctor searched everywhere for some sort of resin which might serve to caulk our boat.

He at last found some which he thought might answer, but as we had only a small iron pot to boil it in, we had to go without our soup or our hot water till the pot was again thoroughly cleaned out. It answered the purpose, however, better than we had expected, and with mosses and dried grass we made up a substance which served instead of oakum. Jack worked as hard as any of us, and was very useful in catching a number of birds, which he salted and dried in the sun.

At length one day, when nearly all our preparations were concluded, the mate said, "And now, Jack Trawl, we must get you to bring your poultry-yard down. We shall not have room for all the fowl, in the boat but I think we can cut down and repair the old hen-coop to hold a good many, and we must kill and salt the rest."

"What! kill my fowl—my old companions!" said Jack. "What! cannot we let them live? They'll soon find food for themselves; they do that pretty well already, and I couldn't bear to see their necks wrung."

"I wish we were able to do without them," said the mate; "but our lives are of more value than those of the fowl. I can enter into your feelings, and we will not ask you to kill any nor to eat them afterwards unless you change your mind. Look you here, Jack; if the savages came to the island they'd kill the fowl fast enough, and perhaps our lives may depend on our having them."

The doctor then said something to the same effect, and at last Jack was talked over to allow some of his fowl to be killed at once, and dried and salted like the other birds.

We brought the hen-coop down to the beach, and by dint

of hard work cut it away so as to hold two dozen fowl closely packed. At night, when the birds had gone to roost, Miles, Coal, Jack, and I went up and took the others while roosting. What a cackling and screeching the poor creatures made on-finding themselves hauled off their perches and having their legs tied ! The noise they made might have been heard over half the island.

We brought them down and stowed them away in the hen-coop. Jack, accompanied by Jim, had before collected a good supply of seeds, which might serve them as food with the help of the cocoanuts and scraps of fish which we might leave. Mr. Griffiths and the doctor had arranged to start the next morning. All hands had agreed to do as they proposed, which was to be up at daylight, and as soon as we had breakfasted launch the boat and go on board.

We lay down, as we hoped, for the last time in our hut. As the island was known to be uninhabited it was no longer thought necessary to keep a watch. All of us slept like tops, recollecting that we should not for many days get another thorough night's rest.

I was the first to wake, and, calling up Jim, he and I agreed to go to the lake and fill our pot with water to boil for breakfast, knowing that the rest would light the fire as soon as they were aroused ready for it. There was just a single streak in the eastern sky, which showed us that it would soon be daylight, and we knew our way so well through the grove that we didn't think it worth while stopping till then. We carried the pot on a stick between us, and as we had to pass among the trees, of course we could not do so as fast as if it had been daylight. It took us some little time before we could reach the place where we could dip the pot in and get the water pure. We filled it, and set off again on our way back. We had just reached the grove of cocoanut-trees. I happened to look up at the hill where I had seen Jack the morning after our arrival, when I saw against the sky the forms of well-nigh a dozen savages.

I rubbed my eyes for a moment, as I at first thought it might be fancy, and then whispered to Jim to look in the same direction and then tell me what he saw.

"Savages," he answered, "no doubt about that."

"Then we must rouse up the rest and be prepared for them," I said.

We ran on among the trees, to which we were close, hoping that we hadn't been seen. Still I thought that the savages must know that we were on the island. We didn' like to abandon our pot, though we spilled some of the water as we hurried along. Our friends were still fast asleep.

"Mr. Griffiths! Dr. Cockle! the savages have landed and are on the hill out there," Jim and I cried out.

They started to their feet in a moment, and Jack and the rest of the men jumped up on hearing our voices. The mate seemed satisfied that what we said was true.

"Then, lads," he said, "we will launch the boat at once; we must at all events avoid a fight, and we can't tell how they'll behave if we remain."

Jack was about the most eager to get the boat in the water, and Horner looked not a little frightened. We soon had her afloat, and then as quickly as we could, running backwards and forwards, put the cargo on board.

The doctor and mate were still on shore, seeing that nothing had been left behind, when loud shrieks reached our ears, and a score or more of tattooed savages, flourishing their war clubs, burst out of the grove and rushed towards us.

"Quick, doctor," cried the mate. "Get on board, and I'll follow you."

He stood, as he spoke, with his musket in his hand

pointed towards the savages, and then slowly retreated, while Dr. Cockle sprang on board. We had our oars ready to shove off as soon as the mate was safe.

"Come on, Mr. Griffiths, come on," cried several others.

The savages were scarcely a dozen yards from us as the mate threw himself over the bows, and we quickly shoved the boat into deep water, while the savages stood yelling and heaving stones at us from the beach.

Just, however, as we got the boat's head to sea we saw, coming round a point to the eastward, four or five large canoes. It seemed impossible that we could escape them.

CHAPTER XXVIII.

ESCAPE FROM THE ISLAND AND THE EVENTS WHICH FOLLOWED.

"GIVE way, lads! give way!" shouted Mr. Griffiths: "if the worst comes we must fight for it, and try to save our lives, but I want, if we can, to avoid fighting." The men bent to their oars; the wind was ahead, so that it was useless to hoist the sail. The savages on shore howled and shrieked as they saw us getting off, and hurled stones at us. The big double canoes came round the point, two more appearing astern. They were close on a wind, and rapidly skimming the water.

"There's an outlet from the bay to the westward, I marked it yesterday, we will make for it," said Mr. Griffiths.

The canoes were to the eastward, but it seemed very doubtful whether we could reach the outlet the mate spoke of before they would be up with us. We pulled for our lives, for there could be no doubt, from the behaviour of the savages on shore, how those in the canoes would be inclined to treat us. While the mate steered, the doctor and I got the muskets ready; the rest of the crew were rowing, Horner helping the stroke oar. On the canoes came, nearer and nearer. We observed the sea breaking over the reef, but there was a clear channel between it and the shore. The savages had left the beach and were rushing towards the point which they knew we must pass; probably, as we supposed, to enjoy the satisfaction of seeing us overtaken and massacred. As the mate altered our course to steer for the channel, we found the wind on our starboard bow; should it shift a point or two more, it would come right ahead, and even the canoes, though they sail closer to the wind than any ordinary craft, would be unable to get through it; but they were already within one hundred fathoms of us, and coming on rapidly. I counted seven of them. One took the lead of the rest, and was coming up hand over hand with us. We could see the warriors on the raised deck dancing and leaping and flourishing their clubs, and hear them shouting and shrieking like their companions on shore. I looked anxiously at the channel. Soper was pulling bow oar. The mate told Horner to take it, and directed Soper to keep a look-out for reefs ahead. The leading canoe was now within fifty fathoms astern.

"Give them a shot, doctor," said the mate; "but fire over their heads. It will show them that we are armed, but I don't want to kill any one."

"Ay, ay!" answered the doctor; and shouting to the savages to make them understand what he was about to do, he fired. The first shot seemed to have no effect. Still the big canoe came on. We were as far from the passage as we were from them. Our men were straining every nerve, and could make the boat go no faster. The doctor waited till I had reloaded the first musket. He again fired, still aiming high, as the mate told him to do. The next instant down came the yard and sail of the canoe. The bullet must have cut the slings right in two.

"It was a chance shot, and a fortunate one," said the doctor, as he saw its effect. The canoe still glided on, but the next, unable to alter her course, ran right into her, and the others, also coming up, were thrown into confusion. Our men cheered as they saw what had happened. The channel was reached before our pursuers could get clear of each other. Then on they came again. Before, however, they had come far, the wind shifted a point and then blew right ahead. First one lowered her sail, and then another and another, while we pulled through the channel, Soper keeping a bright look-out for sunken rocks. I caught sight of the savages on shore rushing along the beach, but we had passed the point before they had gained it, and there they stood shrieking, shouting, and gesticulating at us. We pulled away in the wind's eye, knowing that we should thus have a better chance of keeping ahead of our pursuers. They had not yet, however, given up the chase. We saw them at length coming through the channel urged on by their paddles. They could thus move but slowly. Once outside, however, they might again hoist their sails, and, by standing first on one tack and then on the other, come up with us.

As we got away from the island we found the wind blowing steadily from the southward, while in shore it still came from the westward. This gave us a great advantage.

"We'll hoist the sail, lads," said Mr. Griffiths, "and see if a whale-boat can beat a double canoe."

The men, who were streaming from every pore, gladly obeyed. The mast was set up in an instant, the sail hoisted, and "*Young Hopeful*," as the doctor called our boat, glided rapidly over the dancing waters.

We had made good way before we saw the sails of the canoes once more hoisted, standing, as far as we could make out, for the north-west.

Now we had got the wind, it would take them a long time to come up with us. The wind was too fresh to allow the oars to be of any use. We trusted, however, to the good providence of God to carry us clear. All that we could do was to sit quiet and hope that the wind would continue steady. We could see the canoes in the north-east hull down, and we hoped that we might keep ahead till night should hide us from their sight. The mate said he was sure that they would not then attempt to follow us farther.

"But, I say, is any one hungry?" exclaimed Horner. "We've had no breakfast, you'll remember."

We had all been too excited to think of eating, but the mention of food excited our appetites, and the mate told the doctor to serve out provisions.

The occupation of eating assisted to pass the time, and to raise our spirits. The mate told us that he and the doctor had determined to steer for the Pellew Islands, the inhabitants of which, though uncivilised, were supposed to be of a mild disposition, and likely to treat us kindly. Even had we intended to steer for Guam, the canoes in that direction would have prevented us doing so.

From the Pellew Islands we should have a long voyage round to Manilla. When once there we should be sure of finding European vessels on board of which we should be able to obtain a passage to some English settlement. Every now and then, while we were eating, I took a look at the canoes, but the sight of them didn't spoil my appetite, nor that of the rest of us, as far as I could judge.

"They are getting no nearer," I observed.

"Wait till they come about," said Horner; "they'll then be up with us fast enough, and this may be the last meal we shall ever eat."

"Haul in the slack of that, you young croaker!" cried the mate, in an angry tone. "You would like to make the others as much afraid as you are yourself."

Horner could not say he was not afraid, for he looked it. The breeze freshened, and the boat made good way in spite of being heavily laden, standing up well to all the sail we could set. For another hour or more we could see the canoes.

At last the mate, standing up, took a look at them and then cried,

"Hurrah! they have gone about, and are steering for the land."

Just as the sun set they disappeared, and we had no longer any fear of being followed. The mate now set a regular watch ;—the rest of us lay down as we best could along the thwarts, or at the bottom of the boat, with some of Jack's matting for pillows. We were rather crowded, to be sure, but we were thankful to have escaped our enemies, and hoped, in spite of its length, that we should have a prosperous voyage.

Day after day we sailed on. Mr. Griffiths maintained good discipline among us. Everything was done with as much regularity as if we were aboard ship. He got us to spin yarns and sing songs. I thus heard more of Jack's adventures than I ever since have been able to get out of him. He corroborated all that Miles Soper had told me, and added much more. Sam Coal told us how he had once been a slave in the Southern States of America, and made his escape, and being followed, was nearly caught, and how a kind Quaker sheltered him, at the risk of his own life, and got him away on board a ship, where he found that he had not changed much for the better in some respects; but then, as he said,

"Dis nigger feel dat he was a free man, and dat make up for all de rest."

The wind was fair and the sea calm. Our chief fear was that we might run short of water, so Mr. Griffiths thought it wise to put us upon an allowance at once. Several times flying-fish fell aboard, which we didn't despise, although we had to eat them raw, or rather dried in the sun. If we had had fuel we might have managed to make a fire and cook them, but in our hurry to get off we had come away without any spare wood.

"Never mind, lads," said the mate ; "we'll get some at

the Pellew Islands, and after that we'll have a hot meal every other day at least."

Brown was always on the look-out with his harpoon, ready to strike any large fish which might come near us, but they seemed to know what we were about, and kept at a respectful distance. Now and then a shark would come up and have a look at us, and the men would call him all manner of names. One day, as we were running along at the rate of about five knots an hour, we saw a black fin coming up astern; it sheered off under the counter and then floated up abreast of us, just coming near enough to show us its wicked eye. It kept too far off, however, for Brown to strike it, or it might have paid dearly for its curiosity. At last, cocking its eye, it gave a turn of its tail, and off it went like a shot, followed by our roars of laughter.

"'Pend on it, Jack Shark find dat we not going to make dinner for him dis day!" cried Sam Coal, "so he tink better go look out sumber else."

Such were the trifling incidents which afforded us amusement and assisted to keep up our spirits. It was trying work, thus to sit all day and day after day in an open boat with nothing to do, and unable to move about freely. We were very thankful, however, to be favoured by such fine weather.

At last Mr. Griffiths stood up in the stern sheets, and, after shading his eyes for some time—for the sun had already passed the zenith, said quietly, "Lads, we have made a good landfall. I'm much mistaken if we have not the Pellew Islands in sight. I make out a dozen or more blue hillocks rising above the horizon. Sit quiet, however, for you won't see them just yet. We shall have to heave-to to-night outside the reef which surrounds them, but I hope we shall get ashore in the morning."

This news cheered us up, for we were beginning to get

somewhat downcast, and some of us thought that we must have passed the islands altogether, and might make no other land till we reached the Philippines. We ran on till dark, by which time we could make out one large island and a number of smaller ones, some to the northward and some to the southward, with a reef marked by a line of white foam surrounding them. As it would be dangerous to attempt looking for a passage through the reef except in daylight, we hove-to, and the watch below lay down—or "turned in," as we used to call it—rejoicing in the hope of setting our feet on dry ground the next morning, and getting a plentiful supply of provisions. I had to keep the middle watch with Jim. I took good care not to let my eyes close, for we were at no great distance from the reef, and I knew the danger of being drifted on it. Now I looked to windward to make sure that no vessel was approaching to run us down, now at the reef to find out whether we were drifting nearer it than was safe. After a long silence Jim spoke to me.

"There's something on my mind, Peter," he said. "I'm afraid that now you have found your brother Jack you'll not be caring for me as you used to do, for the whole of the last day you have not opened your lips to me, while you have been talking away to him."

"Don't let such an idea rest on your mind, Jim," I answered. "I very naturally talked to Jack, for of course I wanted to hear everything he had been about since he first went to sea, and it's only lately I have been able to get him to say much. I don't think that anything will make me forget your affection for me. Though Jack is my brother, you've been more than a brother, and as brothers we shall remain till the end of life."

In this way I did my best to satisfy Jim's mind. It hadn't before occurred to me that there was any spice of jealousy in him, and I determined in future to do my best to prevent him having any such feeling. We talked on just as we used to do after that.

The wind was light, and except a slight swell coming from the eastward, the sea was perfectly smooth. If it hadn't been for the talking I should have found it a hard matter to keep my eyes open. After I lay down, I had been for some time asleep, as I fancied, when I heard the mate cry,

"Out oars, lads! Pull for your lives!"

I jumped up in a moment.

The strong current into which the boat had got was carrying her along at the rate of five knots an hour towards the reef, over which the sea was breaking and rising up in a wall of white foam.

There was now not a breath of wind, but a much greater swell was coming in than before.

We all bent to our oars, and had good reason to be thankful that we had got them to help us, for a sailing vessel would very quickly have been dashed to pieces on the reef, and every soul aboard lost.

The mate headed the boat off from the shore in a diagonal course, so that we hoped soon to get out of the current. Still, notwithstanding all our efforts, we appeared to be drawing nearer and nearer the reef as the current swept us along, and I began to think that, notwithstanding all we had gone through, we were doomed to be lost at last. The mate, however, cheered us up.

Daylight soon broke. As the sun rose the wind increased, and presently, a fresh breeze springing up, he hauled aft the sheet, and with the help of the oars the boat moved quickly along till we got out of the current.

We were now able to venture close enough to the reef to look out for a safe opening. At last we found one a little to the southward of the largest island, and hauling up, we steered for it.

The sea broke on either side of the passage, which was large enough for a good-sized vessel to venture through. We stood on, keeping a look-out for dangers ahead.

We were soon inside, where the water was perfectly smooth. Seeing a snug little harbour, we ran for it. As we approached, we saw a number of natives coming down, darkish-skinned fellows, though not so black as those of the Caroline Islands all of them without a stitch of clothing on except a loin cloth; but they were pleasant-looking, and we saw no weapons among them.

The mate, however, kept the muskets concealed in the stern-sheets, ready for use in case they were only acting treacherously, and should suddenly rush down upon us with clubs and spears. Still, as we got nearer, and waved our hands, they showed no inclination to attack us, and made every sign to let us understand that they wished to be friends.

We therefore lowered the sail, and pulled the boat gently towards the beach. On this they came down, and when we jumped out, helped us to haul her up. There was one man who seemed to be the chief. He came up and shook hands with Mr. Griffiths, the doctor, and me, and then ordered six of his people to stay by the boat, as we supposed to guard her. He made no objection when the mate and the doctor went back to get the muskets, but seemed to think it very natural that they should wish to be armed amongst so many strangers.

The other people were in the meantime making friends with the rest of our party. The chief now invited us up to his house. It was built of trunks of small trees and bamboo canes, and thatched with palm leaves, much in the same style as the huts of other South Sea islanders, though of a fair size. It was also very clean, and the floors were covered with mats. He begged us to sit down near him, while he squatted on a mat at one end of the room.

As we could only talk by signs we didn't say much. Presently a number of girls appeared, bringing clay dishes, with fish and fowl and vegetables. As soon as they were placed on the ground, he told us to fall to, and a very good meal we enjoyed, after the uncooked food we had lived on so long.

The mate made signs that we had come from the eastward, and were bound west for the Philippines, of which he seemed to have heard.

After dinner he took us down to the shore, and showed us some fine large canoes, with the stems and sterns well carved. They were used for going about between the islands, but I don't think they could have done much in a heavy sea. Some were large enough to hold thirty or forty men. He then had a look at our boat, and seemed to wonder that we had come so far in her.

The mate explained to him that, though she was shorter, she had much higher sides, and was much lighter built than his canoes. From the way he behaved we had no doubts as to his friendly intentions, or any anxiety about the men who were attended to by other natives.

In the evening he gave us another feast, and then took us to a clean new hut, which by his signs we understood we were to occupy. From the way he behaved we agreed that, though he looked liked a native savage, he was as civilised a gentleman as we could wish to meet. The rest of our party were billeted in huts close to us, and from the sounds of laughter which came from them we guessed that they and their hosts were mightily amused with each other. The chief, after making signs to us to lie down and go to sleep, took his leave, and we were left alone.

"I hope our fellows will behave well, and not get into any quarrel with the natives," observed the doctor.

"I don't think there's any chance of that, though it would be a serious matter if they did," answered Mr. Griffiths

"If you'll give me leave, sir, I'll go and speak to them," I said. "I'm sure Jim and my brother Jack will behave properly, and so I should think would Brown."

"It doesn't do always to trust men," said the mate. "Just tell them to be careful. I would rather that we had been all together, but it won't do to show that we're suspicious of the natives."

I accordingly got up, and, directed by the sounds I heard, went to the other huts. I found Jack and Jim in one of them, with a number of natives sitting round them, examining their dresses and trying to imitate their way of speaking.

I advised them to let their friends know that they were sleepy, and wanted to lie down. As soon as they did this, the natives got up in the politest way possible, and spread mats for them at one side of the room. In the next hut I found Miles Soper and Sam Coal. I said to them what I had said before to Jack and Jim, and I then went on to another hut, the natives in each behaving in precisely the same manner.

When I told the mate, he was perfectly satisfied, and said that we must trust the natives. We were not mistaken. Early the next morning a plentiful meal was brought us, and during our stay on the island we were treated with the greatest kindness by these mild and courteous people. The doctor said that they were Malays, though very unlike many of their brethren scattered about the Indian seas.

Having recovered completely from the effects of being cramped up so long in the boat, and the unwholesome food we had lived on, we were anxious to prosecute our voyage.

The chief looked very sorrowful when the mate told him we must be going, and that we should be thankful to him for provisions and water for the voyage. When he told his people, they brought us down fowl and vegetables enough to fill the boat. We showed them our hen-coop, in which we could keep a number of the fowl alive, but that we wanted food for them. Off they ran, and quickly came back with a good supply.

By this time we could understand each other wonderfully well, helping out what we said by signs. The chief gave us all a grand feast the last night of our stay, and the next morning, having shaken hands with all round, we went aboard, and once more put to sea. The natives at the same time came off in their canoes, and accompanied us some way outside the reef; then, with shouts and waving of hands, they wished us good-bye.

We had a long passage before us, but we were in good health and spirits, and we hoped to perform it in safety. We had to keep a sharp look-out at night, for, as the mate told us, there were some small islands between the Pellew and the Philippines, and that, he not being certain of their exact position, we might run upon them.

For a whole week we had fine weather, though, as the wind was light, we didn't make much way. At the end of that time clouds began to gather in the horizon, and soon covered the whole sky, while the wind shifted to the northwest, and in a short time was blowing a heavy gale. The sea got up, and the water every now and then, notwithstanding our high sides, broke aboard, and we had to take to baling. Night came on, and matters grew worse.

We all had confidence in Mr. Griffiths's skill; and as he had, by his good seamanship, preserved our lives before, we hoped that we should again escape. At length he determined to try his former plan, and, heaving the boat to, we cast out a raft, formed by the oars, and rode to it. The gale, however, increased, and seemed likely to turn into a regular typhoon.

There was no sleep for any of us that night; all hands had to keep baling, while a heavier sea than we had yet encountered broke aboard and carried away a large portion of our provisions, besides drowning all the fowl in the hen-coop. Most of us, I suspect, began to think that we should never see another sunrise. It seemed a wonder, indeed, that the boat escaped being knocked to pieces. Had it continued long, we must have gone down. Towards morning, however, the wind moderated, and before noon we were able to haul the raft aboard and once more make sail. But there we were on the wide ocean, with but scanty provisions and a sorely battered boat.

The weather still looked unsettled, and we feared that we should have another bad night of it. The greater part of the day had gone by, when Brown, who was at the helm while the mate was taking some rest, suddenly exclaimed,

"A sail! a sail! She's standing this way."

We all looked out to the northward, and there made out a large vessel steering directly for us.

CHAPTER XXIX.

ON BOARD OUR OLD SHIP—HER VOYAGE THROUGH EASTERN SEAS.

THE doctor awoke Mr. Griffiths to tell him the good news. He at once hove the boat to. We sat eagerly watching the stranger. She could not possibly at present see us, and might alter her course before she came near enough to do so. Her topsails rose above the horizon, then in a short time her courses were seen, and then her hull itself as she came on swiftly before the breeze. I saw Mr. Griffiths several times rub his eyes, then he stood up and looked fixedly at her.

"Brown," he said, "did you ever see that ship before?"

"Well, I was thinking that the same sailmaker cut her topsails that cut the *Intrepid's;* but there's no wonder in that," answered Brown.

"What do you say to that white patch in the head of her foresail?" asked the mate. "It looks to me like one we put in when we were last at the Sandwich Islands. To be sure it's where the sail is likely to get worn, and another vessel may have had one put in like it; still, the *Intrepid's* foresail had just such a patch as that."

"What! do you mean to say that she's the *Intrepid?*" exclaimed the doctor, interrupting him.

"I mean to say that she's very like her, if she's not her," answered the mate.

We all of us now looked with even greater eagerness than before at the approaching vessel.

"Let draw the foresail," cried the mate.

We stood on so that we might be in the best possible position for running alongside the whaler, for such she was, as soon as she hove to.

"We're seen!—we're seen!" shouted several of our crew.

We waved our hats, and shouted.

"She is the *Intrepid!*" cried Mr. Griffiths.

Presently she came to the wind, and we, lowering our sail and getting out our oars, were soon alongside her. There stood Captain Hawkins—there the second mate, with many other faces we knew. I never saw people look so astonished as we sprang up the side, while our boat was hooked on and hoisted on board.

"Why, Griffiths!—Cockle! where have you come from?" exclaimed Captain Hawkins. "I had given you up for lost long ago."

They gave a brief account of our adventures, but there was not much time for talking, for we had not been aboard five minutes before all hands were employed in shortening sail, and the gale came down upon us with even greater strength than on the previous night. Had we been exposed to it in our open boat there would have been little chance of our escape. We had thus much reason to be thankful to Heaven that we had got aboard in time.

There being plenty of sea room, the *Intrepid* was hove to. Even as it was, the sea broke aboard and carried away one of her boats and did other damage. She had been nearly wrecked on the reef during the gale when we were on the island; and Captain Hawkins, believing that we had been lost, stood for Guam, where he had been detained for want of proper workmen and fresh hands. Had it not been for this she would long before have been on her homeward voyage.

For some time I felt very strange on board, often when half asleep fancying myself still in the boat, and the air below seemed close and oppressive.

The mate declared that he had caught cold from sleeping in a bed after not having been in one for so many months.

The doctor suggested that his bed might have been damp. However, the gale being over, the sun came out brightly, and he soon got rid of his chill.

The captain took no more notice of me than he did before, and did not even speak to Jack. His idea was to keep us at a proper distance, I suppose. He had heard, I have no doubt, of our adventures from Dr. Cockle or the mate. It mattered very little to us, though I was afraid that he might take it into his head to turn Jack out of the ship at some place or other, on the plea that he did not belong to her.

I advised my brother, therefore, to keep out of his sight as much as possible, especially when in harbour. Jim and I agreed that if he was sent ashore we would go also, wherever it might be.

"So will I," said Miles Soper, who had heard us talking about the matter.

"And I no stop eider, and den he lose four good hands. He no like dat," said Sam Coal.

Brown, hearing from Jim of my apprehensions, said he would go likewise if the captain attempted to play any tricks of that sort.

Three days after the gale we hove to off three small islands surrounded by a reef. Brown, Miles Soper, two Africans and the New Zealander, the second mate and I, were sent on shore to catch turtle. We hauled the boat up and waited till the evening, at which time the creatures land to lay their eggs.

Darkness approached, and we concealed ourselves behind some rocks, and watched for their coming. Presently one landed, and crawled slowly up the beach. Sam declared that she was as big as the boat. She was certainly an enormous creature. Then another and another came ashore, and commenced scraping away in the sand to make holes for their eggs. We waited till some thirty or forty had come ashore.

"Now is your time," cried the mate; and rushing out, grasping the handspikes with which we were armed, we got between them and the sea, and turned them over on their backs, where they lay kicking their legs, unable to move. We had brought ropes to assist us in dragging them down to the water and hauling them on board. We had turned a dozen or more, when I said to Jim.

"We mustn't let that big one go we first saw land."

She and the other turtles still on their feet, had taken the alarm, and were scuttling down the beach. We made her out and attempted to turn her, but that was more than we could do.

"She'll be off," cried Jim.

We hove the bight of a rope over her head.

"Hold on, Peter!" he cried; and he and I attempted to haul the turtle back, all the time shouting for help, for she was getting closer and closer to the water. At last in she got, dragging us after her. We could not stop her before, and there was very little chance of our doing so now.

"Let her go, Jim," I cried out.

"We shall lose the rope," he answered, still holding on.

We were already up to our middles in the water.

"It's of no use. Let go! let go!" I cried out, "or we shall be dragged away to sea!"

Supposing that he would do as I told him, I let go at the

same moment, when what was my dismay to see Jim dragged away out of his depth.

I swam off to him, still shouting loudly. Presently Soper and Sam Coal came up, and seeing what was happening, dashed into the water. Our united strength, however, could not stop the turtle, and Sam, who had a sharp knife in his pocket, drawing it, cut the rope, and we got Jim back to shore.

The mate rated Jim for losing the rope, though Brown and the rest declared that he had behaved very pluckily, and that if help had come in time we should have saved the turtle. As it was we had turned more than we could carry off.

Having been ordered not to attempt to regain the ship during the night, we turned the boat up and slept under it, while a couple of hands remained outside to watch the turtles and see that they did not manage to get on their feet again and escape.

In the morning we loaded the boat, and pulled back with our prizes.

The mate said nothing about the lost rope, as he knew the notion Brown and the rest had formed of Jim's courage.

We sighted after this several small islands, and then made the coast of New Guinea.

The captain, seeing a good place for landing, sent a boat ashore with the doctor and most of us who had been engaged in catching turtle.

It seemed a beautiful country, with magnificent trees, and birds flying about in numbers among them.

"This is a perfect paradise," said the doctor, as we approached the beach.

Just then a number of natives came rushing out from the forest, brandishing clubs and spears. They were the ugliest set of people I ever saw, their bodies nearly naked and their heads covered with hair frizzled out like huge mops. They had also bows at their backs, but they did not point their arrows at us.

The doctor and mate agreed that it would be folly to land amongst them, so we lay on our oars while the mate held up bottles and bits of iron hoops, beads and knives, and a few old clothes, to show them that we wished to trade. After a considerable time they seemed to understand what we wanted, and some of them going away returned with numbers of stuffed birds of a delicate yellow with long tails. We made signs that only those who wanted to trade must come near us. At last several came wading into the water bringing their birds. They set a high price on them, and we only bought a dozen or so. As the rest of the people behaved in as threatening a manner as before, as soon as the trading was over we pulled off, not wishing to risk an encounter with them.

The doctor said that the birds were birds of paradise, and that they were such as the ladies of England wore in their hats. The curious thing was that none of the birds had feet.

"Of course not," said the second mate, when I pointed this out to him; "they say that the birds come down from the skies and live in the air, and as they never perch, they don't want feet. That's why they're called birds of paradise."

The doctor laughed. "That's a very old notion," he remarked, "but it's a wrong one notwithstanding, and has long since been exploded. They have legs and claws like other birds, though the natives cut them off and dry the birds as these have been over a hot fire. It's the only way they have of preserving them."

The captain said we were very right not to land, as the natives might have been tempted to cut us off for the sake of possessing themselves of the articles in our boat.

As we sailed along the coast the country seemed to be thickly populated, and the boat was frequently sent to try and land, but we always met with the same inhospitable reception. The moment we drew near the shore the black-skinned natives would rush down, apparently to prevent our landing.

This was a great disappointment, for the captain was anxious to obtain fresh provisions, as several of the men, from having lived a long time on salt meat, were suffering from scurvy. Curiously enough, we, who had been in the boat, were free from it. At one place, however, we traded with the natives, and bought several more of the stuffed paradise birds, and a number of live lories, which we kept in cages, and beautiful little creatures they were. Our hope was to carry them safely home, but, either from improper food or change of climate, they all shortly died.

Rounding New Guinea, and passing the island of Mysole, we came to a small island called Gely, at the south-east end of Gillolo, lying exactly under the equator. It contains a magnificent and secure harbour, in which we brought up. There being an abundance of good water, and trees from which spars can be cut, it is an excellent place for repairing damages. The second mate said that those suffering from scurvy would now have an opportunity of being cured.

The plan he proposed was to bury them up to their necks in the sand, and to leave them there for some hours. The doctor was unwilling to try the experiment, though he did not deny that it might be effectual. Two of our men suffering from the complaint were, however, perfectly willing to submit to the remedy, and, our boats having to go on shore to fill the water-casks, we carried them with us. Holes were dug, and the poor fellows, being stripped naked, were covered up side by side in the warm sand, leaving only their heads above the surface, so that they could not possibly extricate themselves. The captain, I should have said, approved of the plan, having before seen it tried with success; but the doctor, declaring that he would have nothing to do with the matter, went with Jack and another man in an opposite direction. Horner and I had charge of the watering party. The stream from which we filled our casks was at some distance from the place where the men were buried. I undertook to see to the casks being filled if Horner would remain by the men. We had just finished our work and were rolling the casks down to the boat when Horner came rushing up, with his eyes staring and his hair almost on end.

"What's the matter? What has happened?" I asked, thinking he had gone out of his mind.

"I can't bear it!" he exclaimed. "It's too dreadful. I couldn't help it."

"What is dreadful? What could you not help?" I inquired.

"The brutes of crocodiles. Poor fellows," he stammered out. "There won't be a bit of them left presently!" and he pointed to where we had buried our poor shipmates, and where he ought to have been watching.

The men and I set off running to the spot. A dreadful sight met our eyes. The body of one man lay half eaten on the sand. A huge crocodile was dragging off the other. He had dragged it under the water before we could reach the spot. We could do nothing but shout at the crocodiles. Horner confessed that he had gone to a distance for a short time, during which the brutes had landed and killed the two men. We returned very sad to the boat. As for Horner, it was a long time before he could get over the horror he felt for his neglect of duty. Several canoes filled with natives came into the harbour from Gillolo, bringing potatoes and other vegetables. One of them brought a number of clam-shells of various sizes. One which we hoisted on board weighed four hundred-weight, and we afterwards saw on shore one which must have weighed a quarter of a ton. The natives use them as tubs; I saw a woman bathing a child in one. The meat of the creature when fried is very palatable. I also obtained some beautiful specimens of coral, which I wanted to carry home to Mary and my Shetland relations. I bought also two gallons of nutmegs for an old file, and a large number of shells for some old clothes. The harbour swarmed with sharks, which prevented us from bathing. We here cut some splendid spars for the use of the ship. I may mention that the inner harbour, from its perfect security, has obtained the name of "Abraham's Bosom." Were it not for the sharks and crocodiles the place would be perfect.

All the crew having recovered from scurvy, and the ship being refitted, we once more put to sea. The weather was delightful, and we sailed on over the calm ocean with a light breeze.

We had to keep a constant look-out for rocks and reefs.

I can assert, though it is often denied, that when passing under the lee of the Spice Islands, the scent which came off from the shore was perfectly delicious. Whether this arises from the flowers of the cloves and nutmegs, or from the nature of the soil, I cannot determine.

Though we generally had a light breeze, we were sometimes completely becalmed, on which occasions, when near shore, we ran the risk of being driven on the rocks by the currents, and more than once we had all the boats towing ahead to keep her off them till the breeze should spring up. We continued our course, passing to the eastward of Ceram and Banda, and steering for Timor, to the north-west of Australia. We had other dangers besides calms and currents.

We had just left the Serwatty Islands astern when the wind dropped, and we lay becalmed.

Though there was little chance of catching whales, we always kept a look-out for them from the masthead, as we could stow one or two more away. We were most of us on deck whistling for a breeze, when the look-out aloft shouted that he saw three craft stealing up from behind the island to the eastward. The second mate went up to have a look at them through his glass, and when he returned on deck he reported that they were three large proas, pulling, he should say, twenty oars or more, and full of men, and that he had no doubt they were pirates. Those seas, we knew, were infested with such gentry—generally Malays, the most bloodthirsty and cruel of their race. Many a merchant vessel has been captured by them and sunk, all hands being killed.

"Whatever they are, we must be prepared for them!" cried Captain Hawkins. "I'll trust to you, lads, to fight to the last; and I tell you that if they once get alongside us we shall find it a difficult job to keep them off. We will have the arms on deck, Mr. Griffiths, for if we don't get a breeze, as they pull fast, they'll soon be up to us."

All the muskets were at once brought up and arranged in order; our two guns were loaded, and the armourer and carpenter set to work to sharpen the blubber-spades, harpoons, and spears. We had thus no lack of weapons; our high bulwarks also gave us an advantage; but the pirates, we knew, would probably out-number us by ten to one.

However, we did not lose heart; Captain Hawkins looked cool and determined, and the mates imitated his example. I didn't think about myself, but the fear came over me that, after all, Jack might be killed, and that I should not have the happiness of taking him home.

As the pirates approached, we made all necessary preparations for defending ourselves. Muskets and ammunition were served out to the men most accustomed to firearms; the others had the blubber-spades and spears put into their hands. The two mates took charge of the guns, which were loaded to their muzzles, and matches were got ready for firing them. The doctor provided himself with a couple of muskets and a sword. The captain told him he must not run the risk of being wounded, as he might be required to bind up the hurts of the rest of us. He laughed, and said that the first thing to be done was to drive back our enemies should they attempt to board the ship.

The pirates came closer and closer. The captain looked anxiously round the horizon, for though, like a brave man, he was prepared to defend his ship to the last, he had no wish for a fight. As I looked over the sides I saw some cats-paws playing along the surface of the water. The pirates by this time were not a quarter of a mile astern. Presently the lighter canvas, which had hung down against the masts, bulged out, and then the topsails filled.

"All hands trim sails!" shouted the captain.

The breeze came from the eastward; the yards were squared, and the *Intrepid* began to move through the water. She glided on but slowly; the pirates were still gaining on us. The wind, however, freshened.

As we watched our pursuers, first one raised a mast and a long taper yard, then another, and they were soon under all sail standing after us. The breeze increased; we gave a cheer, hoping soon to get well ahead of them. Still on they came, and it seemed very doubtful whether we should succeed. I believe that some of the crew would rather have had a fight than have escaped without it.

The pirates, by keeping their oars moving, still gained on us. To look at the captain, one might have supposed that it was a matter of indifference to him whether they came alongside or not, but our cargo was too valuable to risk the chance of being lost. We had soon studding-sails rigged below and aloft. Again the wind dropped, and the pirates were now almost within musket shot.

"We will slew round one of our guns, and run it through the after port, Griffiths," said the captain. "A shot or two will teach the rascals what to expect should they come up to us."

Just, however, as we had got the gun run out the wind again freshened. The *Intrepid*, deep in the water though she was, showed that she had not lost her power of sailing. Though the pirates were straining every nerve, we once more drew ahead of them. The more the breeze increased the faster we left them astern, and by the time the sun had set we had got fully four miles ahead, but still by going aloft we could see them following, evidently hoping that we should be again becalmed, and that they might get up with us. During the night we continued our course for Timor. At the usual hour the watch below turned in, though the captain remained on deck, and a sharp look-out was kept astern. However, as long as the breeze continued we had no fear of being overtaken.

It was my morning watch. As soon as it was daylight I went aloft, and saw the proas the same distance off that they had been at nightfall. I told Mr. Griffiths when I came below.

"The rascals still expect to catch us," he said, "but we must hope that they'll be disappointed. However, we're prepared for them."

For some hours the breeze continued steady. Soon after noon it again fell, and our pursuers crept closer to us. It was somewhat exciting, and kept us all alive, though it did not spoil our appetites. The whole of the day they were in sight, but when the wind freshened up again in the evening we once more distanced them. The night passed as the former had done. We could not tell when we went below what moment we might be roused up to fight for our lives. I for one did not sleep the worse for that.

The breeze was pretty steady during the middle watch, and I was not on deck again till it was broad daylight. The second mate, who had been aloft, reported that the pirates were still in sight, but farther off than they were the day before, and the breeze now freshening, their hulls sank beneath the horizon, and we fully expected to see no more of them. We sighted Timor about three weeks after leaving Gely, and in the evening brought up in a small bay, with a town on its shore, called Cushbab. Our object was to obtain vegetables and buffalo meat.

The natives are Malays, and talk Portuguese. Nearly all those we met on shore carried creeses, or long, sharp knives, in their belt, which they use on the slightest provocation. Every boy we saw had a cock under his arm. The people seemed to spend all their time in cock-fighting. They are very fond of the birds, which are of enormous size; considerably larger than any English cocks. Being unable to obtain any buffaloes here, we got under way, and anchored in another bay some way to the west, where we obtained twelve animals.

At first they were very wild when we got them on board, but in a few hours became tame, and would eat out of our hands. They were destined, however, for the butcher's knife. Some of the meat we ate fresh, but the larger quantity was salted down for sea stores. The unsalted meat kept for a very short time, and we had to throw a large piece overboard. The instant it reached the water up came two tiger sharks, which fought for it, seizing each other in the most ferocious manner possible, and struggling together, although there was enough for both of them.

After leaving Timor we steered along the south-east coast of Java, and then shaped a course across the Indian Ocean for the Cape of Good Hope. The wind was fair, the sea smooth, and I never remember enjoying a longer period of fine weather. In consequence of the light winds our passage was lengthened more than we had expected, and we were running short of provisions of all sorts. There were still two casks of bread left, each containing about four hundredweight.

"Never mind," observed the second mate, "we shall have enough to take us to the Cape."

At length the first was finished, and we went below to get up the second. It was marked bread clearly enough, but when the carpenter knocked in the head, what was our dismay to find it full of new sails, it having been wrongly branded! The captain at once ordered a search to be made in the store-room for other provisions. The buffalo meat we had salted had long been exhausted, part of it having turned bad; and besides one cask of pork, which proved to be almost rancid, a couple of pounds of flour, with a few other trifling articles, not a particle of food remained in the ship. Starvation stared us in the face.

CHAPTER XXX.

THE VOYAGE HOME, AND HOW IT ENDED.

ON hearing of the alarming scarcity of food on board, the captain called the crew aft.

"Lads," he said, "I don't want to hide anything from you. Should the wind shift to the westward, it may be a month or more before we reach the Cape, so if you wish to save your lives, you must at once be put on a short allowance of food and water. A quarter of a pint of water, two ounces of pork, and half an ounce of flour is all I can allow for each man, and the officers and I will share alike with you."

Not a word was said in reply, and the men went forward with gloomy looks. To make the flour go farther we mixed whale oil with it, and, though nauseous in the extreme, it served to keep body and soul together.

At first the crew bore it pretty well, but they soon took to grumbling, saying that it was owing to the captain's want of forethought in not laying in more provisions that we were reduced to this state.

Hitherto the wind had been fair, but any day it might change, and then, they asked, what would become of us? Most of them would have broken into open mutiny had not they known that the mates and doctor, Jack and I, Jim, and probably Brown and Soper, would have sided with the captain, though we felt that they were not altogether wrong in their accusation.

I heard the doctor tell Mr. Griffiths that he was afraid the scurvy would again appear if we were kept long on our present food. Day after day we glided on across the smooth ocean with a cloudless sky, our food and water gradually decreasing.

We now often looked at each other, wondering what would be the end. At last, one night, when it was my middle watch on deck, Jim came aft to me.

"I'm afraid the men won't stand it any longer," he said. "They vow that if the captain don't serve out more food and water they'll take it. I know that it will be death to all of us if they do, or I would not tell on them. You let Mr. Griffiths know; maybe he'll bring them to a right mind. They don't care for Jack or me, and Brown, Soper, and Sam seemed inclined to side with the rest. Jack says whatever you do he'll do."

"Thank you, Jim," I answered. "You try to show them what folly they'll commit if they attempt to do as they propose. They won't succeed, for the captain is a determined man, and there'll be bloodshed if they keep to their purpose."

Jim went forward, and I took a turn on deck to consider what was best to be done. It was the second mate's watch, and it had only just struck two bells. I did not wish to say anything to him. I waited for a little, and then asked the second mate to let me go below for a minute, for I could not quit the deck without his leave.

"You may go and turn in if you like," he said. "There's no chance of your being wanted on a night like this."

"Thank you, sir," I answered, and at once ran down to Mr. Griffiths's cabin.

He awoke when I touched his shoulder, and I told him in a low voice what I had heard.

"You have acted sensibly, Peter," he answered "I'll

be on deck in a moment. When the men see that we are prepared for them they'll change their minds."

I again went on deck, and he soon appeared, with a brace of pistols in his belt, followed by the captain and the doctor, with muskets in their hands.

At that moment up sprang from the fore hatchway the greater part of the crew, evidently intending to make their way to the after store room, where the provisions and water were kept.

"What are you about to do, lads?" shouted the captain. "Go below, every one of you, except the watch on deck, and don't attempt to try this trick again."

His tall figure holding a musket ready to fire cowed them in an instant, and they obeyed without uttering a word. The captain said that he should remain on deck, and told Mr. Griffiths and the doctor that he would call them if they were wanted.

Some time afterwards, going forward, I found Jim, who told me that they had all turned in.

The night passed away without any disturbance. As soon as it was daylight the captain ordered me to go aloft and take a look round. I obeyed, though I felt so weak that I could scarcely climb the rigging. I glanced round the horizon, but no vessel could I see. A mist still hung over the water.

I was just about to come down when the sun rose, and at the same moment I made out over our quarter, away to the southward, a white sail, on which his rays were cast, standing on the same course that we were.

"Sail ho!" I shouted in a joyful tone, and pointed out in the direction in which I saw her.

The captain, immediately I came down, ordered me to rouse up all hands, and every sail the ship could carry being set, we edged down to the stranger, making a signal that we desired to speak her. She was an English barque, also bound for the Cape.

As we got close together, a boat being lowered, Mr. Griffiths and I went on board and stated our wants. Her captain at once agreed to supply us with everything he could spare, and we soon had our boat loaded with a cask of bread, another of beef, and several other articles, and in addition a nautical almanack, for we had run out our last one within a week before this. We had a second trip to make, with casks to fill with water. As may be supposed, we had quenched our own thirst on our first visit. When we again got back we found the cook and two hands assisting him busily employed in preparing breakfast, and a right hearty one we had.

We kept our charitable friends in sight till we reached the Cape, by which time we had expended all the provisions with which they had furnished us.

In a few days, from the abundance of fresh meat and vegetables which we obtained from the shore, our health and strength returned, and I for one was eager once more to put to sea, that Jack and I might the sooner reach home. We had got so far on our way that it seemed to me as if we were almost there. We were, however, detained for several days refitting and provisioning the ship.

Once more, however, the men showed their mutinous disposition, for when they were ordered to heave up the anchor they refused to man the windlass, on the plea that they had had no liberty on shore. Though this was the case, there having been work for all hands on board, there was no real excuse for their conduct, as they were amply supplied with provisions, and had not been really over-worked.

"We shall see, my fine fellows," exclaimed the captain, on seeing them doggedly standing with their arms folded in a group forward.

At once ordering his boat, which was pulled by Jack and Jim, Miles Soper and Brown, he went on shore. He soon returned, with the deputy captain of the port, who, stepping on board, called the men aft, and inquired what they had to complain of. As they were all silent, Captain McL—— made them a speech, pointing out to them that they were fortunate in being aboard a well-found and well-provisioned ship.

"And, my lads," he continued, "you need not have any fear of falling sick, for the captain has an ample supply for you of anti-scorbutics."

As none of the mutineers had a notion what this long word meant, they were taken completely aback; and after staring at him and then at each other, first one and then another went forward to the windlass, and we soon had the ship under way.

Whenever during the voyage any of us talked about the matter, we always called Captain McL—— "Old Anti-Scorbutic." I felt happier than I had been for a long time when the ship's head was directed northward, and as we had a fresh breeze the men declared that their friends at home had got hold of the tow-rope, and that we should soon be there.

On running down to St. Helena we were followed for several days by some black whales of immense length. Sometimes they were so close to the ship's side that we might have lanced them from the deck. The fourth day after we saw them the second mate and Horner took it into their heads wantonly to fire musket-shots at them. At last one of the poor creatures was hit, when it dived, the others following its example, and we saw them no more. The only object of interest we met with crossing the north-east trades was the passage through the Gulf Stream, or Sargasso Sea, as it is sometimes called. It was curious to find ourselves surrounded by thick masses of seaweed as far as the eye could reach on every side, so that no clear water could be seen for miles away. I can compare it to nothing else than to sailing through a farmyard covered with deep straw.

The first land we made was Fyal. Thence we ran across to Pico, where we obtained provisions and water. If we had got nothing else it would have been well, but the crew managed to smuggle on board a quantity of new rum, the effects of which were soon visible.

Leaving Pico, we shaped a course for old England. The wind was now freshening, and all sail was made, as the captain was in a hurry to get the voyage over. In the evening, when the watch was called, not a man came on deck, every one of them being drunk, while most of the men in the other watch, who had managed to slip down every now and then, were in no better condition. The captain, who had been ailing, was in bed. Mr. Griffiths, the doctor and I, Jim and Brown, were the only sober ones. The second mate evidently did not know what he was about. Mr. Griffiths advised him to turn in. I was very sorry to see my brother Jack nearly as bad as the rest, though he afterwards told me that, having been so long without spirits, they had had an unexpected effect upon him. We sober ones had to remain all night on deck, running off when a puff of wind struck the sails. It was a mercy that it didn't come on to blow hard, for we could never have managed to shorten sail in time to save the spars. Indeed, very probably the masts would have gone. Brown, Jim, and I took it by turns to steer till morning broke, by which time some of the rest of the crew began to show signs of life. As we got into northern latitudes a strong north-easterly breeze made the weather feel bitterly cold to us, who had been for so long a time accustomed to a southern climate.

During all that period I had not worn shoes. For the sake of warmth I now wanted to put on a pair, but my feet had so increased in size that I could not find any large enough in the slop-locker.

At last the wind shifted to the south-west, and we ran before it up Channel.

The first object we made was the Owers light-vessel, about ninety miles from the Downs. Having made a signal for a pilot, one boarded us out of a cutter off Dungeness. How eagerly all of us plied the old fellow for news, though as he was a man of few words it was with difficulty that the captain or mates could pump much out of him. We remained but a few hours in the Downs to obtain provisions, of which we were again short, and thence proceeded to the Thames, where we dropped our anchor for the last time before going into dock to unload.

Jim and I, although we had been kept on board against our will and had never signed articles, found that we could claim wages. Though I had no reason to like Captain Hawkins, yet I felt that I ought to wish him good-bye.

To my surprise, he seemed very friendly, and said that if I ever wished to go to sea again he should be very glad to have me with him, as well as my brother and Jim. Poor man! he had made his last voyage, for I heard of his death shortly afterwards. I was very sorry to part from Mr. Griffiths and Dr. Cockle. They invited me to come and see them, both of them saying that they never intended again to go afloat, though I heard that Mr. Griffiths got the command of a fine ship shortly afterwards; so I supposed that like many others similarly situated he was induced to change his mind and tempt once more the dangers of the ocean.

"We will meet again, Peter," said Miles Soper; "and I hope that if you and Jack go to sea, we shall all be aboard the same ship."

Brown said the same thing, but from that day to this I have never been able to learn what became of him. Such is often the case in a sea life. For years people are living on the most intimate terms, and separate never to meet again in this life.

After remaining a week in London for payment of our wages, Jim and I each received five-and-twenty pounds, Jack also obtaining nearly half that amount. Our first care before we set off for Portsmouth, to which we were eager to return, was, our clothes being worn out, to supply ourselves with decent suits of blue cloth and other necessaries.

At daylight the morning after we were free, carrying our bundles and the various treasures we had collected, a pretty load altogether, we went to the place from which the coach started for Portsmouth, and finding three seats on the top, off we set with light hearts, thinking of the friends we should meet on our arriving there. Jack confessed that he had forgotten the appearance of most of them, though he longed to see Mary and to give her the curiosities he had brought. We had a couple of parrots, three other beautifully coloured birds, a big basket of shells, and a whole bundle of bows, and arrows, and darts, and a lot of other things.

Rattling down the Portsmouth High Street, we at last dismounted and set off for Mr. Gray's house, where I fully expected I should still find Mary living. As we walked along, the boys gathered round us to look at our birds, and some asked where we had come from with so many curious things.

"From round the world," answered Jim, "since we were last at home," which was not a very definite answer.

In vain we looked about expecting to see some old acquaintances, but all the faces we set eyes on were strange. No wonder, considering how long we had been away, while certainly no one would have recognised us. It was not quite an easy matter to find our way to Mr. Gray's house, and we had to stop every now and then while Jim and I consulted which turning to take, for we were ashamed to ask any one. At last, just as we got near it, we saw an old gentleman in a Quaker's dress coming along the road. He just glanced at us, as other people had done; when I, looking hard at him, felt sure he must be Mr. Gray. I nudged Jim's shoulder.

"Yes, it's he, I'm sure," whispered Jim.

So I went up to him, and pulling off my hat said,

"Beg pardon, sir; may I be so bold as to ask if you are Mr. Gray?"

"Gray is my name, young man," he answered, looking somewhat surprised, "Who art thou?"

"Peter Trawl, sir; and this Jim Pulley, and here is my brother Jack."

If the kind Quaker had ever been addicted to uttering exclamations of surprise he would have done so on this occasion, I suspect, judging from the expression of astonishment which came over his countenance.

"Peter Trawl! James Pulley! Why, it was reported that those two lads were lost in the North Sea years ago," he said.

"We are the lads, sir, notwithstanding," I answered; and I briefly narrated to him how we had been picked up by the *Intrepid* and carried off to the Pacific, and how I had there found my brother Jack.

"Verily, this is good news, and will cheer the heart of thy young sister, who has never ceased to believe that thou wouldst turn up again some day or other," he said.

"Is Mary well, sir? is she still with you?" I inquired, eagerly.

"Yes, Peter, thy sister is as one of my family. Though greatly pressed by her newly-found relatives in Shetland to go there and reside with them, she has always replied that she was sure thou wast alive, and that thou wouldst come back to Portsmouth to look for her, and that it would grieve thee much not to find her."

"How kind and thoughtful!" I exclaimed. "Do let me go on, sir, at once to see my young sister."

"Stay, lad, stay," he answered. "The surprise might be too great for her. I will go back to my house and tell her that thou hast returned home safe. Thou art so changed that she would not know thee, and therefore thou and thy companions may follow close behind."

We saw Mr. Gray go to his door and knock. It was opened by a woman-servant, who I was sure, when I caught sight of her countenance, was Nancy herself. She saw me at the same moment, and directly Mr. Gray had entered, came out on the doorstep, and regarded me intently.

"Yes, I'm sure it is!" she exclaimed. "Peter, Peter, aren't you Peter, now? I have not forgotten thy face, though thee be grown into a young man!" and she stretched out her arms, quite regardless of the passers-by, ready to give me such another embrace as she had bestowed on me when I went away. I could not restrain myself any longer, but, giving the things I was carrying to Jack, sprang up the steps.

"Here he is, Miss Mary, here he is!" cried Nancy, and I saw close behind her a tall, fair girl.

Nancy, however, had time to give me a kiss and a hug before I could disengage myself, and the next moment my sweet sister Mary had her arms round my neck, and, half crying, half laughing, was exclaiming,

"I knew you would come, I knew you would, Peter; I was sure you were not lost!"

My brother Jack and Jim were, meantime, staying outside, not liking to come in till they were summoned. Nancy did not recognise them, and thought that they were two shipmates who had accompanied me to carry my things.

A JOYOUS MEETING.

Page 346.

The Voyage Home, and How it Ended.

At last, when I told Mary that I had not only come myself, but had brought back our brother Jack, she was eager to see him, though she was so young when he went away that she had no recollection of his countenance, and scarcely knew him from Jim.

Mary had let me into the parlour. I now went and beckoned them in. Nancy, when she knew who they were, welcomed them warmly, but did not bestow so affectionate a greeting on them as she had done on me. Jim stood outside the door while I brought Jack in. Though Mary kissed him, and told him how glad she was to see him, it was easy to see that she at first felt almost as if he were a stranger.

Mr. Gray left us to ourselves for some time, and then all the family came in and welcomed us kindly, insisting that Jack should remain with me in the parlour, while Nancy took care of Jim in the kitchen, where he was much more at his ease than he would have been with strangers. Jack, indeed, looked, as he afterwards confessed to me he felt, like a fish out of water in the presence of so many young ladies.

Though I had twice written to Mary, and had directed my letters properly, neither had reached her; yet for all these years she had not lost hope of seeing me.

After supper, Jack and I were going away, but Mr. Gray insisted that we should remain, as he had had beds arranged for us in the house.

"I must not let you lads be exposed to the dangers and temptations of the town," he said in a kind tone. "You must stay here till you go to sea again."

Mary at once wrote to Mr. Troil to tell him of my return, and of my having brought my brother Jack back with me.

While waiting for an answer, one day Jack and Jim and I were walking down the High Street, when we saw a large, placard stating that the *Thisbe* frigate, commissioned by Captain Rogers, was in want of hands.

"I shouldn't wonder but what he was my old skipper," observed Jack. "And you fine young fellows couldn't do better than join her," exclaimed a petty officer, who was standing near, clapping Jack on the back.

"Why I think I know your face," he added.

"Maybe. I'm Jack Trawl. I'm not ashamed of my name," said my brother.

"Jack Trawl!" exclaimed the man-of-war's man; "then you belong to the *Lapwing*. We all thought you were lost with the rest of the boat's crew."

"No, I wasn't; Miles Soper and I escaped. Now I look at you, ain't you Bill Bolton?"

"The same," was the answer. "Tell us how it all happened."

Jack in a few words told his old shipmate what is already known to the reader. While he was speaking, who should come up but Miles Soper himself, come down to Portsmouth to look out for a berth, accompanied by Sam Coal. The long and the short of it was that they all three agreed to enter aboard the *Thisbe*, and did their best to persuade Jim to follow their example.

I had no notion of doing so myself, for I knew that it would break Mary's heart to part with me again so soon, and I feared, indeed, that she would not like Jack's going. Still, taking all things into consideration, he could not do better I thought—for having been so long at sea, he felt, as he said, like a fish out of water among so many fine folks.

Jim made no reply, but drawing me aside, said,

"Peter, I can't bear the thoughts of leaving you, and yet I know you wouldn't like to ship before the mast again; but if I stay ashore what am I to do? I've no fancy to spending my days in a wherry, and haven't got one if I had. I've taken a liking to Jack, and you've many friends,

The Voyage Home, and How it Ended.

and can do without me, so if you don't say no I'll ship with the rest."

I need not repeat what I said to Jim. I was sure that it was the best thing he could do, and advised him accordingly.

"I'm with you, mates," he said, in a husky tone, going back to the rest, and away they all went together, while I returned to Mr. Gray's.

"I wish the lads had shipped on board a peaceable merchantman," he observed when I told him, "but I can't pretend to dictate to them. I am glad thou hast been better directed, Peter."

Jack and Jim came to see us before the ship went out of harbour. Jack said he knew that he must work for his living, and that he would rather serve aboard a man-o'-war than do anything else.

"I'll look after him as I used to do you, Peter," said Jim. "And I hope some day we'll come back with our pockets full of gold, and maybe bear up for wherever you've dropped your anchor."

A few days after this a letter came from Mr. Troil, inviting Mary, Jack, and me to Shetland. Mary was very unwilling to leave her kind friends, but Mr. Gray said that it would be to our advantage, and advised Mary and me to go.

He was right, for when we arrived Mr. Troil received us as relatives. Mary became like a second daughter to him. I assisted in managing his property, and in the course of a few years Maggie, to whom he left everything he possessed, became my wife, while Mary married the owner of a neighbouring estate.

Some few years after a small coaster came into the Voe. I went down to see what she had on board. A sailor-looking man, with a wooden leg, and a woman, stepped ashore

"That's him—that's him!" I heard them exclaim, and in

a moment I was shaking hands with Jim and Nancy, who had become his wife. He had got his discharge, and had come, he said, to settle near me. I several times heard from my brother Jack, who, after serving as bo'sun on board a line-of-battle ship, retired from the service with a pension, and joined our family circle in Shetland, where he married, and declared that he was too happy ever to go to sea again.

THE END.

www.ingramcontent.com/pod-product-compliance
Lightning Source LLC
Chambersburg PA
CBHW031423230426
43668CB00007B/408